Math in Focus®

Singapore Math®
by Marshall Cavendish

Student Edition

Program Consultant and Author
Dr. Fong Ho Kheong

Authors
Chelvi Ramakrishnan
Michelle Choo

Grade 1B

Marshall Cavendish
Education

U.S. Distributor

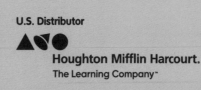

Houghton Mifflin Harcourt.
The Learning Company™

Contents

▶ Hands-on Activity

9 Length and Weight

▶ Hands-on Activity

Chapter

10 Numbers to 120

▶ Hands-on Activity

Addition and Subtraction Within 100

▶ Hands-on Activity

© 2020 Marshall Cavendish Education Pte Ltd

Graphs

Chapter Opener 311

How can you collect, organize, and show data in a picture graph and tally chart?

RECALL PRIOR KNOWLEDGE 312
Showing information with pictures

▶ Hands-on Activity

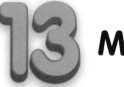

Chapter

13 Money

Hands-on Activity

Manipulative List

10–sided die

Balance bucket

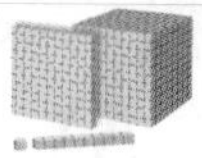

Base-ten blocks

Base-ten unit

Base-ten rod

Coin set

Color number cubes

Connecting cubes

Craft sticks

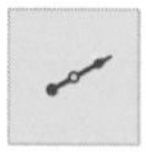

Spinner

Transparent counters

Preface

Welcome!

Math in Focus® is a program that puts **you** at the center of an exciting learning experience! This experience is all about helping you to really understand math and become a strong and confident problem solver!

What is in your book?

Each chapter in this book begins with a real-world example of the math topic you are about to learn.

In each chapter, you will see these features:

THINK provides a problem for the whole section, to get you thinking. If you cannot answer the problem right away, you can come back to it a few times as you work through the section.

ENGAGE contains tasks that link what you already know with what you will be learning next. You can explore and discuss the tasks with your classmates.

LEARN introduces you to new math concepts using examples and activities, where you can use objects to help you learn.

Hands-on Activity gives you the chance to work closely with your classmates, using objects or drawing pictures, to help you learn math.

TRY gives you the chance to practice what you are learning, with support.

INDEPENDENT PRACTICE allows you to work on different kinds of problems, and to use what you have learned to solve these problems on your own.

Additional features include:

RECALL PRIOR KNOWLEDGE	Math Talk	MATH SHARING	GAME
Helps you recall related concepts you learned before, accompanied by practice questions	Invites you to talk about your thinking and communicate your ideas to your classmates and teachers	Encourages you to create strategies, discover methods, and share them with your classmates and teachers using mathematical language	Helps you to really master the concepts you learned, through fun partner games
LET'S EXPLORE	MATH JOURNAL	PUT ON YOUR THINKING CAP!	CHAPTER WRAP-UP
Extends your learning through investigation	Allows you to reflect on your learning when you write down your thoughts about the concepts learned	Challenges you to apply the concepts to solve problems in different ways	Summarizes your learning in a flow chart and helps you to make connections within the chapter
CHAPTER REVIEW	Assessment Prep	PERFORMANCE TASK	STEAM
Provides you with a lot of practice in the concepts learned	Prepares you for state tests with assessment-type problems	Assesses your learning through problems that allow you to demonstrate your understanding and knowledge	Promotes collaboration with your classmates through interesting projects that allow you to use math in creative ways

Let's begin your exciting learning journey with us! Are you ready?

Addition and Subtraction Within 40

We have 24 bottles of juice in the trolley.
We need 30 bottles of juice.
How many more bottles do we need?

What is 30 – 24?

24, 25, 26, 27, 28, 29, 30
We need 6 more bottles!

How can you add or subtract two numbers?
What ways can you use?

Name: _____   Date: _____

Adding within 20

a Add by counting on.
$11 + 4 = ?$

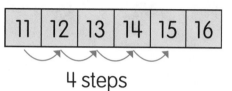

4 steps

$11 + 4 = 15$

b Add by making a 10.
$8 + 5 = ?$

$8 + 5 = 13$

$8 + 2 = 10$
$10 + 3 = 13$

▶ **Quick Check**

Add.
Count on from the greater number.
Use the counting tape to help you.

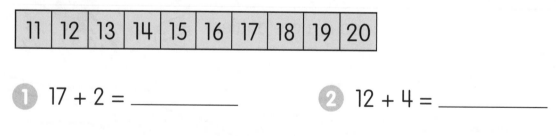

| 11 | 12 | 13 | 14 | 15 | 16 | 17 | 18 | 19 | 20 |

1 $17 + 2 =$ _____

2 $12 + 4 =$ _____

Make a 10.
Then, add.

3 8 + 7 = _____

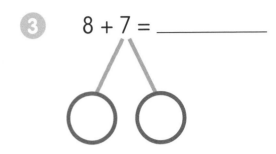

4 9 + 5 = _____

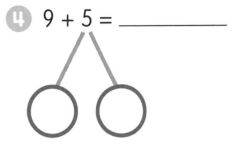

Subtracting within 20

a Subtract by counting back.
16 − 3 = ?

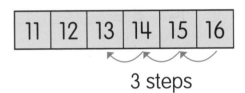

| 11 | 12 | 13 | 14 | 15 | 16 |

3 steps

16 − 3 = 13

b Subtract by grouping into a 10 and ones.
16 − 7 = ?

16 − 7 = 9

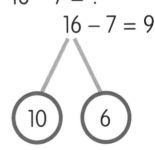

10 − 7 = 3
3 + 6 = 9

▶ **Quick Check**

Subtract.
Count back from the greater number.
Use the counting tape to help you.

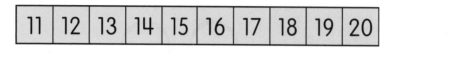

| 11 | 12 | 13 | 14 | 15 | 16 | 17 | 18 | 19 | 20 |

⑤ 13 − 2 = _____

⑥ 19 − 3 = _____

Group each number into a 10 and ones.
Then, subtract.

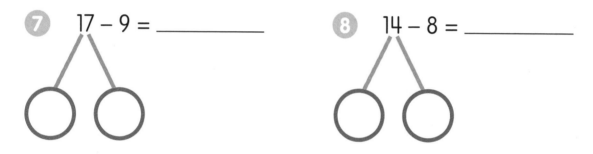

⑦ 17 − 9 = _____

⑧ 14 − 8 = _____

Related addition and subtraction facts

Each addition sentence has a related subtraction sentence.
4 + 5 = 9 ----------------- 9 − 4 = 5   or   9 − 5 = 4

Each subtraction sentence has a related addition sentence.
9 − 5 = 4 ----------------- 5 + 4 = 9   or   4 + 5 = 9

▶ **Quick Check**

Write a related addition or subtraction sentence.

⑨ 8 + 5 = 13 _____

⑩ 16 − 9 = 7 _____

1 Addition Without Regrouping

Learning Objectives:
- Add ones to a 2-digit number without regrouping.
- Add tens to a 2-digit number.
- Add ones and tens to a 2-digit number without regrouping.

New Vocabulary
digit

THINK

Find each missing digit.

Tens	Ones
1	5
+ ☐	☐
2	7

Talk about how you find the answers with your partner.

ENGAGE

Write a number between 21 and 25.

Use 🧊 to show this number.

Show how you would add 4 to your number.

What number do you have now?

Write it down.

Talk about how you added the two numbers with your partner.

LEARN Add ones to a 2-digit number without regrouping

1. 24 + 3 = ?

▶ **Method 1**

Count on from the greater number.

| 24 | 25 | 26 | 27 |

3 steps

24, 25, 26, 27

▶ **Method 2**

Use a place-value chart.

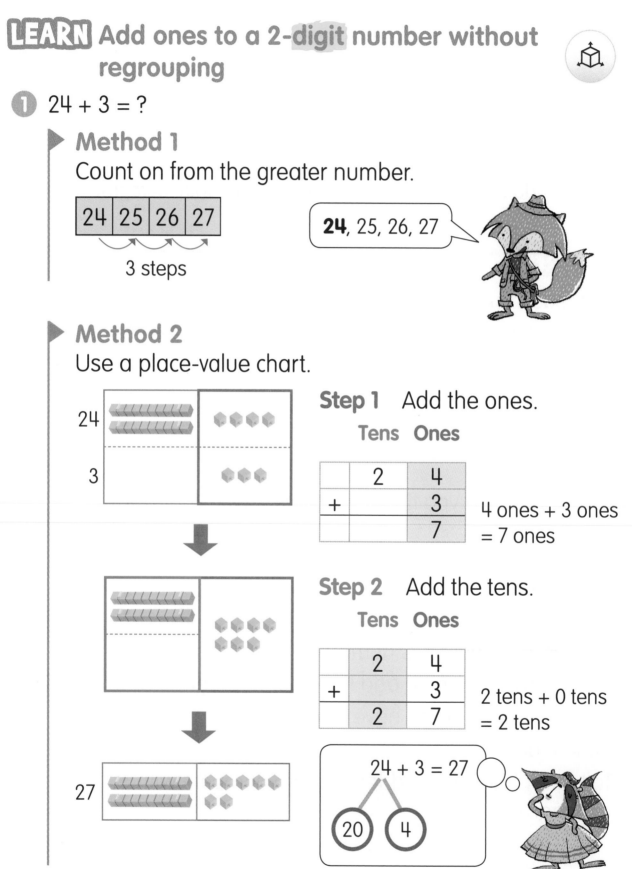

24

3

27

Step 1 Add the ones.

Tens   Ones

	2	4
+		3
		7

4 ones + 3 ones = 7 ones

Step 2 Add the tens.

Tens   Ones

	2	4
+		3
	2	7

2 tens + 0 tens = 2 tens

24 + 3 = 27

20   4

So, 24 + 3 = 27.

TRY Practice adding ones to a 2-digit number without regrouping

Add.

1 36 + 2 = ?

▶ **Method 1**

Count on from the greater number.

| 36 | 37 | 38 |

2 steps

36, _____, _____

▶ **Method 2**

Use a place-value chart.

First, add the ones.
Then, add the tens.

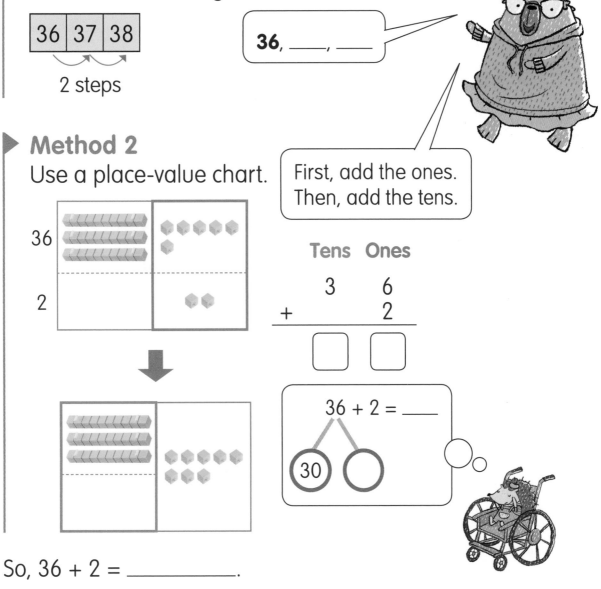

Tens	Ones
3	6
+	2
☐	☐

36 + 2 = _____

30 ◯

So, 36 + 2 = _____.

2 32 + 4 = _____

Count on by 10s to 40.

a What is 10 more than 20?

b What is 10 more than 21?

Talk about how you get your answers with your partner.

LEARN Add tens to a 2-digit number

① 20 + 20 = ?

> 20, …, 30, …, 40

> **Method 1**
> Count on by tens from 20.

> **Method 2**
> Use a place-value chart.

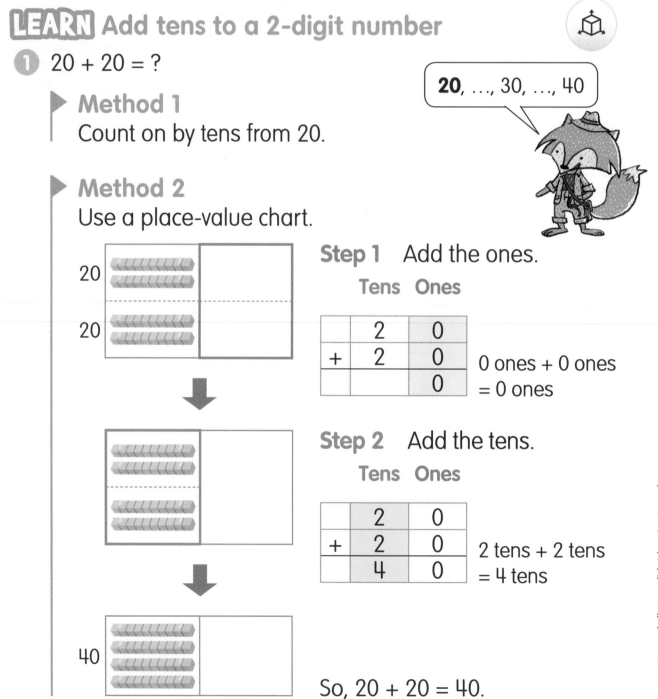

Step 1 Add the ones.

Tens	Ones
2	0
+ 2	0
	0

0 ones + 0 ones
= 0 ones

Step 2 Add the tens.

Tens	Ones
2	0
+ 2	0
4	0

2 tens + 2 tens
= 4 tens

So, 20 + 20 = 40.

2 17 + 20 = ?

▶ **Method 1**
Count on by tens from 17. **17**, …, 27, …, 37

▶ **Method 2**
Use a place-value chart.

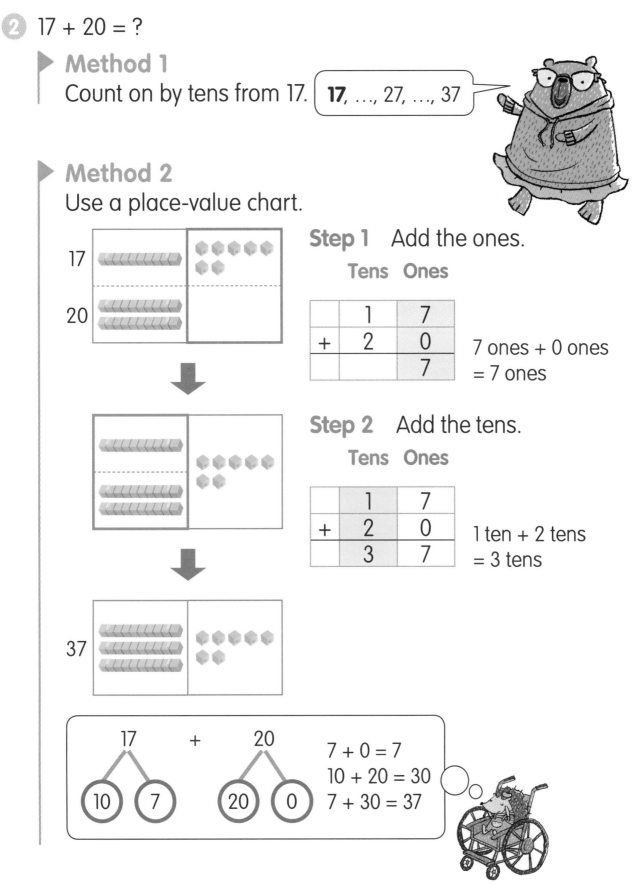

17

20

Step 1 Add the ones.

Tens	Ones
1	7
+ 2	0
	7

7 ones + 0 ones
= 7 ones

Step 2 Add the tens.

Tens	Ones
1	7
+ 2	0
3	7

1 ten + 2 tens
= 3 tens

37

17 + 20

10   7   20   0

7 + 0 = 7
10 + 20 = 30
7 + 30 = 37

So, 17 + 20 = 37.

TRY Practice adding tens to a 2-digit number

Add.

1 20 + 10 = ?

▶ **Method 1**
Count on by tens from 20.

20, ..., _____

▶ **Method 2**
Use a place-value chart.

First, add the ones.
Then, add the tens.

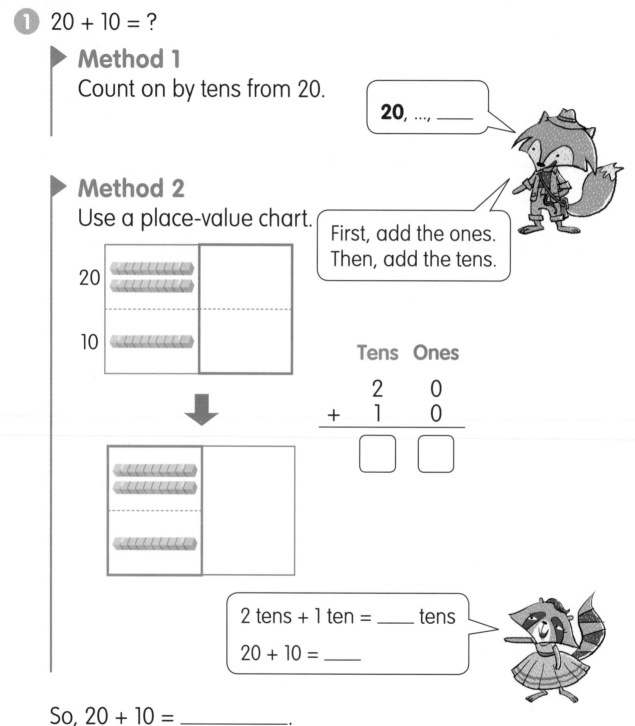

Tens	Ones
2	0
+ 1	0
⬚	⬚

2 tens + 1 ten = _____ tens

20 + 10 = _____

So, 20 + 10 = _____.

2 25 + 10 = ?

▶ **Method 1**
Count on by tens from 25.

25, ..., _____

▶ **Method 2**
Use a place-value chart.

First, add the ones.
Then, add the tens.

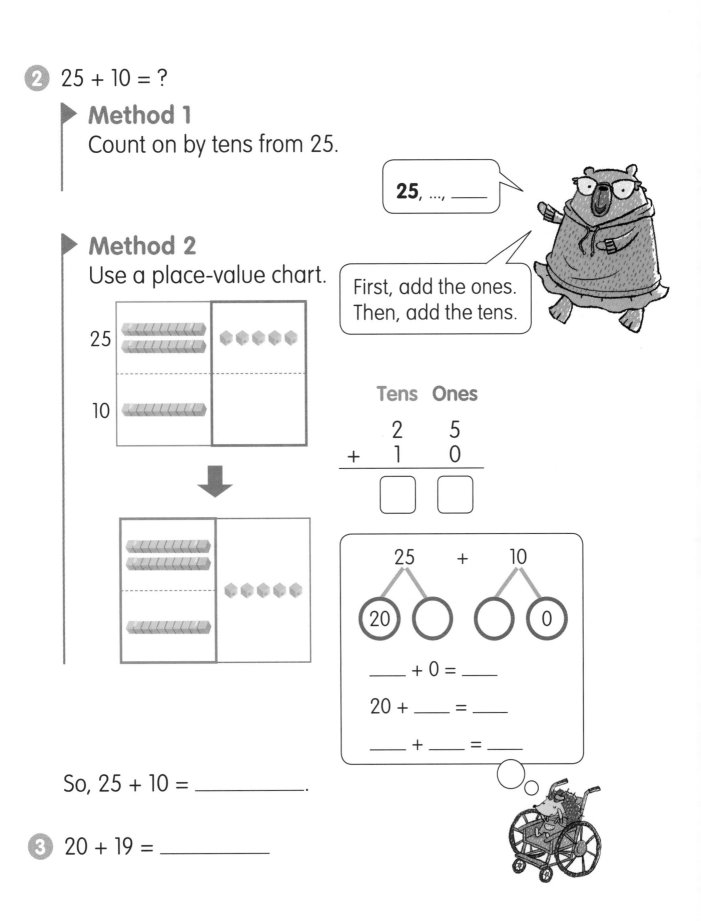

Tens	Ones
2	5
+ 1	0
☐	☐

25 + 10

20 __ __ 0

____ + 0 = ____

20 + ____ = ____

____ + ____ = ____

So, 25 + 10 = _____.

3 20 + 19 = _____

ENGAGE

1 22 + 12 = _____

Draw number bonds to show the tens and ones for each number above.
Add to show the total number of tens and ones.

2 Beth has 24 berries in her basket.
She adds 13 berries to her basket.
How many berries are there now?
Add the tens and ones to find the answer.

LEARN Add ones and tens to a 2-digit number without regrouping

1 14 + 25 = ?

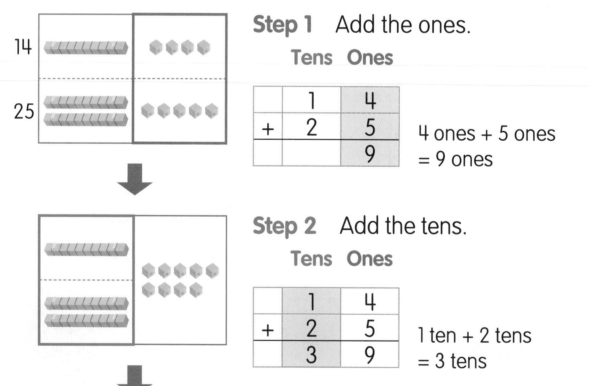

Step 1 Add the ones.

	Tens	Ones	
	1	4	
+	2	5	4 ones + 5 ones
		9	= 9 ones

Step 2 Add the tens.

	Tens	Ones	
	1	4	
+	2	5	1 ten + 2 tens
	3	9	= 3 tens

39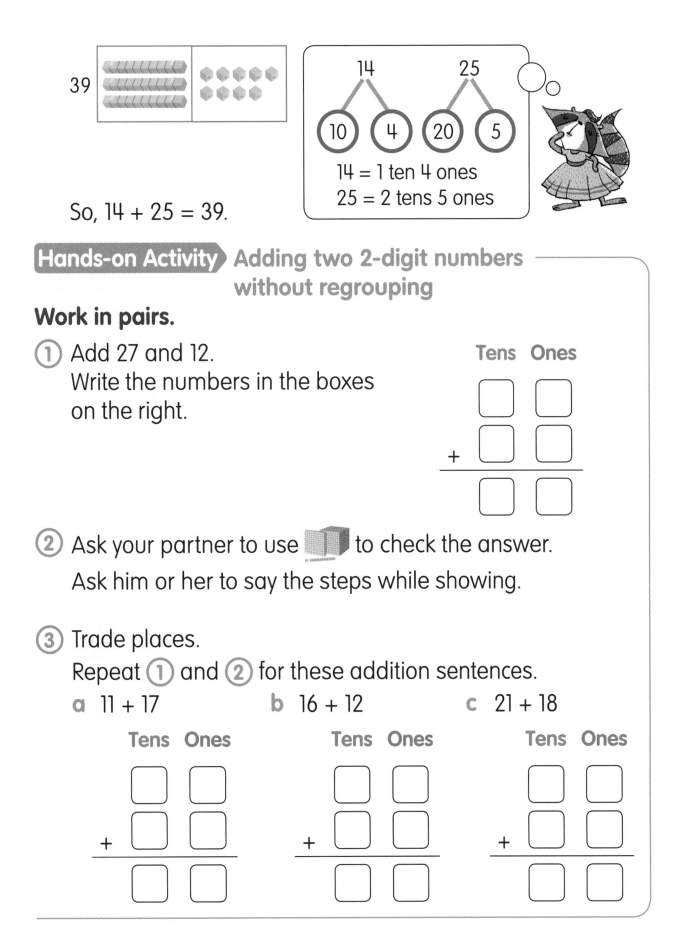

14   25

10 4   20 5

14 = 1 ten 4 ones
25 = 2 tens 5 ones

So, 14 + 25 = 39.

Hands-on Activity Adding two 2-digit numbers without regrouping

Work in pairs.

① Add 27 and 12.
Write the numbers in the boxes on the right.

Tens Ones

+

② Ask your partner to use ☐ to check the answer.
Ask him or her to say the steps while showing.

③ Trade places.
Repeat ① and ② for these addition sentences.

a 11 + 17   b 16 + 12   c 21 + 18

Tens Ones   Tens Ones   Tens Ones

+   +   +

TRY Practice adding ones and tens to a 2-digit number without regrouping

Add.

1 13 + 14 = ?

First, add the ones.
Then, add the tens.

Tens	Ones
1	3
+ 1	4
☐	☐

13
10 ○

14
10 ○

13 = 1 ten ____ ones

14 = 1 ten ____ ones

So, 13 + 14 = _____.

2 22 + 16 = _____

Tens	Ones
2	2
+ 1	6
☐	☐

3 24 + 14 = _____

Tens	Ones
2	4
+ 1	4
☐	☐

INDEPENDENT PRACTICE

Add.
Count on from the greater number.
Draw arrows to help you.

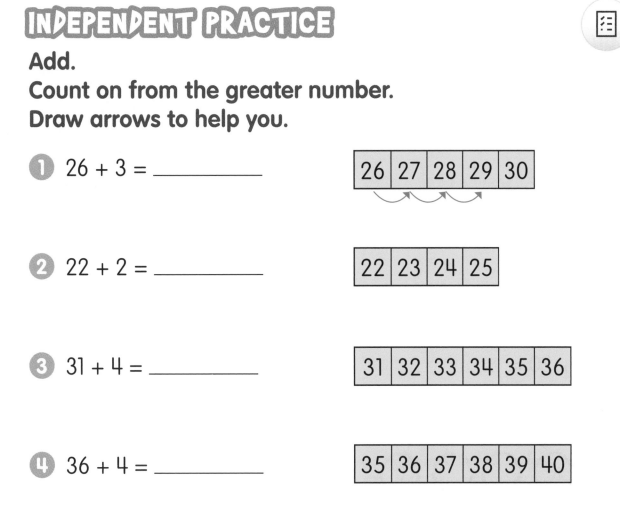

1 26 + 3 = _____

| 26 | 27 | 28 | 29 | 30 |

2 22 + 2 = _____

| 22 | 23 | 24 | 25 |

3 31 + 4 = _____

| 31 | 32 | 33 | 34 | 35 | 36 |

4 36 + 4 = _____

| 35 | 36 | 37 | 38 | 39 | 40 |

Write each missing number.

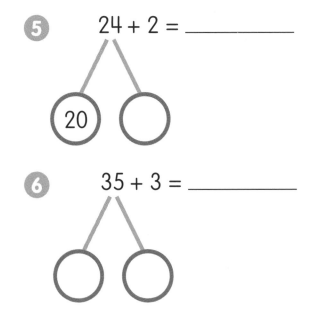

5 24 + 2 = _____

20

6 35 + 3 = _____

Add.
Count on by 10s.

7 16 + 10 = _____

16, ..., _____

8 12 + 20 = _____

12, ..., _____, ..., _____

Write each missing number.

9 11 + 20 = _____

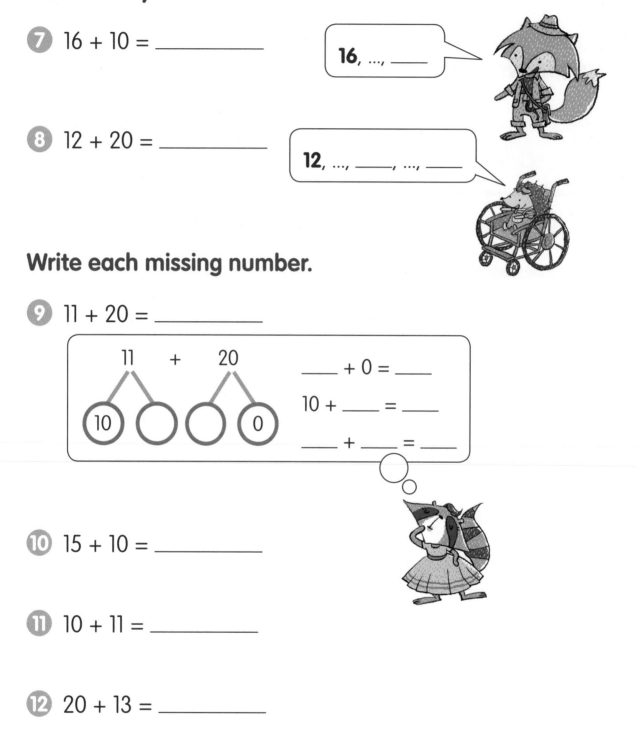

_____ + 0 = _____

10 + _____ = _____

_____ + _____ = _____

10 15 + 10 = _____

11 10 + 11 = _____

12 20 + 13 = _____

Add.
Then, draw lines to match the answers that are the same.

13

Tens	Ones
2	1
+	7
☐	☐

27

Tens	Ones
1	4
+ 2	0
☐	☐

38

Tens	Ones
2	5
+ 1	2
☐	☐

37

28

Tens	Ones
1	8
+ 2	0
☐	☐

34

Write the numbers in the boxes. Then, add.

14 7 + 22 = _____

Tens	Ones
☐	☐
+ ☐	☐
☐	☐

15 13 + 10 = _____

Tens	Ones
☐	☐
+ ☐	☐
☐	☐

16 13 + 16 = _____

Tens	Ones
☐	☐
+ ☐	☐
☐	☐

17 11 + 26 = _____

Tens	Ones
☐	☐
+ ☐	☐
☐	☐

18 15 + 21 = _____

Tens	Ones
☐	☐
+ ☐	☐
☐	☐

19 24 + 15 = _____

Tens	Ones
☐	☐
+ ☐	☐
☐	☐

2 Addition With Regrouping

Learning Objectives:
- Regroup ones into a 10 and ones.
- Add ones to a 2-digit number with regrouping.
- Add ones and tens to a 2-digit number with regrouping.
- Add three numbers with regrouping.

New Vocabulary
regroup

THINK

Find the missing number.

$14 + 9 +$ _____ $= 31$

Talk about how you find the missing number with your partner.

ENGAGE

a   Your teacher will give you some [cubes] and two [ten frames].
Place all your [cubes] on the [ten frame].
Then, complete the sentence.

$10 +$ _____ $=$ _____

How many [cubes] are there?

b   Take 9 [cubes] and 5 green [cubes].
Use the two [ten frames] to find how many [cubes] there are in all.

LEARN Regroup ones into a 10 and ones

1 You can regroup 14 into a 10 and ones.

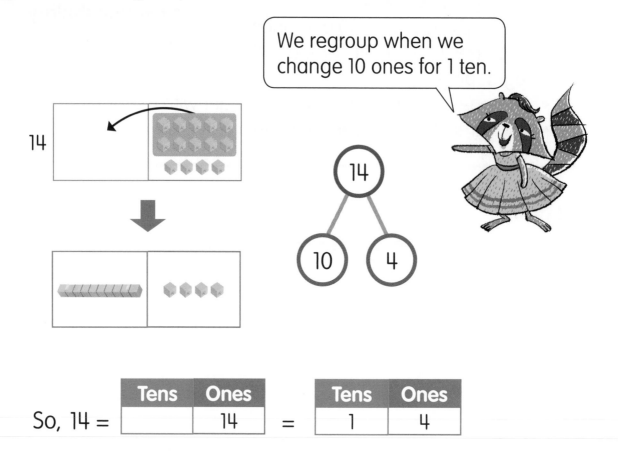

We regroup when we change 10 ones for 1 ten.

Tens	Ones		Tens	Ones
	14	=	1	4

So, 14 =

Hands-on Activity Regrouping ones into tens and ones

Take a 🎲, some 🧊, and a place-value chart.

1 Roll the 🎲.

2 Place this number of 🔲 on the place-value chart.

© 2020 Marshall Cavendish Education Pte Ltd

③ Roll the 🎲🎲 again.
Add to the number of 🟦 on your chart.
If you get 10 or more 🟦, trade 10 of them for 1 ▭.

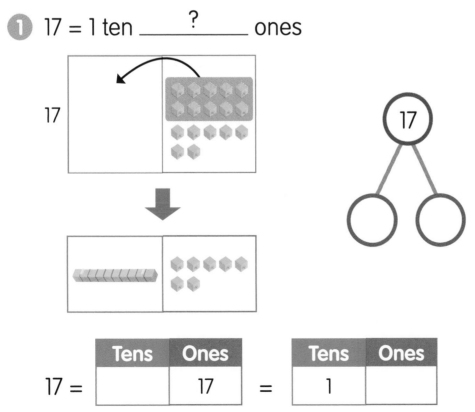

④ Repeat ① to ③ until you get 40.

TRY Practice regrouping ones into a 10 and ones

Regroup the ones.
Then, complete the place-value chart.

① 17 = 1 ten ____?____ ones

Tens	Ones
	17

17 =

Tens	Ones
1	

=

ENGAGE

Your teacher will give you some 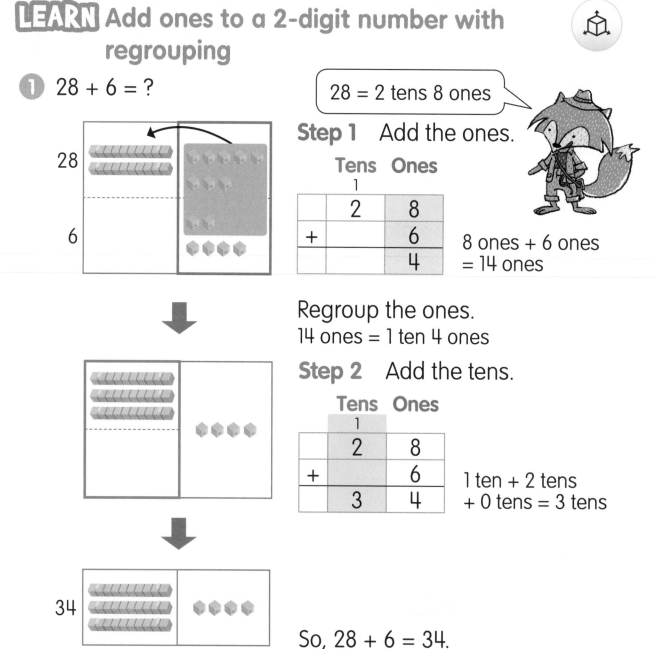 and three ▦.
Use the ◈ and ▦ to help you solve this problem:
Ayden has 15 toy cars.
He gets 7 more toy cars.
How many toy cars does Ayden have now?

LEARN Add ones to a 2-digit number with regrouping

1. 28 + 6 = ?

> 28 = 2 tens 8 ones

Step 1 Add the ones.

Tens	Ones
1	
2	8
+	6
	4

8 ones + 6 ones
= 14 ones

Regroup the ones.
14 ones = 1 ten 4 ones

Step 2 Add the tens.

Tens	Ones
1	
2	8
+	6
3	4

1 ten + 2 tens
+ 0 tens = 3 tens

34

So, 28 + 6 = 34.

TRY Practice adding ones to a 2-digit number with regrouping

Add and regroup.

1 25 + 7 = ?

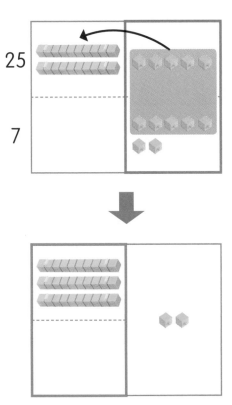

25

7

First, add the ones.
Regroup the ones into a 10 and ones.
Then, add the tens.

Tens	Ones
2	5
+	7
☐	☐

So, 25 + 7 = _____.

2 29 + 6 = _____

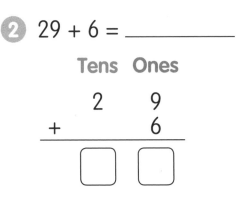

Tens	Ones
2	9
+	6
☐	☐

3 36 + 4 = _____

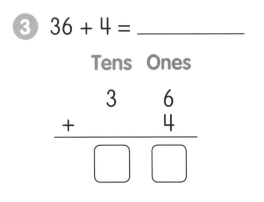

Tens	Ones
3	6
+	4
☐	☐

ENGAGE

Your teacher will give you some 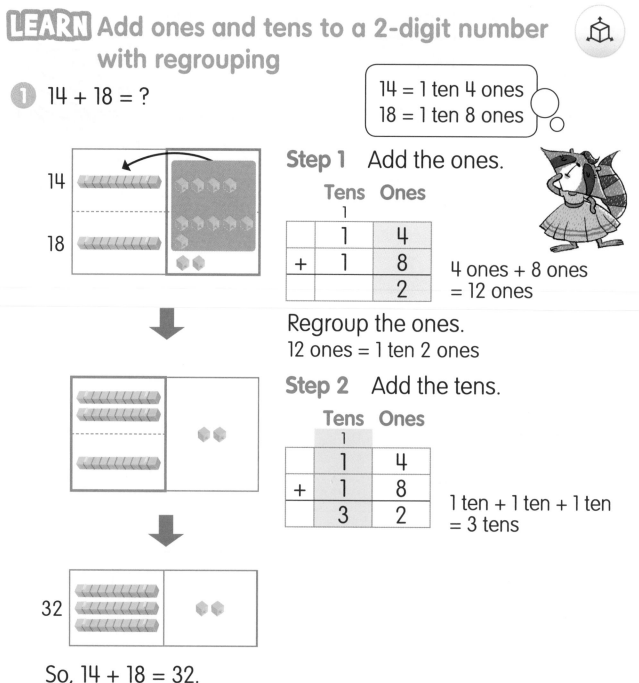 and four ⬜⬜⬜⬜.
How do you add 18 and 17?
Show two different ways.
Then, complete the sentence: 18 + 17 = 30 + _____

LEARN Add ones and tens to a 2-digit number with regrouping

① 14 + 18 = ?

> 14 = 1 ten 4 ones
> 18 = 1 ten 8 ones

Step 1   Add the ones.

	Tens	Ones
	1	
	1	4
+	1	8
		2

4 ones + 8 ones
= 12 ones

Regroup the ones.
12 ones = 1 ten 2 ones

Step 2   Add the tens.

	Tens	Ones
	1	
	1	4
+	1	8
	3	2

1 ten + 1 ten + 1 ten
= 3 tens

So, 14 + 18 = 32.

Hands-on Activity Adding two 2-digit numbers with regrouping

Work in pairs.

① 19 + 19 = ?
Add the ones, then regroup.
Next, add the tens.

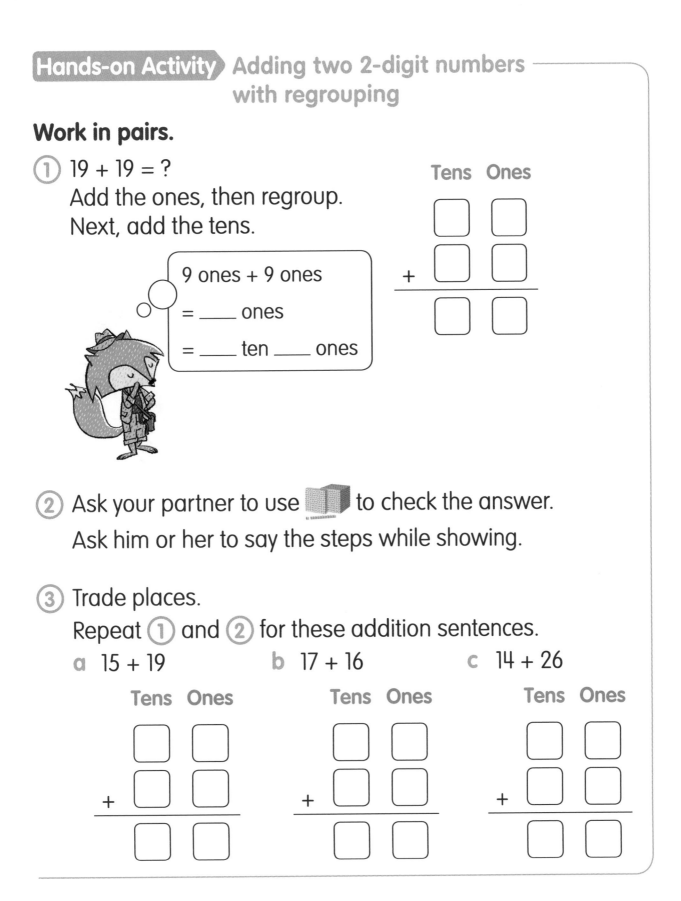

9 ones + 9 ones

= ____ ones

= ____ ten ____ ones

Tens Ones

+

② Ask your partner to use ▨ to check the answer.
Ask him or her to say the steps while showing.

③ Trade places.
Repeat ① and ② for these addition sentences.

a 15 + 19   b 17 + 16   c 14 + 26

Tens Ones   Tens Ones   Tens Ones

+   +   +

TRY Practice adding ones and tens to a 2-digit number with regrouping

Add and regroup.

1 15 + 15 = ?

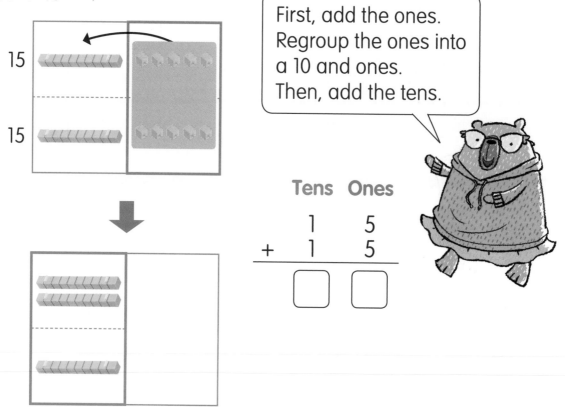

First, add the ones.
Regroup the ones into a 10 and ones.
Then, add the tens.

Tens	Ones
1	5
+ 1	5
☐	☐

So, 15 + 15 = _____.

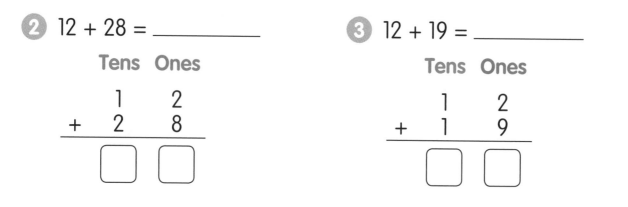

2 12 + 28 = _____

Tens	Ones
1	2
+ 2	8
☐	☐

3 12 + 19 = _____

Tens	Ones
1	2
+ 1	9
☐	☐

Mathematical Habit **3** **Construct viable arguments**

John shares with his classmates his way of adding 19 and 18.

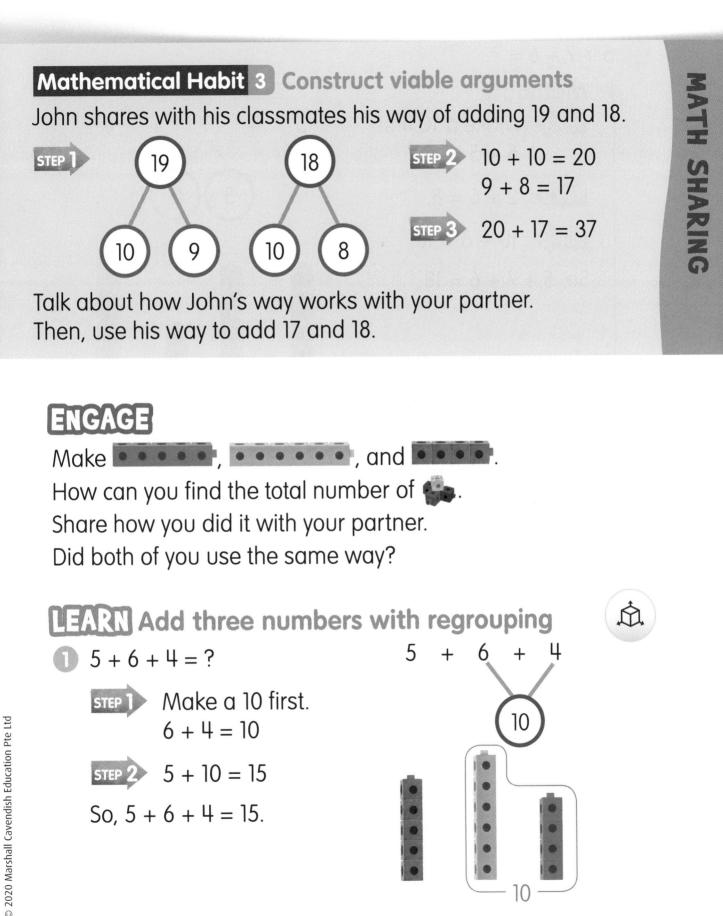

STEP **1**

19 → 10, 9

18 → 10, 8

STEP **2** 10 + 10 = 20
9 + 8 = 17

STEP **3** 20 + 17 = 37

Talk about how John's way works with your partner.
Then, use his way to add 17 and 18.

ENGAGE

Make ▭, ▭, and ▭.
How can you find the total number of ▦.
Share how you did it with your partner.
Did both of you use the same way?

LEARN Add three numbers with regrouping

1 5 + 6 + 4 = ?

STEP **1** Make a 10 first.
6 + 4 = 10

STEP **2** 5 + 10 = 15

So, 5 + 6 + 4 = 15.

5 + 6 + 4
       ↘ ↙
       10

② $5 + 7 + 6 = ?$

▶ **Method 1**

STEP 1 ▶ Make a 10 first.
$5 + 5 = 10$

STEP 2 ▶ $2 + 6 = 8$

STEP 3 ▶ $10 + 8 = 18$

So, $5 + 7 + 6 = 18$.

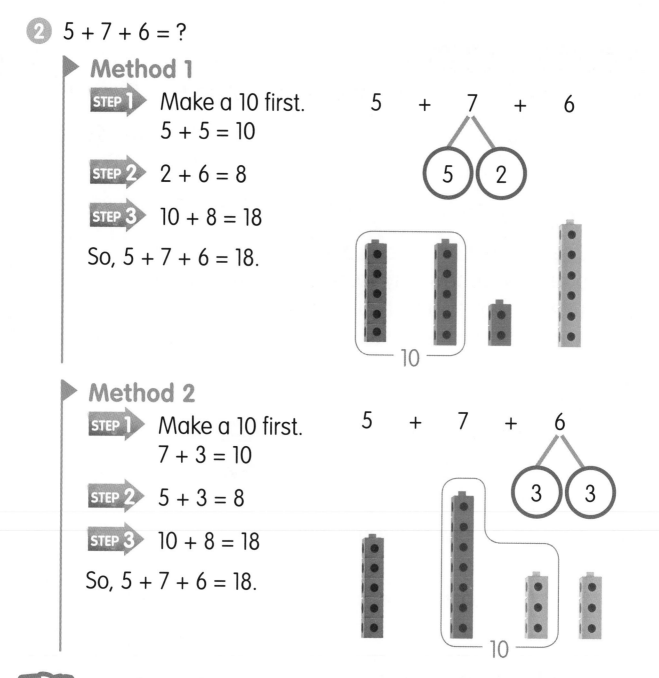

▶ **Method 2**

STEP 1 ▶ Make a 10 first.
$7 + 3 = 10$

STEP 2 ▶ $5 + 3 = 8$

STEP 3 ▶ $10 + 8 = 18$

So, $5 + 7 + 6 = 18$.

TRY Practice adding three numbers with regrouping

Make a 10.
Then, add.

① $3 + 7 + 4 =$ _____

② $6 + 8 + 3 =$ _____

INDEPENDENT PRACTICE

**Regroup the ones into tens and ones.
Then, fill in each missing number.**

①

Tens	Ones
	13

=

Tens	Ones
	3

②

Tens	Ones
	27

=

Tens	Ones
	17

Add.

③

Tens	Ones
2	8
+	3
☐	☐

④

Tens	Ones
1	7
+	4
☐	☐

⑤

Tens	Ones
	9
+ 1	2
☐	☐

⑥

Tens	Ones
1	9
+ 1	1
☐	☐

⑦

Tens	Ones
1	8
+ 1	7
☐	☐

⑧

Tens	Ones
1	3
+ 1	9
☐	☐

The Jones family is having a tour at the safari.
What animals does the Jones family see?
Add.
Then, color the circles with the answers on the next page to find out.

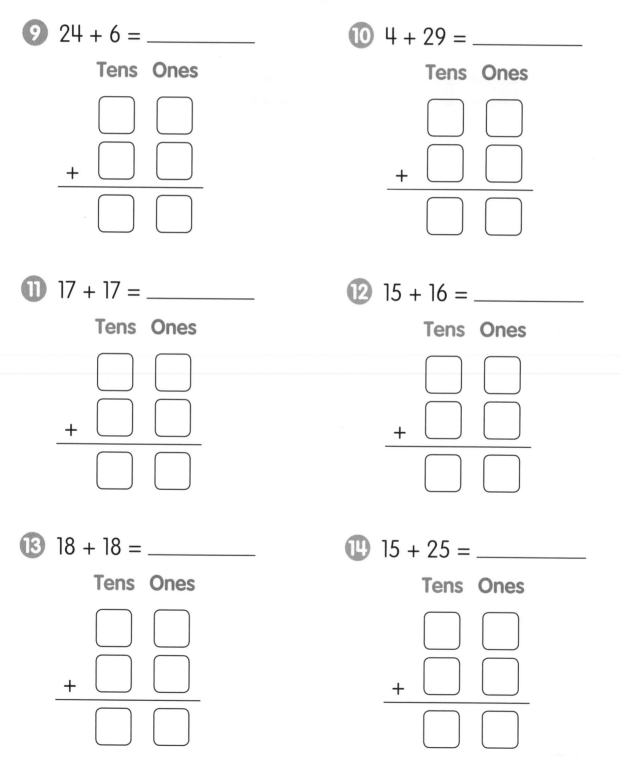

9 24 + 6 = _____

Tens Ones

+

10 4 + 29 = _____

Tens Ones

+

11 17 + 17 = _____

Tens Ones

+

12 15 + 16 = _____

Tens Ones

+

13 18 + 18 = _____

Tens Ones

+

14 15 + 25 = _____

Tens Ones

+

tigers 35

leopards 36

lions 31

elephants 37

baboons 30

hippos 28

crocodiles 39

impalas 33

buffaloes 32

zebras 40

giraffes 34

monkeys 38

Trace the route the Jones family takes.
What animals do they see?

Make a 10.
Then, add.

15

$$5 + 5 + 9 = \underline{\hspace{2cm}}$$

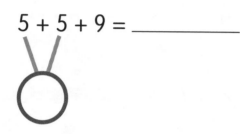

Make a 10.
Then, add.

16 $1 + 9 + 4 = \underline{\hspace{2cm}}$

17 $8 + 4 + 6 = \underline{\hspace{2cm}}$

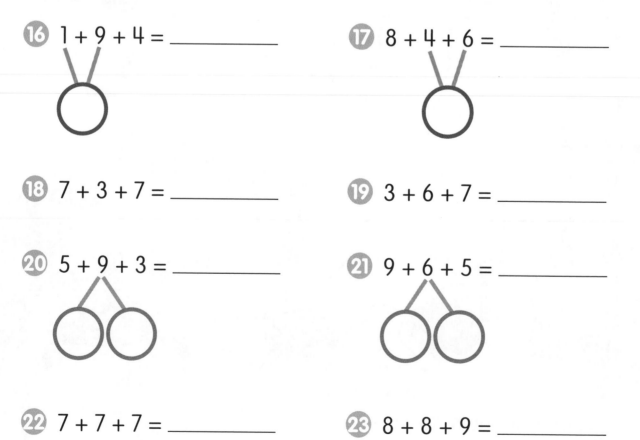

18 $7 + 3 + 7 = \underline{\hspace{2cm}}$

19 $3 + 6 + 7 = \underline{\hspace{2cm}}$

20 $5 + 9 + 3 = \underline{\hspace{2cm}}$

21 $9 + 6 + 5 = \underline{\hspace{2cm}}$

22 $7 + 7 + 7 = \underline{\hspace{2cm}}$

23 $8 + 8 + 9 = \underline{\hspace{2cm}}$

3 Subtraction Without Regrouping

Learning Objectives:
- Subtract ones from a 2-digit number without regrouping.
- Subtract tens from a 2-digit number.
- Subtract ones and tens from a 2-digit number without regrouping.

 THINK

Find each missing digit.

Tens	Ones
3	6
− ☐	☐
1	5

Talk about how you find the answers with your partner.

ENGAGE

Use 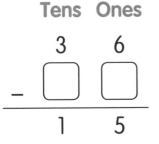 to show 27.
How can you subtract 4?
Show two different ways.
Share what ways you used with your partner.

LEARN Subtract ones from a 2-digit number without regrouping

1. 27 – 4 = ?

▶ **Method 1**

Count back from the greater number.

| 23 | 24 | 25 | 26 | 27 |

4 steps

27, 26, 25, 24, 23

▶ **Method 2**

Use a place-value chart.

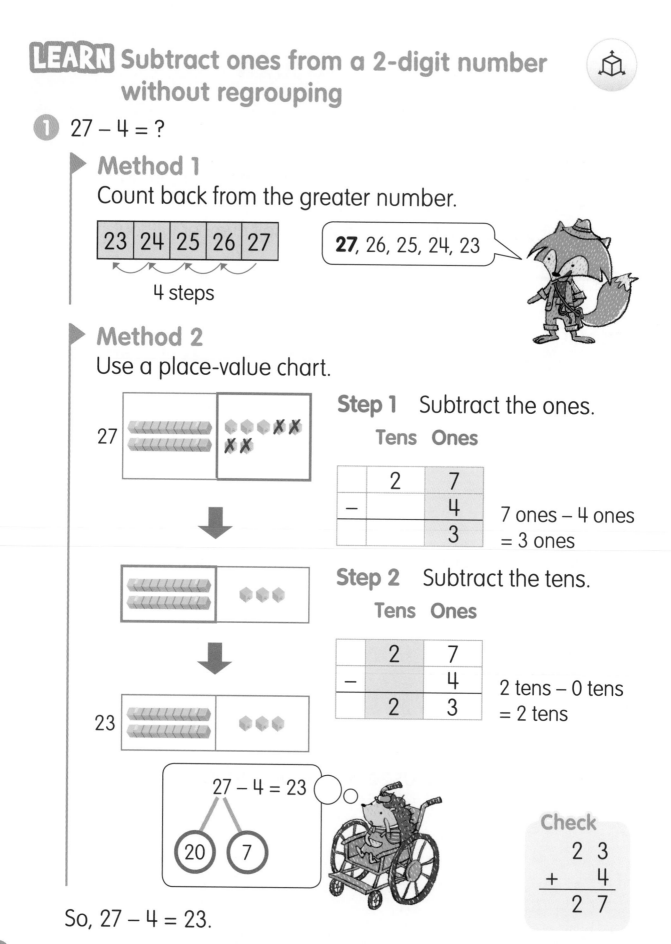

27

Step 1 Subtract the ones.

Tens	Ones
2	7
–	4
	3

7 ones – 4 ones
= 3 ones

Step 2 Subtract the tens.

Tens	Ones
2	7
–	4
2	3

2 tens – 0 tens
= 2 tens

23

27 – 4 = 23

20   7

Check

```
  2 3
+   4
  2 7
```

So, 27 – 4 = 23.

TRY Practice subtracting ones from a 2-digit number without regrouping

Subtract.

1 36 − 3 = ?

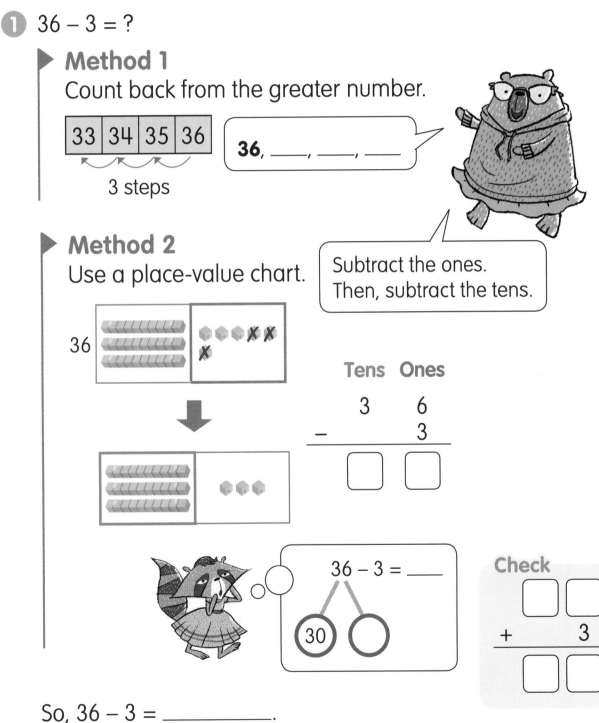

▶ **Method 1**
Count back from the greater number.

| 33 | 34 | 35 | 36 |

3 steps

36, _____, _____, _____

▶ **Method 2**
Use a place-value chart.

Subtract the ones.
Then, subtract the tens.

36

Tens   Ones
  3   6
−   3
 ☐   ☐

36 − 3 = _____
(30)   ( )

Check
☐ ☐
+   3
☐ ☐

So, 36 − 3 = _____.

2 37 − 2 = _____

ENGAGE

Count back by 10s from 40.

40, ..., _____, ..., _____, ..., _____

How is counting back a way of thinking about subtraction?
Share your thinking with your partner.

LEARN Subtract tens from a 2-digit number

1 30 – 10 = ?

▶ **Method 1**
Count back by tens from 30.

30, ..., 20

▶ **Method 2**
Use a place-value chart.

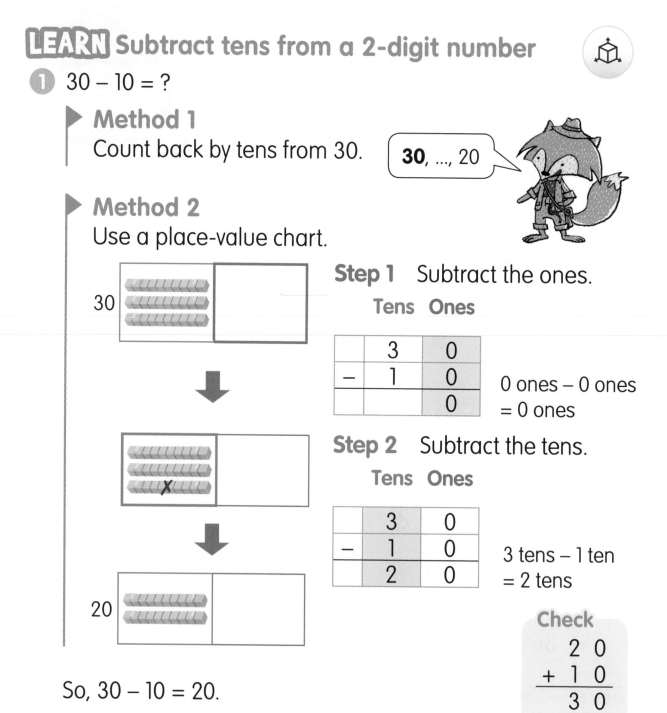

Step 1 Subtract the ones.

Tens	Ones
3	0
– 1	0
	0

0 ones – 0 ones
= 0 ones

Step 2 Subtract the tens.

Tens	Ones
3	0
– 1	0
2	0

3 tens – 1 ten
= 2 tens

Check

```
   2 0
 + 1 0
 ─────
   3 0
```

So, 30 – 10 = 20.

2 34 − 20 = ?

▶ **Method 1**
Count back by tens from 34.

34, ..., 24, ..., 14

▶ **Method 2**
Use a place-value chart.

34

Step 1 Subtract the ones.

Tens	Ones
3	4
− 2	0
	4

4 ones − 0 ones
= 4 ones

Step 2 Subtract the tens.

Tens	Ones
3	4
− 2	0
1	4

3 tens − 2 tens
= 1 ten

14

34   −   20

(30) (4) (20) (0)

4 − 0 = 4
30 − 20 = 10
10 + 4 = 14

Check

```
  1 4
+ 2 0
  3 4
```

So, 34 − 20 = 14.

© 2020 Marshall Cavendish Education Pte Ltd

TRY Practice subtracting tens from a 2-digit number

Subtract.

1 30 − 20 = ?

> ▶ **Method 1**
> Count back by tens from 30.

30, ..., _____, ..., _____

> ▶ **Method 2**
> Use a place-value chart.

Subtract the ones.
Then, subtract the tens.

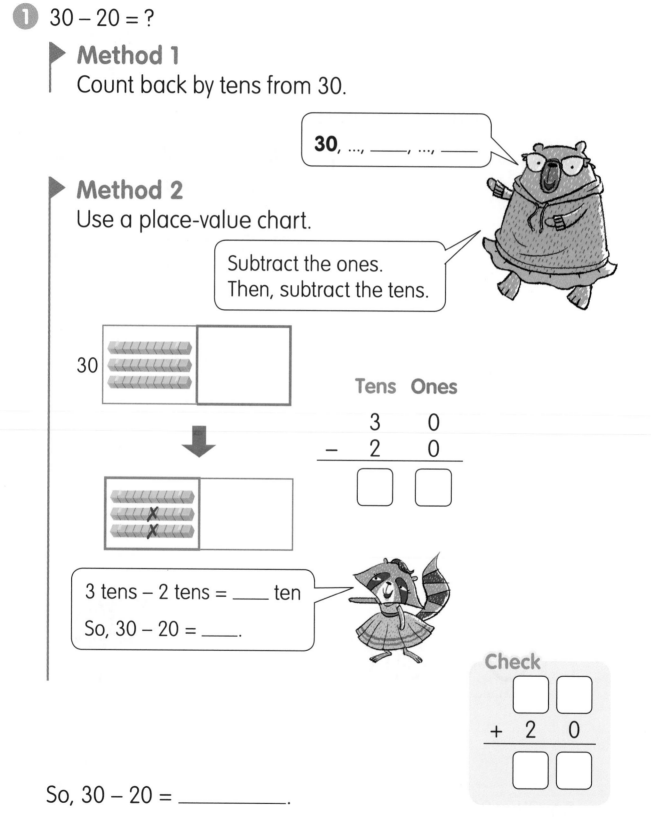

30

Tens	Ones
3	0
− 2	0
☐	☐

3 tens − 2 tens = _____ ten

So, 30 − 20 = _____.

Check

	☐	☐
+	2	0
	☐	☐

So, 30 − 20 = _____.

2 35 – 20 = ?

▶ **Method 1**
Count back by tens from 35.

35, ..., _____, ..., _____

▶ **Method 2**
Use a place-value chart.

First, subtract the ones.
Then, subtract the tens.

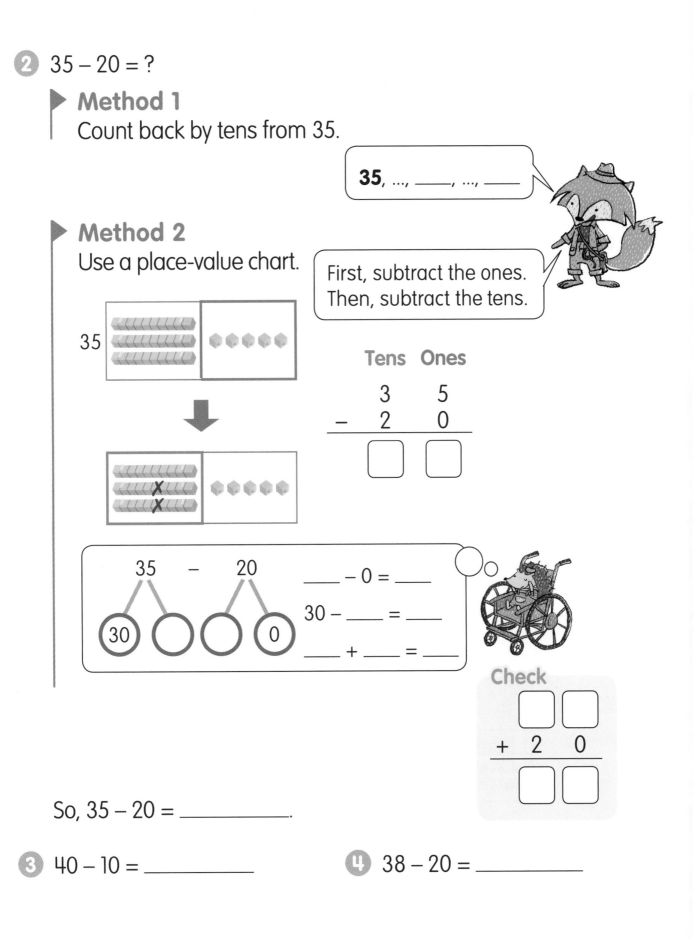

35

	Tens	Ones
	3	5
–	2	0
	☐	☐

35 – 20

(30) ( ) ( ) (0)

_____ – 0 = _____

30 – _____ = _____

_____ + _____ = _____

Check

	☐	☐
+	2	0
	☐	☐

So, 35 – 20 = _____.

3 40 – 10 = _____

4 38 – 20 = _____

ENGAGE

For **a** to **c**, place 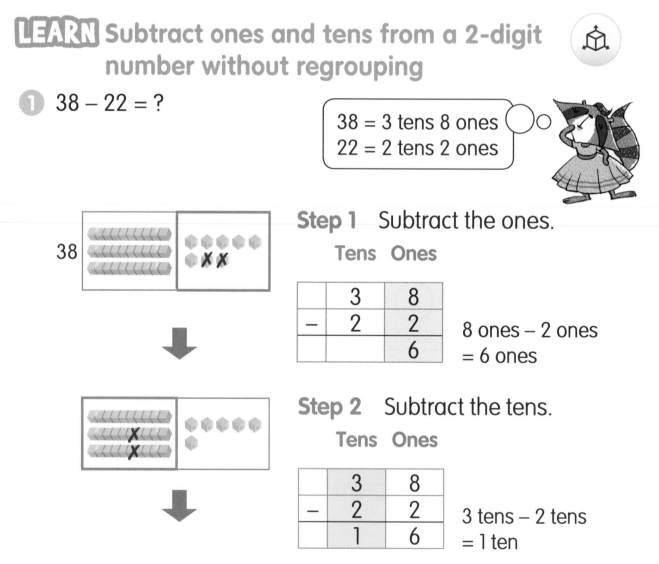 on a place-value chart to show 35. Then,

a   show how you would subtract 3 in two different ways.

b   show how you would subtract 20 in two different ways.

c   show how you would subtract 23.

Talk about the steps you took from **a** to **c** with your partner.

LEARN Subtract ones and tens from a 2-digit number without regrouping

① 38 – 22 = ?

38 = 3 tens 8 ones
22 = 2 tens 2 ones

38

Step 1   Subtract the ones.

Tens   Ones

	Tens	Ones
	3	8
–	2	2
		6

8 ones – 2 ones
= 6 ones

Step 2   Subtract the tens.

Tens   Ones

	Tens	Ones
	3	8
–	2	2
	1	6

3 tens – 2 tens
= 1 ten

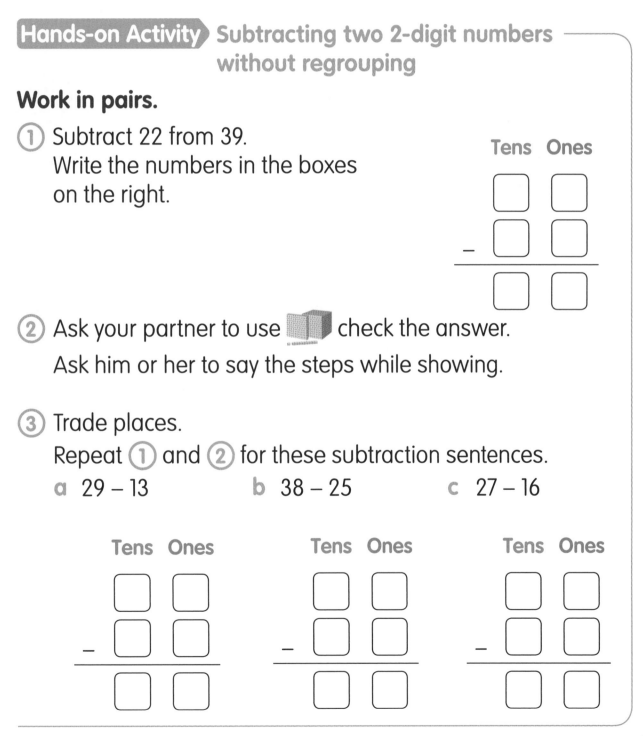

16

So, 38 − 22 = 16.

Check

```
    1 6
  + 2 2
    3 8
```

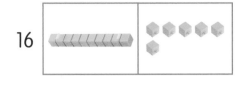 Subtracting two 2-digit numbers without regrouping

Work in pairs.

① Subtract 22 from 39.
Write the numbers in the boxes
on the right.

Tens   Ones

② Ask your partner to use 🧊 check the answer.
Ask him or her to say the steps while showing.

③ Trade places.
Repeat ① and ② for these subtraction sentences.

a 29 − 13   b 38 − 25   c 27 − 16

Tens   Ones   Tens   Ones   Tens   Ones

TRY Practice subtracting ones and tens from a 2-digit number without regrouping

Subtract.

① 39 – 24 = ?

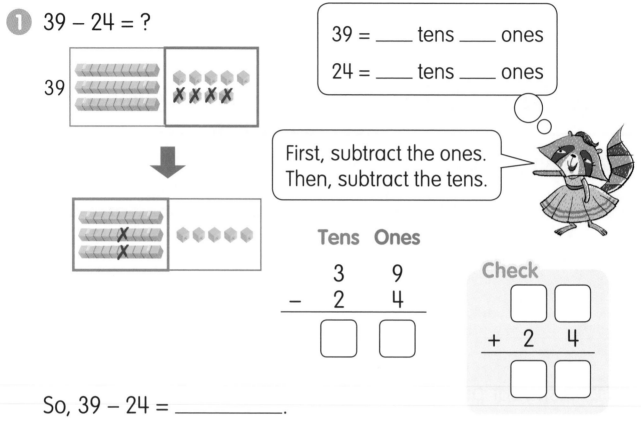

39 = ____ tens ____ ones

24 = ____ tens ____ ones

First, subtract the ones.
Then, subtract the tens.

Tens	Ones
3	9
– 2	4
☐	☐

Check

☐	☐
+ 2	4
☐	☐

So, 39 – 24 = _____.

② 36 – 12 = _____

Tens	Ones
3	6
– 1	2
☐	☐

Check

☐	☐
+ 1	2
☐	☐

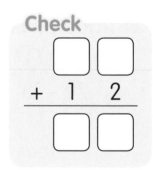

INDEPENDENT PRACTICE

Subtract.
Count back from the greater number.
Draw arrows to help you.

1 25 – 3 = _____

21	22	23	24	25

2 29 – 2 = _____

26	27	28	29

3 33 – 3 = _____

29	30	31	32	33

4 40 – 4 = _____

35	36	37	38	39	40

Write each missing number.

5   28 – 3 = _____

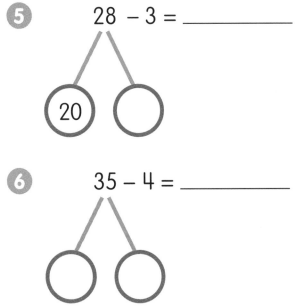

6   35 – 4 = _____

Count back by 10s to subtract.

7 40 − 20 = _____

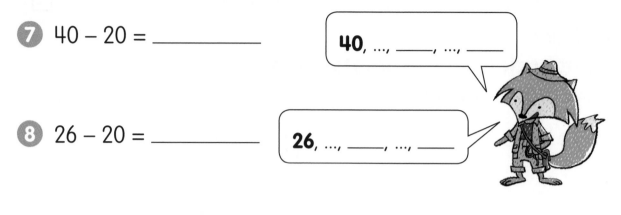

40, ..., _____, ..., _____

8 26 − 20 = _____

26, ..., _____, ..., _____

9 34 − 10 = _____

10 37 − 30 = _____

Subtract.
Show how you check your work.

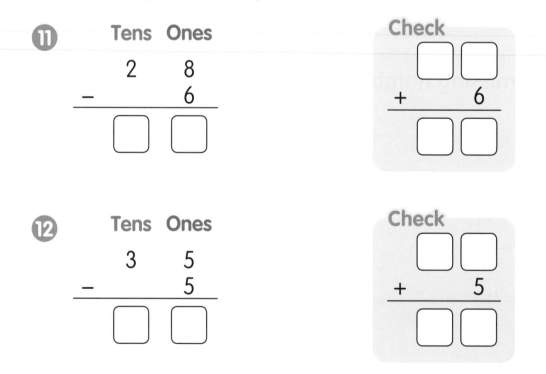

11

Tens	Ones
2	8
−	6
⬚	⬚

Check

⬚	⬚
+	6
⬚	⬚

12

Tens	Ones
3	5
−	5
⬚	⬚

Check

⬚	⬚
+	5
⬚	⬚

13

Tens	Ones
3	1
− 2	0

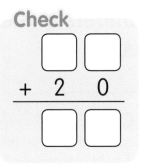

Check

+ 2	0

14

Tens	Ones
3	2
− 2	0

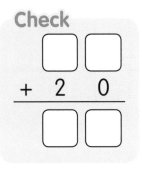

Check

+ 2	0

15

Tens	Ones
2	8
− 1	7

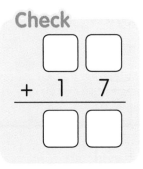

Check

+ 1	7

16

Tens	Ones
3	6
− 1	1

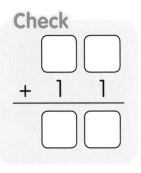

Check

+ 1	1

17

Tens	Ones
3	7
− 1	7

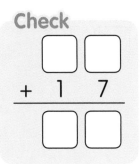

Check

+ 1	7

Write the numbers in the boxes.
Then, subtract.

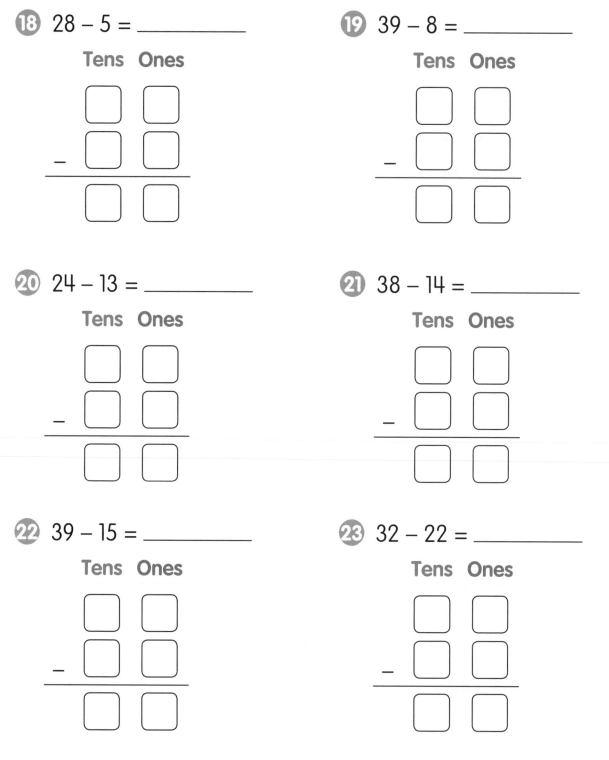

18 28 – 5 = _____

Tens Ones

19 39 – 8 = _____

Tens Ones

20 24 – 13 = _____

Tens Ones

21 38 – 14 = _____

Tens Ones

22 39 – 15 = _____

Tens Ones

23 32 – 22 = _____

Tens Ones

4 Subtraction With Regrouping

Learning Objectives:
- Regroup tens into tens and ones.
- Subtract ones from a 2-digit number with regrouping.
- Subtract ones and tens from a 2-digit number with regrouping.

THINK

Find each missing digit.

	Tens	Ones
	4	0
−	☐	☐
	1	2

Talk about how you find the answers with your partner.

ENGAGE

Make these number trains.

Move the 🧊 between the trains, so that only two trains are left.

One of the trains has only ten 🧊.

How many 🧊 does the other train have?

Share how you do it with your partner.

LEARN Regroup tens into tens and ones

① You can regroup the tens in a number into tens and ones.
26 = 2 tens 6 ones

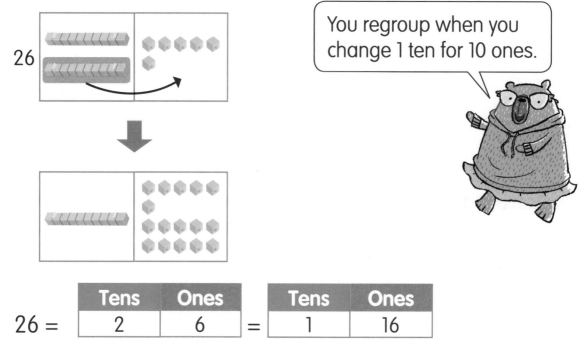

> You regroup when you change 1 ten for 10 ones.

	Tens	Ones		Tens	Ones
26 =	2	6	=	1	16

26 is the same as 1 ten 16 ones.

Hands-on Activity Regrouping tens into tens and ones

Take a 🎲, some 🟦, and a place-value chart.

① Start with four ▭ on your place-value chart.

② Trade one ▭ for 10 ◻.

③ Roll the 🎲.

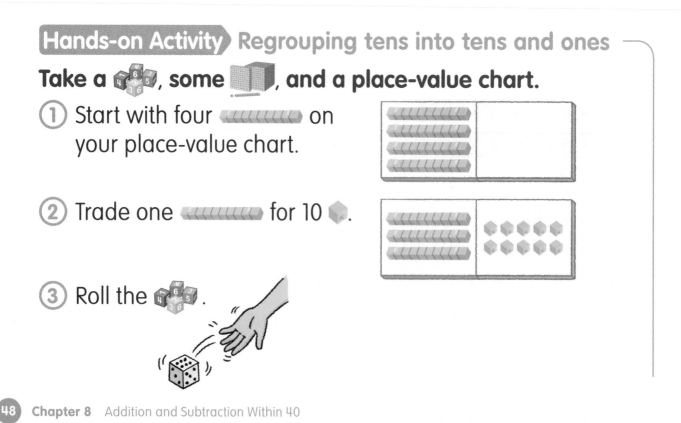

④ Take away this number of 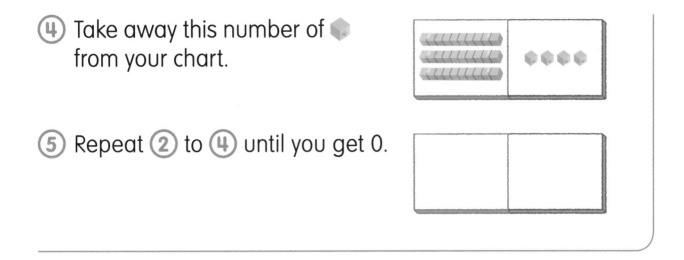 from your chart.

⑤ Repeat ② to ④ until you get 0.

TRY Practice regrouping tens into tens and ones

Regroup the tens and ones.
Then, complete the place-value chart.

① 25 = 1 ten ____?____ ones

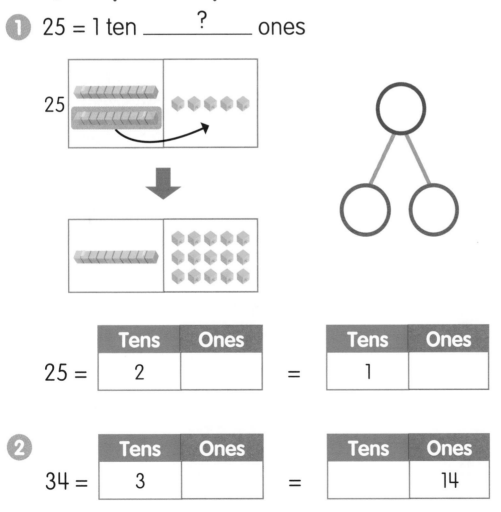

Tens	Ones
2	

=

Tens	Ones
1	

25 =

② 34 =

Tens	Ones
3	

=

Tens	Ones
	14

ENGAGE

Make three towers of 10 on the tens place of a place-value chart.

Next, make a tower of 4 cubes on the ones place of the same place-value chart.

Rearrange the ![] to show how you take away 8 ![]. Share how you did it with your partner.

LEARN Subtract ones from a 2-digit number with regrouping

① 32 − 9 = ?

You cannot take away 9 ones from 2 ones. So, you need to regroup.

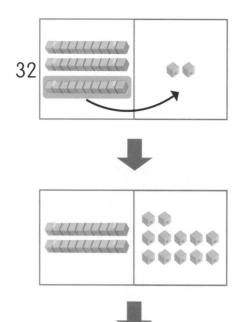

32

Step 1 Regroup the tens and ones.

Regroup the tens in 32.

32 = 3 tens 2 ones

= 2 tens 12 ones

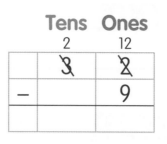

Tens	Ones
2	12
3̶	2̶
−	9

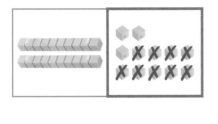

Step 2 Subtract the ones.

	Tens	Ones
	2	12
	~~3~~	~~2~~
−		9
		3

12 ones − 9 ones = 3 ones

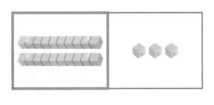

Step 3 Subtract the tens.

	Tens	Ones
	2	12
	~~3~~	~~2~~
−		9
	2	3

2 tens − 0 tens = 2 tens

So, 32 − 9 = 23.

Check

```
   2 3
 +   9
 ─────
   3 2
```

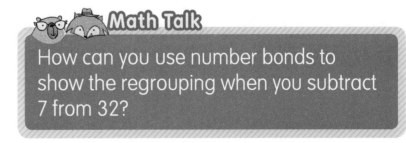

Math Talk

How can you use number bonds to show the regrouping when you subtract 7 from 32?

TRY Practice subtracting ones from a 2-digit number with regrouping

Regroup and subtract.

1 26 − 7 = ?

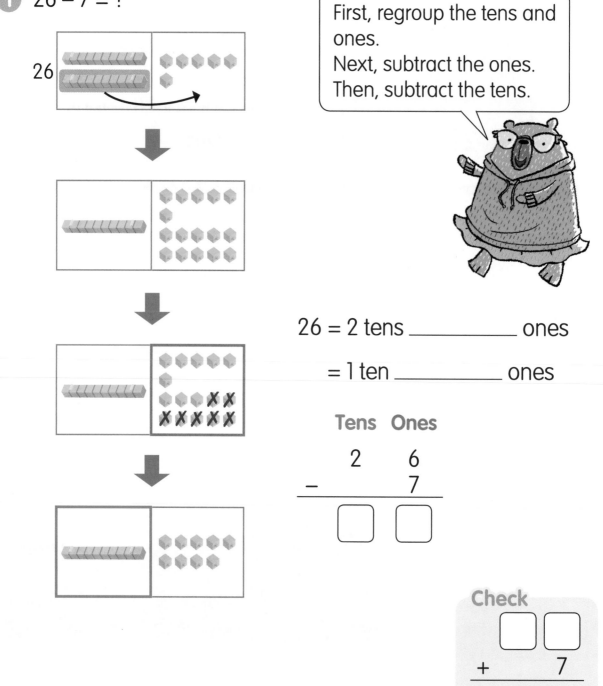

First, regroup the tens and ones.
Next, subtract the ones.
Then, subtract the tens.

26 = 2 tens _____ ones

   = 1 ten _____ ones

Tens	Ones
2	6
−	7
☐	☐

So, 26 − 7 = _____.

Check

☐	☐
+	7
☐	☐

2 34 − 8 = ?

Tens Ones

	3	4
−		8
	☐	☐

34 = 3 tens ___ ones

= 2 tens ___ ones

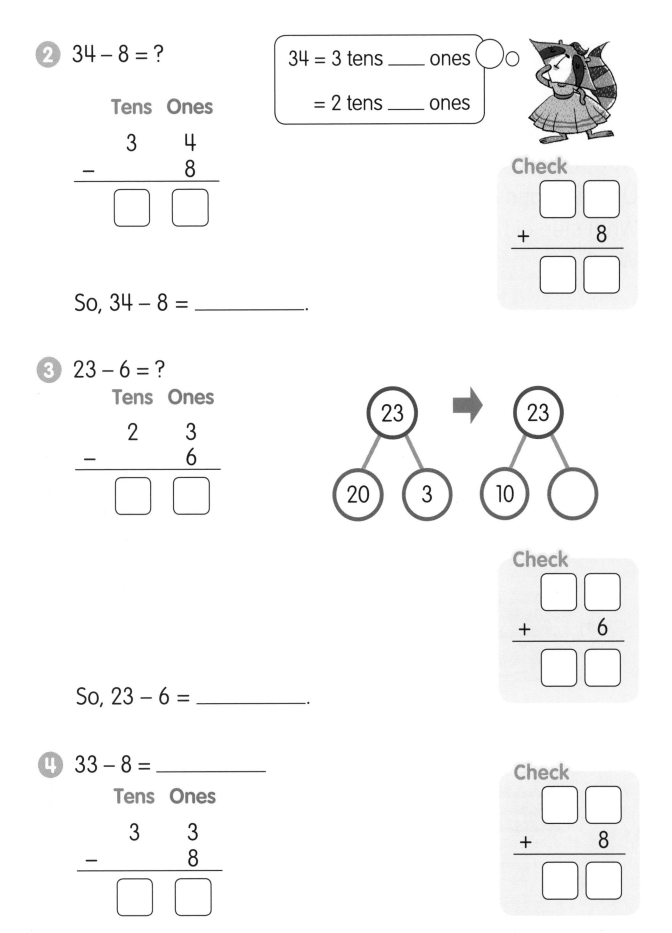

Check

	☐	☐
+		8
	☐	☐

So, 34 − 8 = _____ .

3 23 − 6 = ?

Tens Ones

	2	3
−		6
	☐	☐

23 → 23

20   3   10   ◯

Check

	☐	☐
+		6
	☐	☐

So, 23 − 6 = _____ .

4 33 − 8 = _____

Tens Ones

	3	3
−		8
	☐	☐

Check

	☐	☐
+		8
	☐	☐

ENGAGE

Franco has 40 building blocks.

He gives 18 to Aubree.

How many blocks does Franco have left?

Use 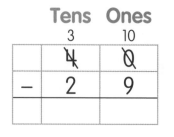 and a place-value chart to show your steps.

What step did you do first?

Why?

LEARN Subtract ones and tens from a 2-digit number with regrouping

1. 40 − 29 = ?

> You cannot take away 9 ones from 0 ones.
> So, you need to regroup.

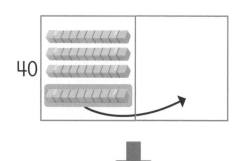

40

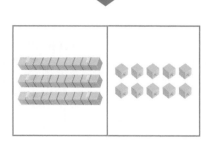

Step 1 Regroup the tens and ones.

Regroup the tens in 40.

40 = 4 tens 0 ones

= 3 tens 10 ones

Tens	Ones
₃4	₁₀0
− 2	9

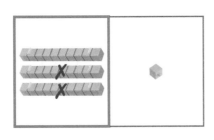

Step 2   Subtract the ones.

	Tens	Ones
	3	10
	4̶	0̶
−		9
		1

10 ones − 9 ones = 1 one

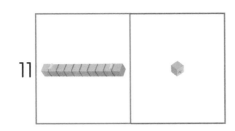

Step 3   Subtract the tens.

	Tens	Ones
	3	10
	4̶	0̶
−	2	9
	1	1

3 tens − 2 tens = 1 ten

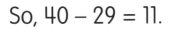

So, 40 − 29 = 11.

Check

```
    1 1
 +  2 9
 ─────
    4 0
```

Math Talk

Talk about how you can use number bonds to help you solve 40 − 28.

Subtracting two 2-digit numbers with regrouping

Work in pairs.

① Subtract 14 from 31.
Write the numbers in the boxes on the right.

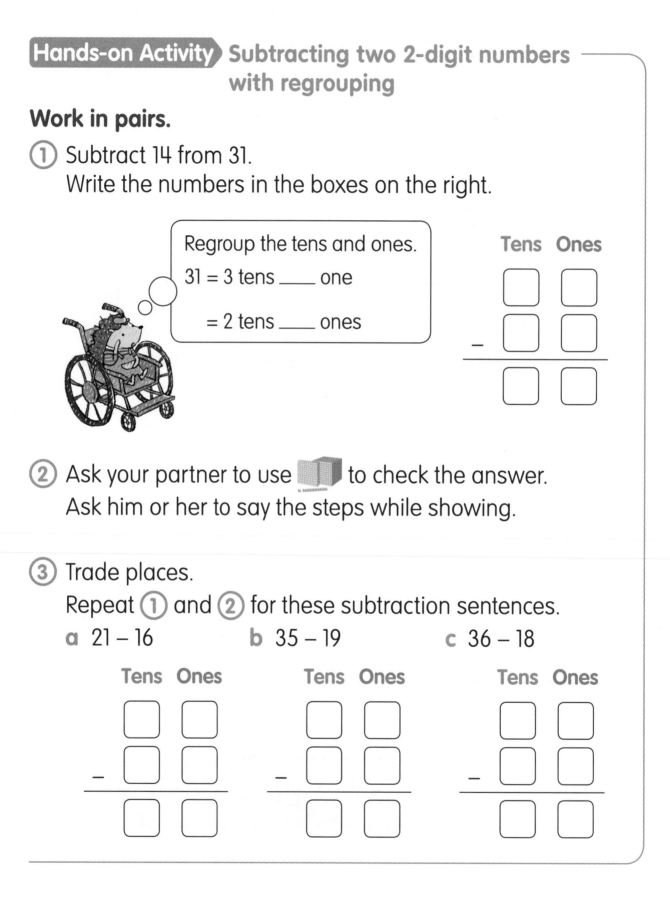

Regroup the tens and ones.

31 = 3 tens ___ one

= 2 tens ___ ones

Tens   Ones

② Ask your partner to use ▨ to check the answer.
Ask him or her to say the steps while showing.

③ Trade places.
Repeat ① and ② for these subtraction sentences.

a 21 − 16   b 35 − 19   c 36 − 18

Tens   Ones   Tens   Ones   Tens   Ones

TRY Practice subtracting ones and tens from a 2-digit number with regrouping

Regroup and subtract.

1 34 − 15 = ?

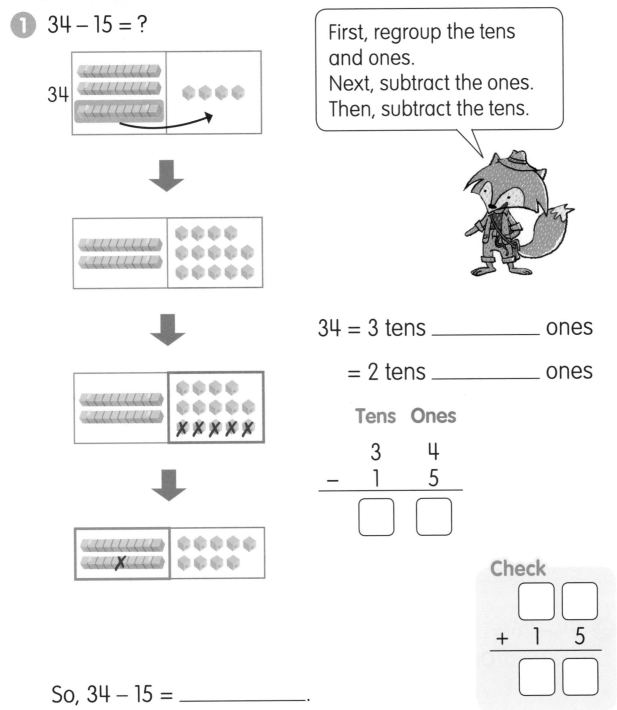

First, regroup the tens and ones.
Next, subtract the ones.
Then, subtract the tens.

34 = 3 tens _____ ones

= 2 tens _____ ones

Tens	Ones
3	4
− 1	5
☐	☐

Check

☐	☐
+ 1	5
☐	☐

So, 34 − 15 = _____.

2 35 − 28 = ?

	Tens	Ones
	3	5
−	2	8
	☐	☐

35 = 3 tens ____ ones

= 2 tens ____ ones

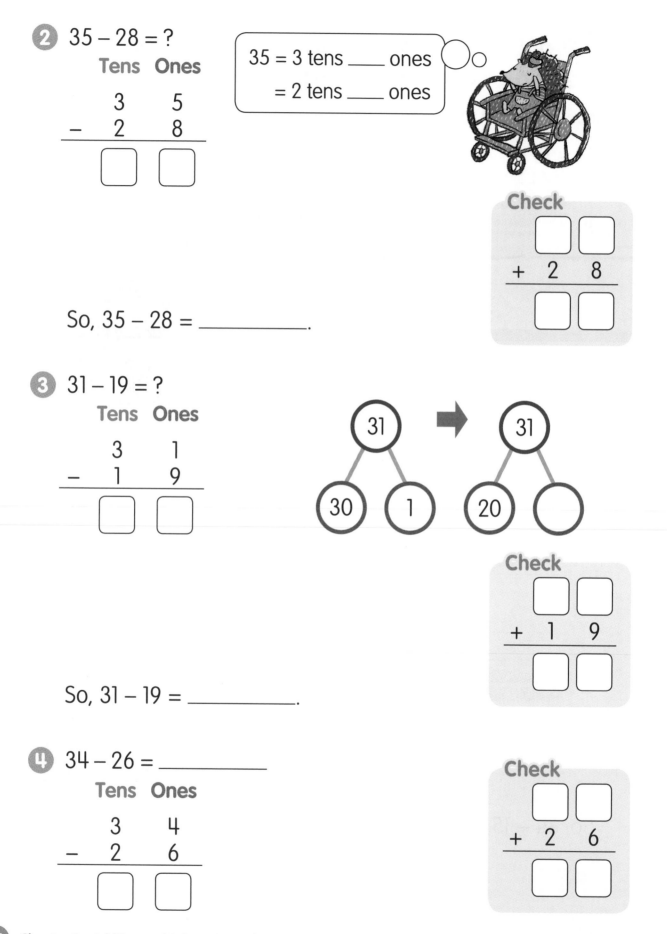

Check

	☐	☐
+	2	8
	☐	☐

So, 35 − 28 = _____.

3 31 − 19 = ?

	Tens	Ones
	3	1
−	1	9
	☐	☐

Check

	☐	☐
+	1	9
	☐	☐

So, 31 − 19 = _____.

4 34 − 26 = _____

	Tens	Ones
	3	4
−	2	6
	☐	☐

Check

	☐	☐
+	2	6
	☐	☐

INDEPENDENT PRACTICE

Regroup.

1

28 =

Tens	Ones
2	

=

Tens	Ones
1	

2

30 =

Tens	Ones
	0

=

Tens	Ones
2	

Regroup and subtract.

3

Tens	Ones
2	4
−	7

◯ ◯

4

Tens	Ones
2	7
−	9

◯ ◯

5

Tens	Ones
3	6
− 2	8

◯ ◯

6

Tens	Ones
2	3
− 1	4

◯ ◯

7

Tens	Ones
3	5
− 1	6

◯ ◯

8

Tens	Ones
4	0
− 2	5

◯ ◯

Luke is at a funfair.
He wants to win a prize.
Which pegs does Luke aim for?
Circle these pegs.

WIN A PRIZE!
Which boards have answers between 15 and 25? Throw rings onto these pegs to win!

9

$30 - 6 =$ _____
Tens Ones

$35 - 9 =$ _____
Tens Ones

$40 - 19 =$ _____
Tens Ones

$30 - 17 =$ _____
Tens Ones

$33 - 19 =$ _____
Tens Ones

$32 - 16 =$ _____
Tens Ones

5 Real-World Problems: Addition and Subtraction

Learning Objectives:
- Solve real-world problems involving addition and subtraction.
- Use related addition and subtraction facts to check answers to real-world problems.
- Solve real-world problems involving the addition of three whole numbers whose sum is less than or equal to 20.

THINK

Luis has some crayons.
He has 3 fewer crayons than Kate.
Both children have 27 crayons in all.
How many crayons does Kate have?
Talk about how you find the answer with your partner.

ENGAGE

Luna has 14 books.
She has 2 more books than Carson.
How many books does Carson have?
Use 🎲 to show the number of books each child has.

LEARN Solve real-world problems involving addition

1. Molly has 15 books.
James has 3 more books than Molly.
How many books does James have?

STEP 1 Understand the problem.

> How many books does Molly have?
> Who has more books?
> What do I need to find?

STEP 2 Think of a plan.
I can use 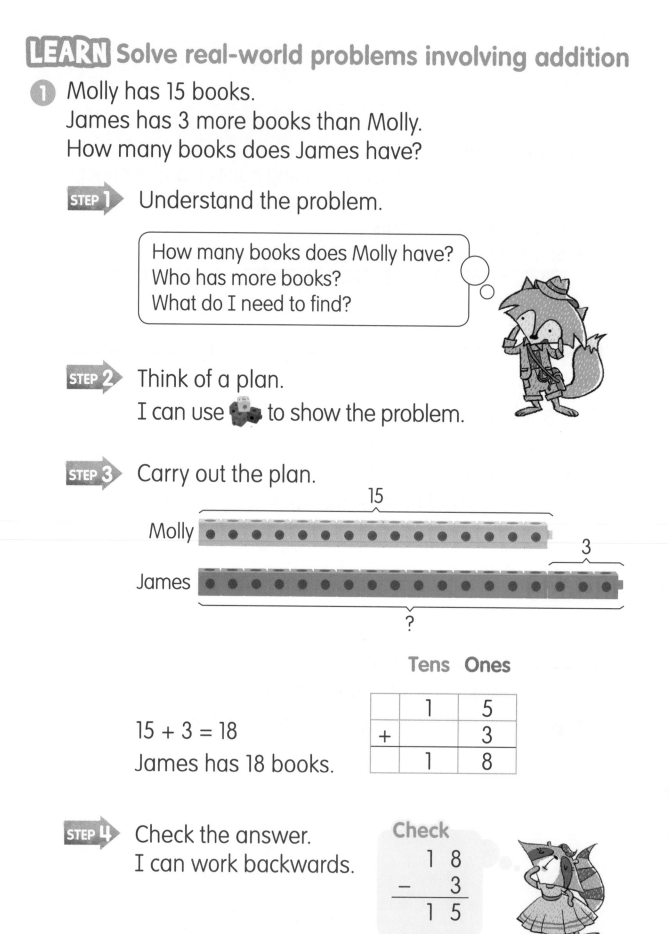 to show the problem.

STEP 3 Carry out the plan.

15

Molly

3

James

?

Tens Ones

	Tens	Ones
	1	5
+		3
	1	8

15 + 3 = 18
James has 18 books.

STEP 4 Check the answer.
I can work backwards.

Check
```
  1 8
-   3
-----
  1 5
```

© 2020 Marshall Cavendish Education Pte Ltd

Work in pairs.

Take some 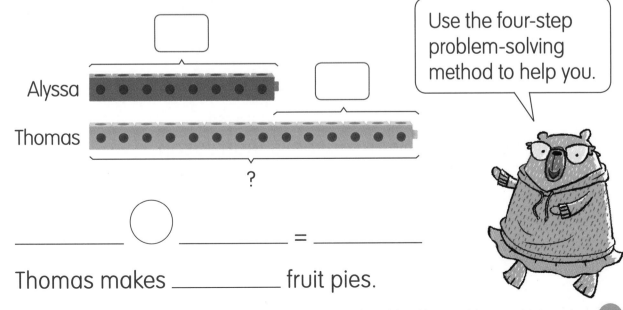.

① Make an addition story.
Use **more** in your story.

② **Mathematical Habit 4** Use mathematical models
Ask your partner to use 🎲 to show the problem.
Then, ask him or her to write the addition sentence.

③ Trade places.
Repeat ① and ②.

TRY Practice solving real-world problems involving addition

Solve.

① Alyssa makes 8 fruit pies.
Thomas makes 6 more fruit pies than Alyssa.
How many fruit pies does Thomas make?

Use the four-step problem-solving method to help you.

Alyssa

Thomas

?

_____ ◯ _____ = _____

Thomas makes _____ fruit pies.

ENGAGE

Rodrigo has 13 stickers.

Ava has 10 stickers.

How many fewer stickers does Ava have than Rodrigo?

Use 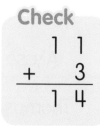 to show the number of stickers each child has.

LEARN Solve real-world problems involving subtraction

1 Jason picks 14 seashells.
Amy picks 11 seashells.
How many fewer seashells does Amy pick than Jason?

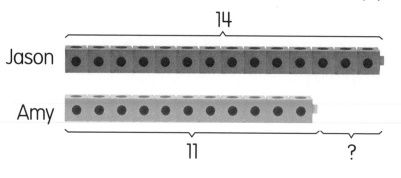

$14 - 11 = 3$

	Tens	Ones
	1	4
−	1	1
		3

Check

```
  1 1
+   3
-----
  1 4
```

Amy picks 3 fewer seashells than Jason.

2 Ellie bakes 19 loaves of bread.
Owen bakes 7 fewer loaves than Ellie.
How many loaves of bread does Owen bake?

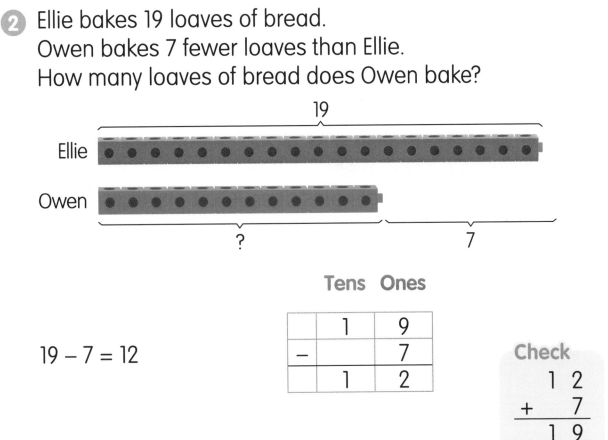

	Tens	Ones
	1	9
−		7
	1	2

$19 - 7 = 12$

Check

```
  1 2
+   7
-----
  1 9
```

Owen bakes 12 loaves of bread.

Hands-on Activity Making subtraction stories

Work in pairs.

Take some 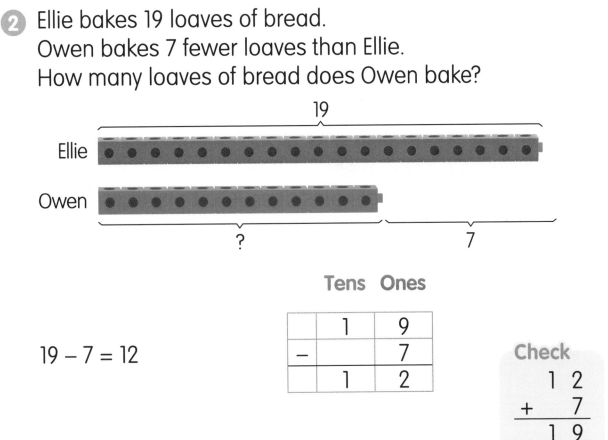.

① Make a subtraction story.
Use **more** or **fewer** in your story.

② **Mathematical Habit 4** Use mathematical models

Ask your partner to use to show the problem.
Then, ask him or her to write the subtraction sentence.

③ Trade places.
Repeat ① and ②.

TRY Practice solving real-world problems involving subtraction

Solve.

1 Ravi bakes 20 apple pies.
Julia bakes 6 apple pies.
How many fewer apple pies does Julia bake than Ravi?

Ravi

Julia

?

_____ ◯ _____ = _____

Julia bakes _____ fewer apple pies than Ravi.

2 Ella has 16 fish.
Pedro has 7 fewer fish than Ella.
How many fish does Pedro have?

Ella

Pedro

?

_____ ◯ _____ = _____

Pedro has _____ fish.

ENGAGE

Stella has 4 red beads, 6 blue beads, and 5 green beads.

Use 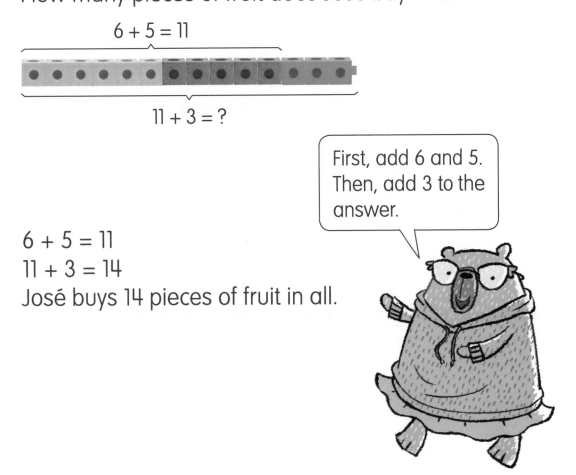 to show the number of beads for each color.

Then, find the number of beads Stella has in all.

Talk about how you add the three numbers with your partner.

LEARN Solve real-world problems involving the addition of three numbers

1 José buys 6 oranges and 5 pears.
He also buys 3 apples.
How many pieces of fruit does José buy in all?

$$6 + 5 = 11$$

$$11 + 3 = ?$$

First, add 6 and 5.
Then, add 3 to the answer.

$6 + 5 = 11$
$11 + 3 = 14$
José buys 14 pieces of fruit in all.

Work in groups.

Take three 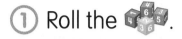 and some .

① Roll the .

② Use the numbers to make an addition story.

③ **Mathematical Habit 4** Use mathematical models
Ask your classmates to use to solve the problem.
Then, ask them to write the addition sentence.

④ Trade places.
Repeat ① to ③.

TRY Practice solving real-world problems involving the addition of three numbers

Solve.

① A pet store has 4 hamsters, 8 rabbits, and 6 cats.
How many pets are there in all?

$$4 + \boxed{} = \boxed{}$$

$$\boxed{} + 6 = ?$$

4 + _____ = _____

_____ + 6 = _____

There are _____ pets in all.

INDEPENDENT PRACTICE

Solve.

1 Jack picks 16 berries.
Leah picks 4 more berries than Jack.
How many berries does Leah pick?

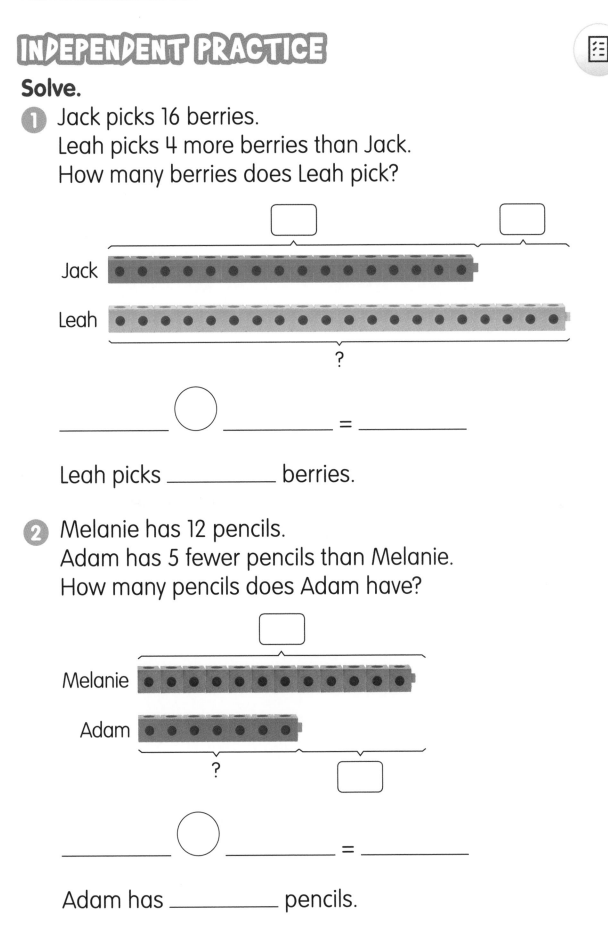

Jack

Leah

?

_____ ◯ _____ = _____

Leah picks _____ berries.

2 Melanie has 12 pencils.
Adam has 5 fewer pencils than Melanie.
How many pencils does Adam have?

Melanie

Adam

?

_____ ◯ _____ = _____

Adam has _____ pencils.

Ana paints 24 flowers.
Robert paints 9 fewer flowers than Ana.
How many flowers does Robert paint?

Robert paints _____ flowers.

4 There are 15 children in the gym.
There are 7 more children in the hall than in the gym.
How many children are there in the hall?

There are _____ children in the hall.

5 Ignacio has 19 toy cars.
Grace has 6 toy cars.
How many toy cars do they have in all?

They have _____ toy cars in all.

6 Angelia reads 12 pages of a book in the morning.
She then reads another 9 pages in the afternoon.
How many pages does Angelia read in all?

Angelia reads _____ pages in all.

7 Tyler buys 30 apples and oranges to make juice.
He buys 15 apples.
How many oranges does Tyler buy?

Tyler buys _____ oranges.

8 There are 24 people on a bus.
At a station, 7 people alighted.
How many people are there left on the bus?

There are _____ people left on the bus.

9 Nicole makes 29 paper boats.
Cotton makes 16 paper boats.
How many fewer paper boats does Cotton make than Nicole?

Cotton makes _____ fewer paper boats than Nicole.

10 Zane sews 25 buttons.
Jess sews 13 buttons.
Who sews more buttons?
How many more?

_____ sews _____ more buttons than _____.

11 June buys 6 erasers from a store.
She then buys another 4 erasers.
Mason buys 6 erasers.
How many erasers do they buy in all?

They buy _____ erasers in all.

12 Bruno makes 8 sandwiches.
Lily makes 5 sandwiches.
Maya makes 7 sandwiches.
How many sandwiches are there in all?

There are _____ sandwiches in all.

Getting Ready for Multiplication

Learning Objectives:
- Use objects or pictures to find the total number of objects in groups of the same size.
- Relate repeated addition to the concept of multiplication.

New Vocabulary
same
groups
rows

THINK

Ariana and Cole are doing an art project.
They paint each of their fingers using a different color.
How many colors do they use in all?

ENGAGE

a Hold up 2 fingers on each hand.
How many fingers are you holding up?
2 groups of 2 fingers is _____ fingers in all.

b Hold up 3 fingers on each hand.
How many fingers are you holding up?
2 groups of 3 fingers is _____ fingers in all.

c What pattern do you notice?
Share what you notice with your partner.

LEARN Add the same number

1

2 toys   2 toys   2 toys

There are 3 groups of toys.
Each group has two toys.

$$2 + 2 + 2 = 6$$
$$3 \text{ twos} = 6$$
$$3 \text{ groups of } 2 = 6$$

There are 6 toys in all.

> 2 + 2 + 2 means
> 3 twos or 3 groups of 2.

2

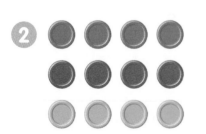

There are 3 rows of 🔵.
Each row has 4 🔵.

$$4 + 4 + 4 = 12$$
$$3 \text{ fours} = 12$$
$$3 \text{ rows of } 4 = 12$$

There are 12 🔵.

3 The picture shows 3 rows of 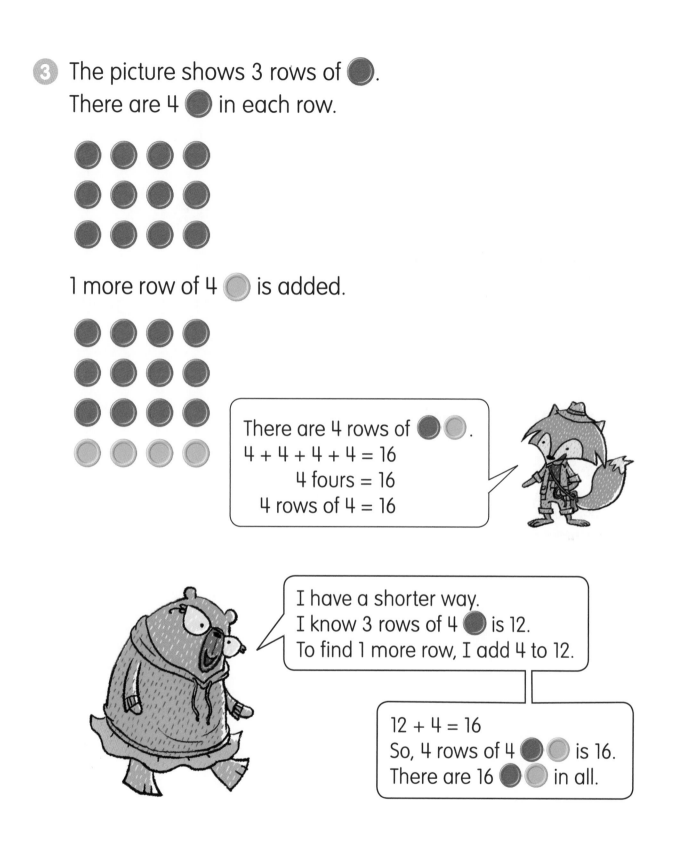.
There are 4 ⬤ in each row.

1 more row of 4 ⬤ is added.

There are 4 rows of ⬤⬤.
$4 + 4 + 4 + 4 = 16$
4 fours = 16
4 rows of 4 = 16

I have a shorter way.
I know 3 rows of 4 ⬤ is 12.
To find 1 more row, I add 4 to 12.

$12 + 4 = 16$
So, 4 rows of 4 ⬤⬤ is 16.
There are 16 ⬤⬤ in all.

Work in pairs.

① Take some 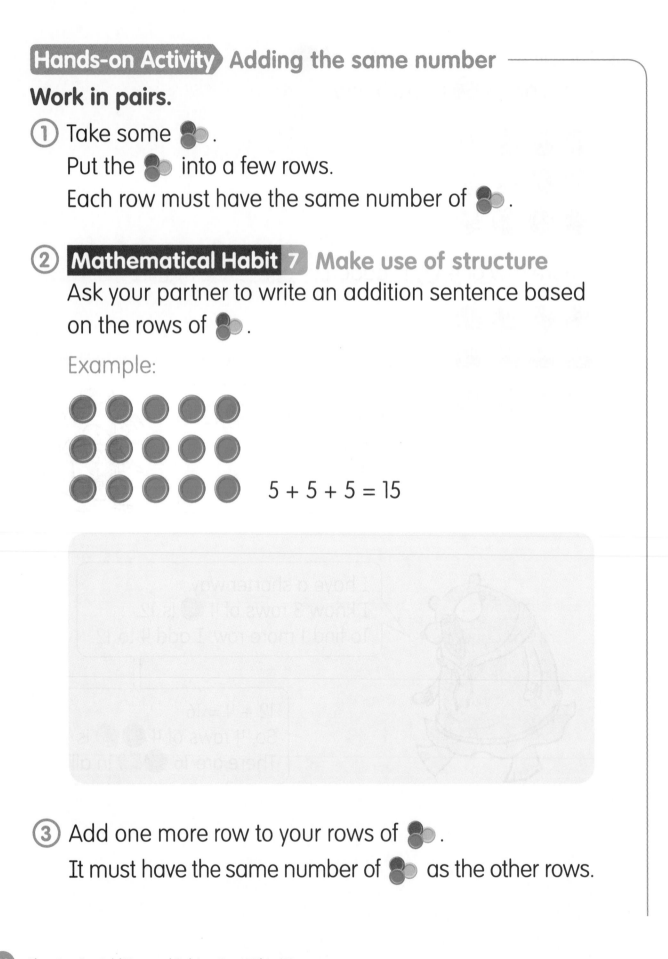.
Put the into a few rows.
Each row must have the same number of .

② **Mathematical Habit 7** Make use of structure
Ask your partner to write an addition sentence based
on the rows of .

Example:

$5 + 5 + 5 = 15$

③ Add one more row to your rows of .
It must have the same number of as the other rows.

④ **Mathematical Habit** 7 **Make use of structure**

Ask your partner to write another addition sentence about it.

Example:

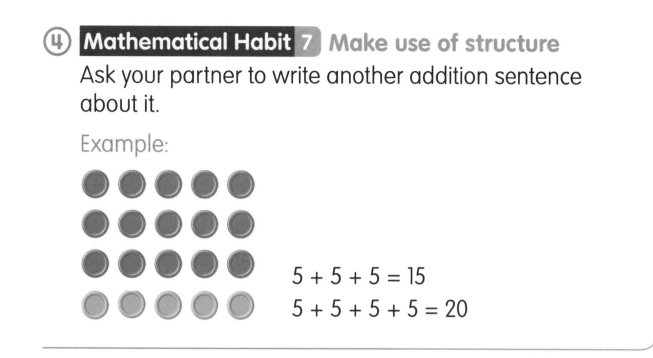

$5 + 5 + 5 = 15$

$5 + 5 + 5 + 5 = 20$

TRY Practice adding the same number

Fill in each blank.

1

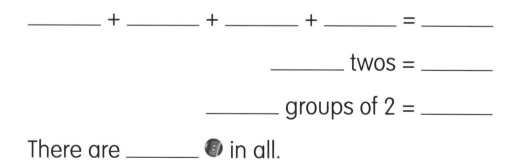

There are _____ groups.

Each group has _____ .

_____ + _____ + _____ + _____ = _____

_____ twos = _____

_____ groups of 2 = _____

There are _____ in all.

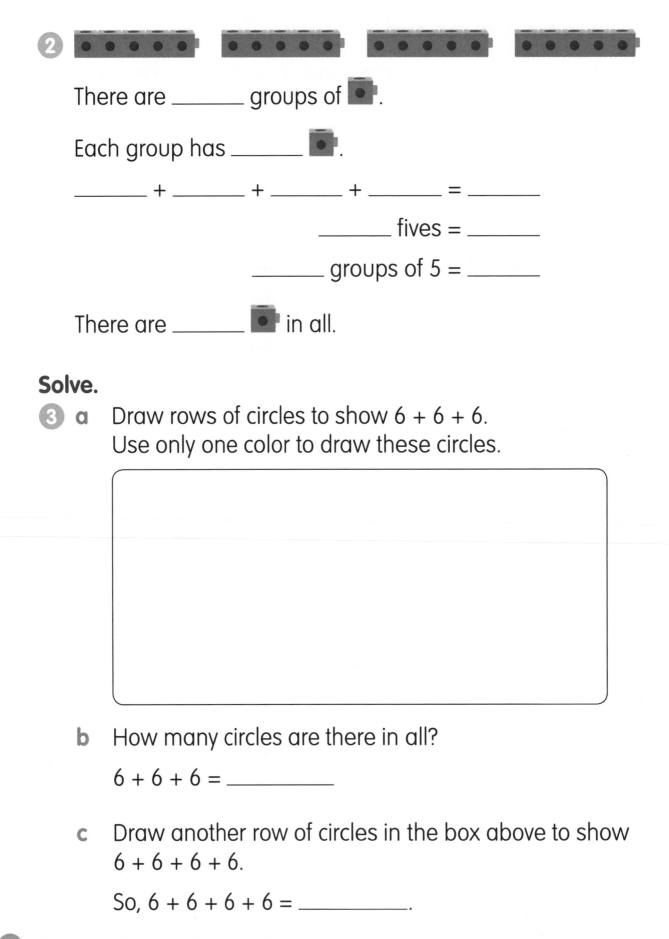

2

There are _____ groups of .

Each group has _____ .

_____ + _____ + _____ + _____ = _____

_____ fives = _____

_____ groups of 5 = _____

There are _____ in all.

Solve.

3 **a** Draw rows of circles to show 6 + 6 + 6.
Use only one color to draw these circles.

b How many circles are there in all?

6 + 6 + 6 = _____

c Draw another row of circles in the box above to show
6 + 6 + 6 + 6.

So, 6 + 6 + 6 + 6 = _____.

INDEPENDENT PRACTICE

Fill in each blank.

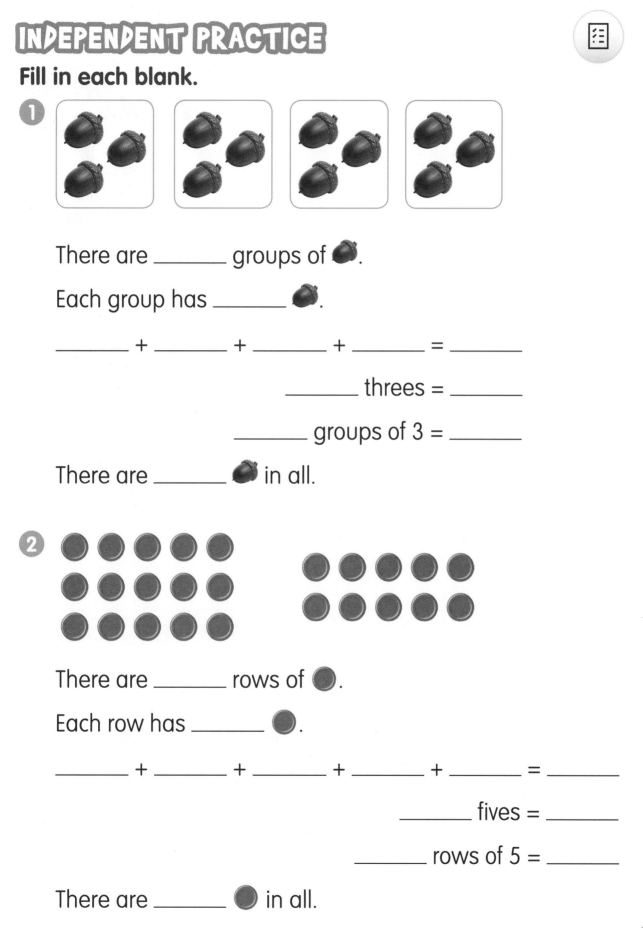

1

There are _____ groups of 🌰.

Each group has _____ 🌰.

_____ + _____ + _____ + _____ = _____

_____ threes = _____

_____ groups of 3 = _____

There are _____ 🌰 in all.

2

There are _____ rows of ⚫.

Each row has _____ ⚫.

_____ + _____ + _____ + _____ + _____ = _____

_____ fives = _____

_____ rows of 5 = _____

There are _____ ⚫ in all.

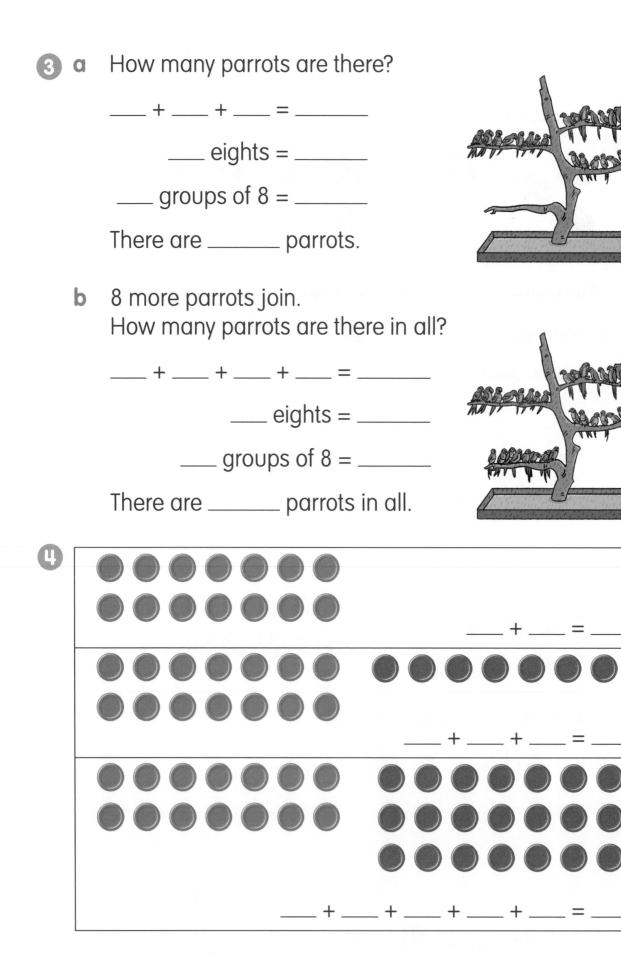

3 **a** How many parrots are there?

___ + ___ + ___ = _____

___ eights = _____

___ groups of 8 = _____

There are _____ parrots.

b 8 more parrots join.
How many parrots are there in all?

___ + ___ + ___ + ___ = _____

___ eights = _____

___ groups of 8 = _____

There are _____ parrots in all.

4

___ + ___ = ___

___ + ___ + ___ = ___

___ + ___ + ___ + ___ + ___ = ___

Name: _____ Date: _____

Mathematical Habit 2 **Use mathematical reasoning**

There are 17 books on Shelf A.
There are 15 more books on Shelf B than on Shelf A.
How many books are there on Shelf B?
Use these ways to solve this problem.

1 Draw pictures.

2 Write an addition sentence.   **3** Work it out.

Tens   Ones

☐   ☐

+   ☐   ☐

☐   ☐

There are _____ books on Shelf B.

Show how you check your answer.

Problem Solving with Heuristics

1 **Mathematical Habit** **1** Persevere in solving problems

a Pick any three numbers shown to complete each addition sentence.
Use a number only once for each sentence.

30   21   12   33   9

_____ + _____ = _____

_____ + _____ = _____

_____ + _____ = _____

_____ + _____ = _____

b Pick any three numbers shown to complete each subtraction sentence.
Use a number only once for each sentence.

9   18   28   19   37

_____ − _____ = _____

_____ − _____ = _____

_____ − _____ = _____

_____ − _____ = _____

② **Mathematical Habit 4** Use mathematical models

Charles has 16 bookmarks.
He has 8 fewer bookmarks than Lydia.
How many bookmarks do they have in all?

Use  to solve the problem.

They have _____ bookmarks in all.

How can you add and subtract two 2-digit numbers? What ways can you use?

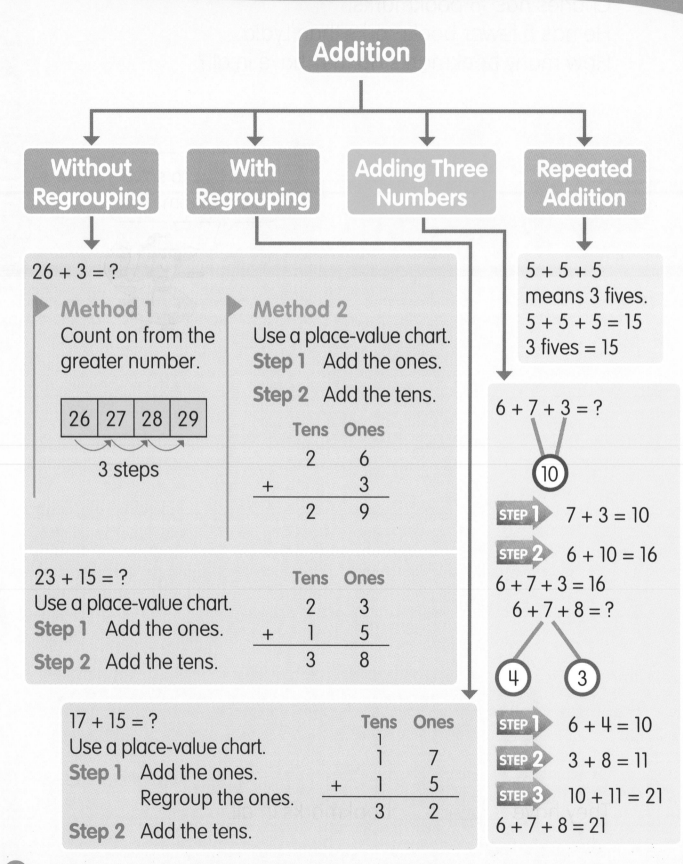

Addition

Without Regrouping

With Regrouping

Adding Three Numbers

Repeated Addition

$26 + 3 = ?$

▶ **Method 1**
Count on from the greater number.

| 26 | 27 | 28 | 29 |

3 steps

▶ **Method 2**
Use a place-value chart.
Step 1 Add the ones.
Step 2 Add the tens.

Tens	Ones
2	6
+	3
2	9

$23 + 15 = ?$
Use a place-value chart.
Step 1 Add the ones.
Step 2 Add the tens.

Tens	Ones
2	3
+ 1	5
3	8

$17 + 15 = ?$
Use a place-value chart.
Step 1 Add the ones.
Regroup the ones.
Step 2 Add the tens.

Tens	Ones
1	
1	7
+ 1	5
3	2

$5 + 5 + 5$ means 3 fives.
$5 + 5 + 5 = 15$
3 fives = 15

$6 + 7 + 3 = ?$

(10)

STEP 1 $7 + 3 = 10$
STEP 2 $6 + 10 = 16$
$6 + 7 + 3 = 16$

$6 + 7 + 8 = ?$

(4)   (3)

STEP 1 $6 + 4 = 10$
STEP 2 $3 + 8 = 11$
STEP 3 $10 + 11 = 21$
$6 + 7 + 8 = 21$

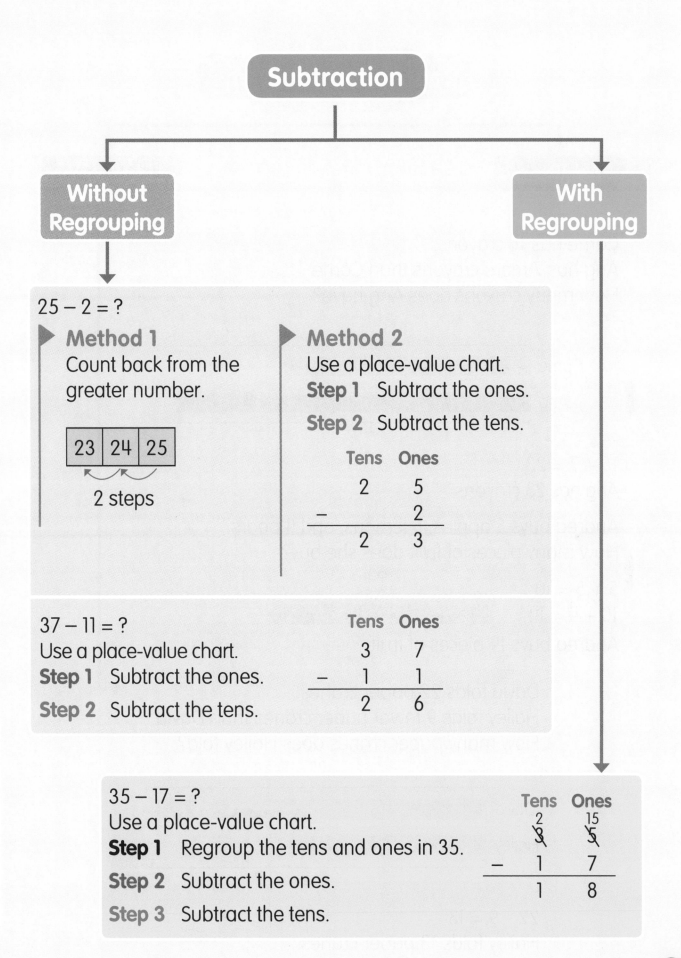

Subtraction

Without Regrouping

25 − 2 = ?

▶ **Method 1**
Count back from the greater number.

23	24	25

2 steps

▶ **Method 2**
Use a place-value chart.
Step 1   Subtract the ones.
Step 2   Subtract the tens.

Tens	Ones
2	5
−	2
2	3

37 − 11 = ?
Use a place-value chart.
Step 1   Subtract the ones.
Step 2   Subtract the tens.

Tens	Ones
3	7
− 1	1
2	6

With Regrouping

35 − 17 = ?
Use a place-value chart.
Step 1   Regroup the tens and ones in 35.
Step 2   Subtract the ones.
Step 3   Subtract the tens.

Tens	Ones
2	15
3̶	5̶
− 1	7
1	8

Real-World Problems

Addition

Subtraction

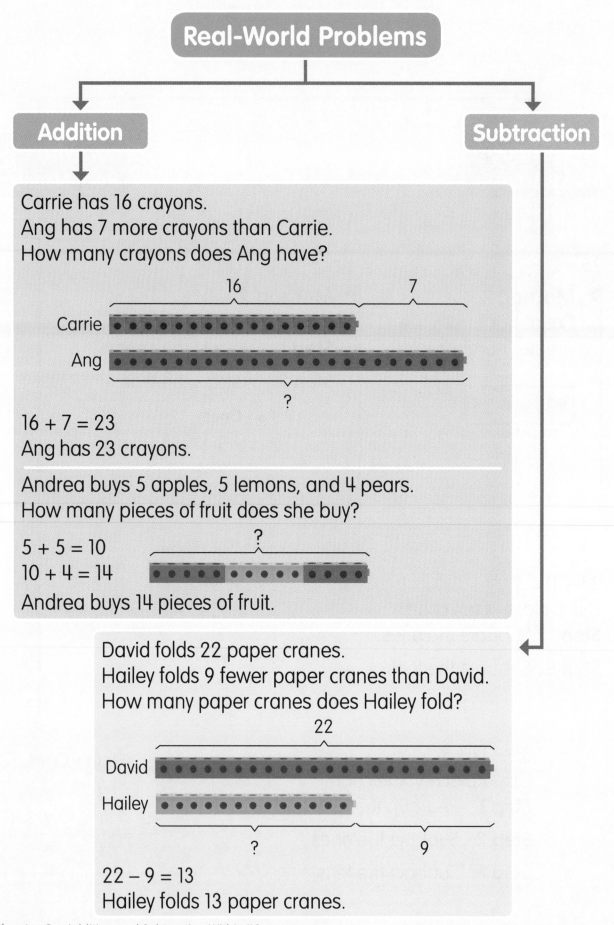

Carrie has 16 crayons.
Ang has 7 more crayons than Carrie.
How many crayons does Ang have?

16

7

Carrie

Ang

?

$16 + 7 = 23$
Ang has 23 crayons.

Andrea buys 5 apples, 5 lemons, and 4 pears.
How many pieces of fruit does she buy?

?

$5 + 5 = 10$
$10 + 4 = 14$
Andrea buys 14 pieces of fruit.

David folds 22 paper cranes.
Hailey folds 9 fewer paper cranes than David.
How many paper cranes does Hailey fold?

22

David

Hailey

?

9

$22 - 9 = 13$
Hailey folds 13 paper cranes.

Name: _____   Date: _____

Add.
Count on from the greater number.
Draw arrows to help you.

1 25 + 3 = _____

| 25 | 26 | 27 | 28 | 29 |

Add.

2 32 + 4 = _____

3 10 + 14 = _____

4 8 + 4 + 6 = _____

5 9 + 7 + 9 = _____

6

Tens	Ones
2	1
+	8
☐	☐

7

Tens	Ones
2	1
+ 1	3
☐	☐

8

Tens	Ones
2	6
+	9
☐	☐

9

Tens	Ones
2	8
+	8
☐	☐

10

Tens	Ones
1	3
+ 2	7
☐	☐

11

Tens	Ones
1	9
+ 1	4
☐	☐

Subtract.
Count back from the greater number.
Draw arrows to help you.

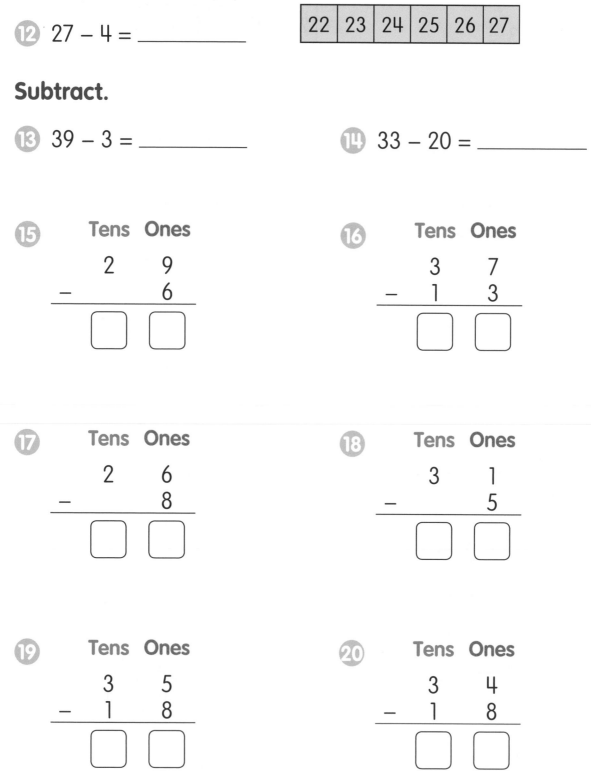

12 27 – 4 = _____

| 22 | 23 | 24 | 25 | 26 | 27 |

Subtract.

13 39 – 3 = _____   14 33 – 20 = _____

15
Tens	Ones
2	9
–	6

☐ ☐

16
Tens	Ones
3	7
– 1	3

☐ ☐

17
Tens	Ones
2	6
–	8

☐ ☐

18
Tens	Ones
3	1
–	5

☐ ☐

19
Tens	Ones
3	5
– 1	8

☐ ☐

20
Tens	Ones
3	4
– 1	8

☐ ☐

Solve.

Mr. Evans bakes 19 pies.
Ms. Young bakes 5 more pies than Mr. Evans.
How many pies does Ms. Young bake?

Ms. Young bakes _____ pies.

Malia has 15 playing cards.
Oliver has 25 playing cards.
How many fewer playing cards does Malia have than Oliver?

Malia has _____ fewer playing cards than Oliver.

Chapter 8 Addition and Subtraction Within 40 **91**

© 2020 Marshall Cavendish Education Pte Ltd

23 There are 6 chickens on a farm.
There are also 7 ducks and 4 horses on the same farm.
How many animals are there on the farm in all?

There are _____ animals on the farm in all.

Which sentence tells the story in the picture?

Color the ⬡ **.**

24

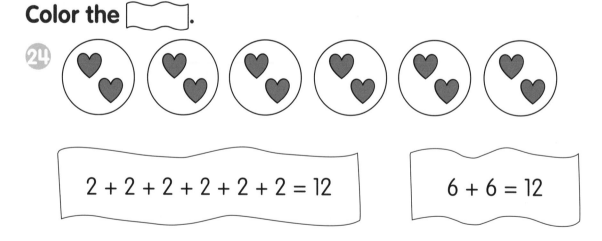

2 + 2 + 2 + 2 + 2 + 2 = 12

6 + 6 = 12

Fill in each blank.

25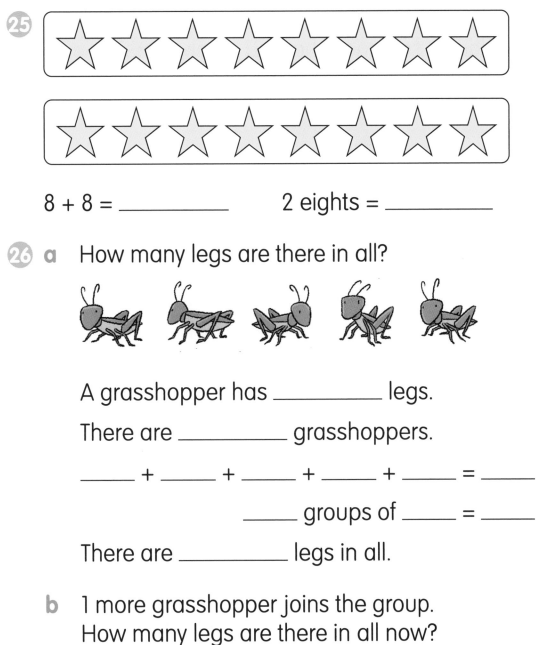

8 + 8 = _____   2 eights = _____

26 **a** How many legs are there in all?

A grasshopper has _____ legs.

There are _____ grasshoppers.

_____ + _____ + _____ + _____ + _____ = _____

_____ groups of _____ = _____

There are _____ legs in all.

b 1 more grasshopper joins the group.
How many legs are there in all now?

There are _____ legs in all now.

Assessment Prep
Answer each question.

27 Which addition sentences have 21 as answers?

21

Color the boxes.

18 + 3	32 − 11
35 − 16	38 − 17

28 Which of the following does not need regrouping to solve?

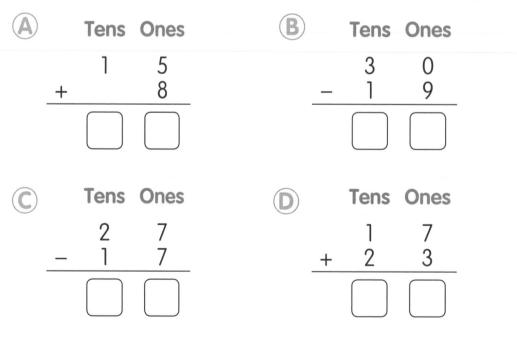

Ⓐ
Tens	Ones
1	5
+	8

Ⓑ
Tens	Ones
3	0
− 1	9

Ⓒ
Tens	Ones
2	7
− 1	7

Ⓓ
Tens	Ones
1	7
+ 2	3

Name: _____ Date: _____

Grocery shopping

1 There are 35 watermelons at a grocery store.

Regroup 35 into tens and ones.

Complete the place-value chart.

Draw ▭ for tens and ☐ for ones.

35 = 2 tens _____ ones =

2 Mr. Garcia needs 17 packets of apple juice for a party.
He also needs 15 packets of orange juice.
How many packets of juice does he need in all?

17 + 15 = _____

Tens	Ones
1	7
+ 1	5
☐	☐

Draw diagrams to help you add.

3 There are 37 packets of potatoes.
Chef Davis buys 18 packets of potatoes for her restaurant.
How many packets of potatoes are left?

Tens	Ones
☐	☐
☐	☐
☐	☐

_____ ◯ _____ = _____

There are _____ packets of potatoes left.

Which related fact will you use to check your answer?

_____ ◯ _____ = _____

4 There are 4 packs of carrots left after a day.
There are 9 carrots in each pack.
How many carrots are there in all?

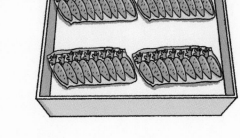

4 packs of _____

= _____ + _____ + _____ + _____

= _____

There are _____ carrots in all.

Rubric

Point(s)	Level	My Performance
7–8	4	• Most of my answers are correct. • I show all my work correctly. • I explain my thinking clearly and completely.
5–6.5	3	• Some of my answers are correct. • I show some of my work correctly. • I explain my thinking clearly.
3–4.5	2	• A few of my answers are correct. • I show little work correctly. • I explain some of my thinking clearly.
0–2.5	1	• A few of my answers are correct. • I show little or no work. • I do not explain my thinking clearly.

Teacher's Comments

Length and Weight

Name: _____   Date: _____

Counting

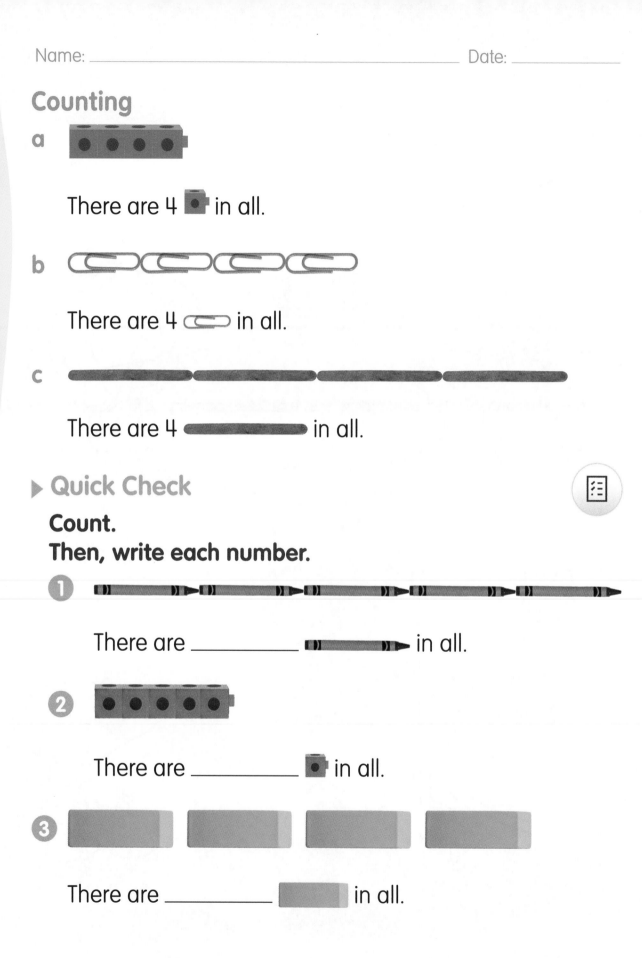

a

There are 4 in all.

b

There are 4 in all.

c

There are 4 in all.

▶ Quick Check

Count.
Then, write each number.

1

There are _____ in all.

2

There are _____ in all.

3

There are _____ in all.

Comparing numbers

8   20   10

Compare the tens.
2 tens is the greatest.
0 tens is the least.
So, 8 is the least number.
20 is the greatest number.

Order the numbers from greatest to least:

20   10   8

greatest   least

▶ **Quick Check**

**Compare the numbers.
Then, fill in each blank.**

18   20   12

Compare the tens.
Then, compare the ones.

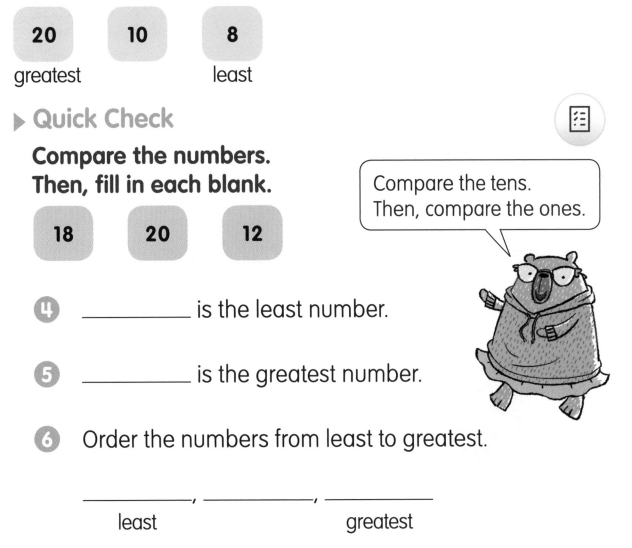

④ _____ is the least number.

⑤ _____ is the greatest number.

⑥ Order the numbers from least to greatest.

_____, _____, _____
   least   greatest

Comparing weights

rock

elephant

These are heavy.

leaf

sponge

These are light.

▶ **Quick Check**

Circle the objects that are heavy.

7

feather

car

table

watermelon

ribbon

strawberry

© 2020 Marshall Cavendish Education Pte Ltd

1 Comparing Lengths

Learning Objective:
- Compare two lengths using the terms "tall," "taller," "long," "longer," "short," and "shorter."

THINK

1. Jacob says a tree is taller than a house.
   Do you agree with him?
2. Natalie says a car is shorter than a bus.
   Do you agree with her?

Share your thinking with your classmates.

ENGAGE

Who is taller?
How can you tell?
Talk about it with your partner.

LEARN Compare two heights and lengths

1

I am tall.

I am taller than Ms. Smith.

I am short.

I am shorter than Emily.

Ms. Smith   Mr. King   Emily   Aki

Math Talk

giraffe

ostrich

How can you tell which animal is taller? Talk about it with your partner.

2 This pencil is long.

This stick is longer than the pencil.

This crayon is short.

This paper clip is shorter than the crayon.

Hands-on Activity

Activity 1   Making towers to compare heights

① Use 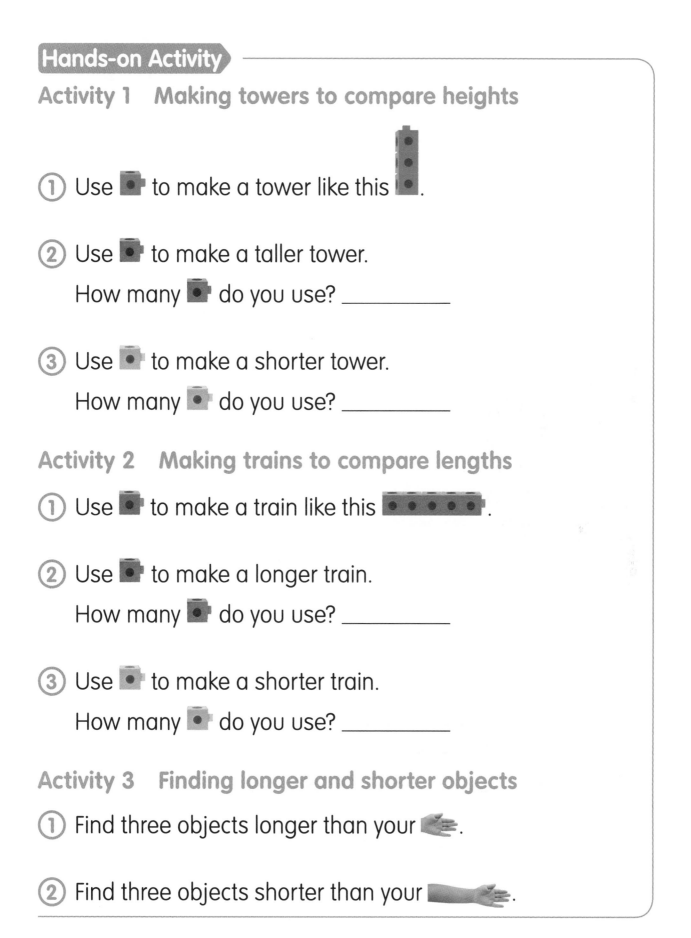 to make a tower like this .

② Use to make a taller tower.
How many do you use? _____

③ Use to make a shorter tower.
How many do you use? _____

Activity 2   Making trains to compare lengths

① Use to make a train like this .

② Use to make a longer train.
How many do you use? _____

③ Use to make a shorter train.
How many do you use? _____

Activity 3   Finding longer and shorter objects

① Find three objects longer than your .

② Find three objects shorter than your .

TRY Practice comparing two heights and lengths

**Look at your desk and your teacher's desk.
Then, answer each question.**

1 Which is taller? _____

2 Which is shorter? _____

**Look at the picture.
Then, answer each question.**

Andrew   Chris

3 Who is taller? _____

4 Who is shorter? _____

tape

rope

5 Which is longer? _____

6 Which is shorter? _____

Name: _____ Date: _____

INDEPENDENT PRACTICE

Look at the pictures.
Then, answer each question.

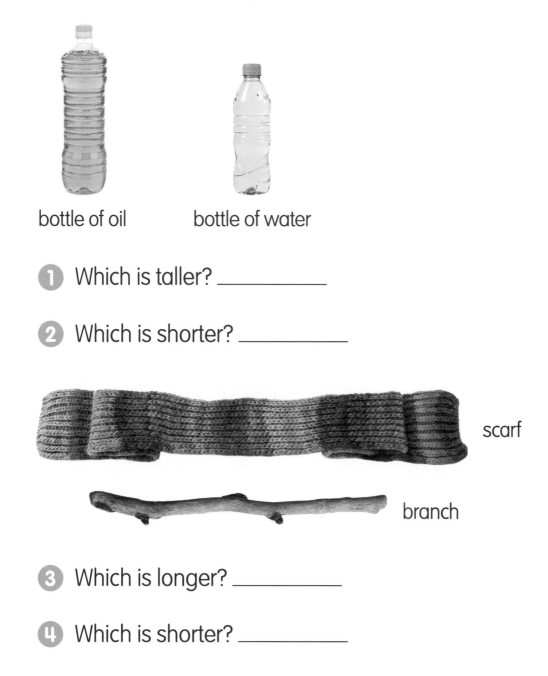

bottle of oil   bottle of water

scarf

branch

1 Which is taller? _____

2 Which is shorter? _____

3 Which is longer? _____

4 Which is shorter? _____

lamp   cupboard

5 Which is taller? _____

6 Which is shorter? _____

7 The cupboard is _____ than the lamp.

8 The lamp is _____ than the cupboard.

ruler

pencil

9 Which is longer? _____

10 Which is shorter? _____

11 The pencil is _____ than the ruler.

12 The ruler is _____ than the pencil.

2 Comparing More Lengths

Learning Objectives:
- Compare two lengths indirectly by comparing each with a third length.
- Compare more than two lengths using the terms "tallest," "longest," and "shortest."

New Vocabulary
tallest
shortest
longest

THINK

A stick is longer than a pen.
The pen is shorter than the pencil.
How can you tell which is the longest?
How can you tell which is the shortest?

ENGAGE

Form a group of three.

① Compare your heights.
Who is the tallest?
Who is the shortest?
How did you decide?

② Compare the lengths of your ▰▰▰.
Who has the longest ▰▰▰?
Who has the shortest ▰▰▰?
How did you decide?

LEARN Compare more than two heights and lengths

1

Amari   Liam   Zoey

Amari is taller than Liam.
Liam is taller than Zoey.
So, Amari is taller than Zoey.

Amari is the tallest.
Zoey is the shortest.

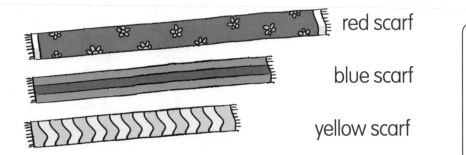

red scarf

blue scarf

yellow scarf

How do you use "shorter" to compare the lengths of the scarves?

The red scarf is longer than the blue scarf.
The blue scarf is longer than the yellow scarf.
So, the red scarf is longer than the yellow scarf.

The red scarf is the longest.
The yellow scarf is the shortest.

© 2020 Marshall Cavendish Education Pte Ltd

Activity 1 Making towers to compare heights

① Use 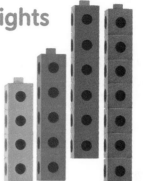 to make these towers.

② Order the towers from shortest to tallest.

③ Make a tower taller than the tallest tower.

How many 🧊 do you use? _____

④ Make a tower shorter than the shortest tower.

How many 🧊 do you use? _____

Activity 2 Finding objects to compare lengths

Look around your classroom.

① Find three objects shorter than your 🦶.

② Arrange them next to one another.

Which is the shortest? _____

③ Find three objects longer than your ✋.

④ Arrange them next to one another.

Which is the longest? _____

TRY Practice comparing more than two heights and lengths

Look at the picture.
Then, answer each question.

Sofia   Hana   Ryan

1 Who is taller, Sofia or Ryan? _____

2 Who is taller, Hana or Ryan? _____

3 Is Hana taller than Sofia? _____

4 Who is the tallest? _____

5 Who is the shortest? _____

6 Who has shorter hair, Hana or Ryan? _____

7 Who has shorter hair, Sofia or Hana? _____

8 Who has the longest hair? _____

9 Who has the shortest hair? _____

INDEPENDENT PRACTICE

Look at the picture.
Then, fill in each blank.
Use the words in the box.

Caleb   Lilian   Lucas

| shorter | shortest | longer | longest | taller | tallest |

1. Caleb is _____ than Lilian.

2. Lucas is _____ than Lilian.

3. Caleb is the _____.

4. Lucas' parrot has a _____ tail than Caleb's parrot.

5. Lilian's parrot has a _____ tail than Lucas' parrot.

6. Caleb's parrot has the _____ tail.

Look at the picture.
Then, answer each question.

Aiden and Karina see some animals.

7 Which is the tallest animal? _____

8 Which is the shortest animal? _____

9 Which animal has a longer neck than the ostrich?

_____

10 Which animal has a shorter neck than the ostrich?

_____

11 Which animal has the shortest neck? _____

3 Using a Start Line

Learning Objective:
- Use a common starting point when comparing lengths.

New Vocabulary
starting line

THINK

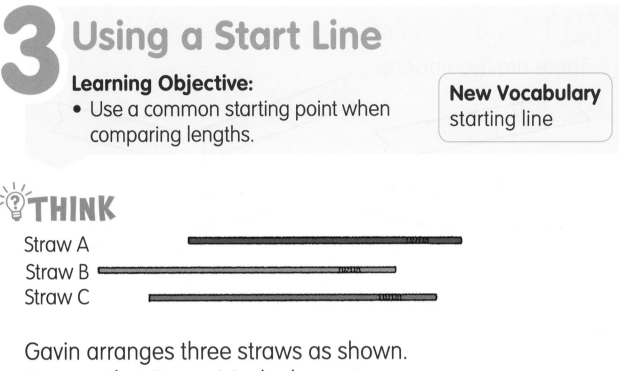

Straw A

Straw B

Straw C

Gavin arranges three straws as shown.
He says that Straw A is the longest.
He also says that Straw B is the shortest.
Is he correct?
Share your thinking with your partner.

ENGAGE

a Your teacher will give you five paper strips of different lengths.
Place the end of each paper strip along the edge of your desk.
Compare their lengths.
Which paper strip is the longest?
Which paper strip is the shortest?

b Why do you need to arrange the paper strips this way?
Share your thinking with your partner.

LEARN Use a start line to compare lengths

1 There are five ribbons.

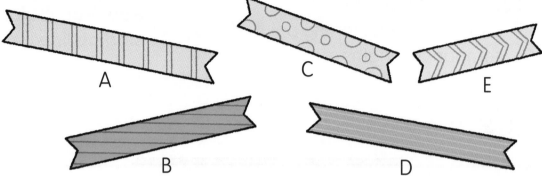

A

C

E

B

D

Which ribbon is the shortest?

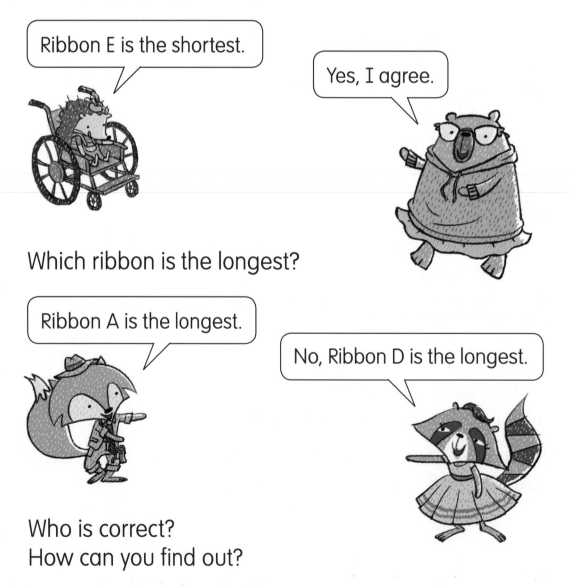

Ribbon E is the shortest.

Yes, I agree.

Which ribbon is the longest?

Ribbon A is the longest.

No, Ribbon D is the longest.

Who is correct?
How can you find out?

You can place objects along a start line to compare their lengths.
Now, can you tell which ribbon is the longest?

So, Ribbon A is the longest, and not Ribbon D.

You can draw the start line like this too.

Hands-on Activity Using a start line to compare lengths

Your teacher will give you a set of 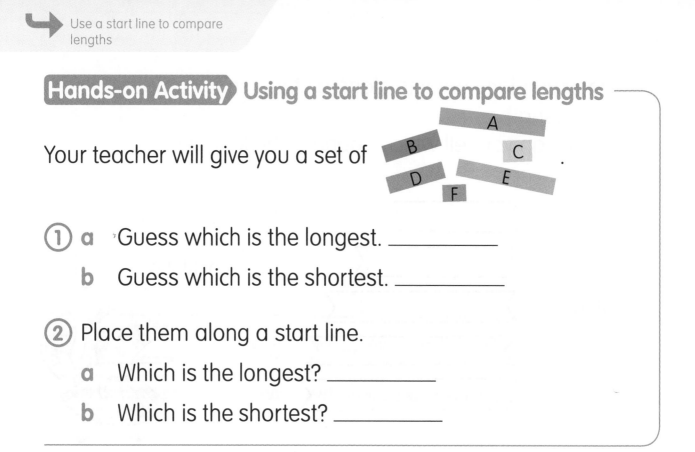 .

① a Guess which is the longest. _____

b Guess which is the shortest. _____

② Place them along a start line.

a Which is the longest? _____

b Which is the shortest? _____

TRY Practice using a start line to compare lengths

Look at the picture.
Then, answer each question.

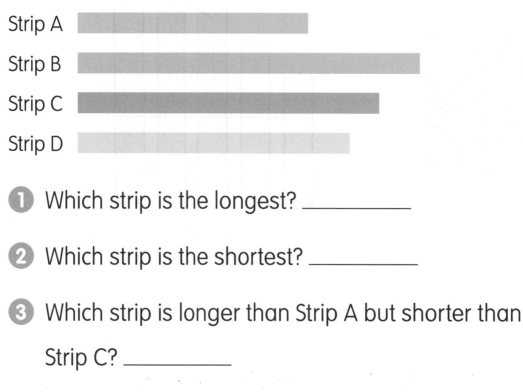

Strip A

Strip B

Strip C

Strip D

❶ Which strip is the longest? _____

❷ Which strip is the shortest? _____

❸ Which strip is longer than Strip A but shorter than

Strip C? _____

© 2020 Marshall Cavendish Education Pte Ltd

INDEPENDENT PRACTICE

Fill in the blank.
Use the scrambled words to help you.

1 Rod A ▭

 Rod B ▭

 Rod C ▭

Bella wants to know which rod is the longest.

She places them on a _____
(srtat lein) to find out.

Fill in each blank.

_____

Ribbon A

_____

2 Which ribbon is longer than Ribbon A?
Name it **Ribbon B**.
Write your answer in the correct blank above.

3 Which ribbon is shorter than Ribbon A?
Name it **Ribbon C**.
Write your answer in the correct blank above.

4 Which ribbon is the longest? _____

5 Which ribbon is the shortest? _____

**Look at the picture.
Then, answer each question.**

P Q R S T

6 Which is the tallest building?

_____

7 Which is the shortest building?

_____

Complete.

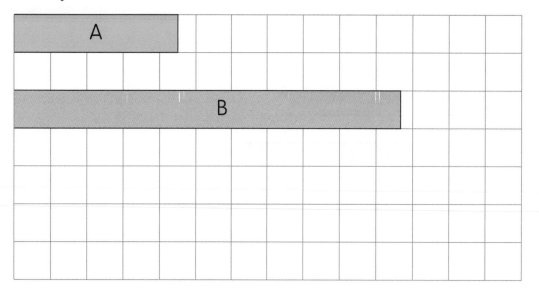

8 Draw a start line.

9 Draw a strip that is longer than A but shorter than B.
Name this **C**.

10 Draw a strip such that it is the shortest.
Name this **D**.

4 Measuring Length

Learning Objectives:
- Measure length using non-standard units.
- Understand that using different non-standard units may give different measurements for the same object.

New Vocabulary
about

THINK

Emma uses 8 ◁▭▷ to measure the length of Bat A.
Connor uses 10 ◁▭▷ to measure the length of Bat B.
Connor says since he uses more crayons, Bat B is longer than Bat A.
Do you agree?
Share your thinking with your partner.

ENGAGE

Take your book.

a   Use ▭ to measure its length.
    How many ▭ do you need?

b   Next, use your ✋ to measure its length.
    How many ✋ do you need?

Talk about the two methods in **a** and **b** with your partner.

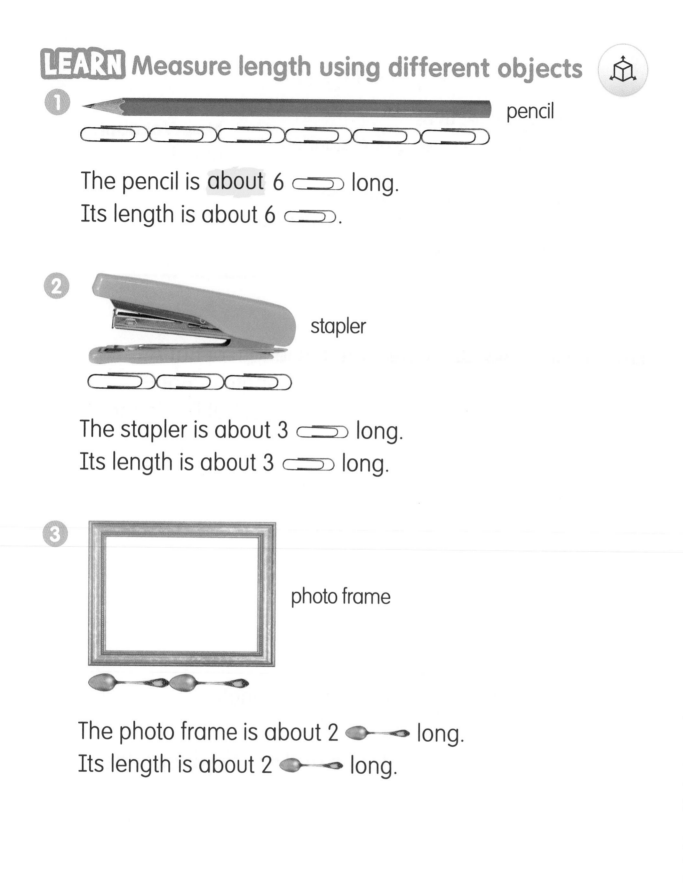

LEARN Measure length using different objects

1
The pencil is about 6 ⬭ long.
Its length is about 6 ⬭.

pencil

2
The stapler is about 3 ⬭ long.
Its length is about 3 ⬭ long.

stapler

3
The photo frame is about 2 🥄 long.
Its length is about 2 🥄 long.

photo frame

Hands-on Activity Using  to measure length

① Use your  to measure the length of the teacher's desk.

② Record the result.

Object	Number of 
Teacher's desk	

③ Repeat ① and ② for these objects.

Object	Number of 
Your desk	
Your book	

④ Answer each question.

a   Which object is the longest? _____

b   Which object is the shortest? _____

c   Is your desk longer than the teacher's desk?

_____

TRY Practice using non-standard units to record length

Look at the pictures.
Then, fill in each blank.

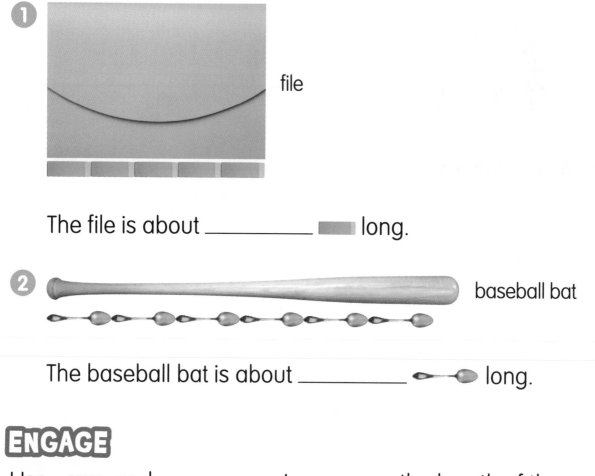

1 file

The file is about _____ ▬ long.

2 baseball bat

The baseball bat is about _____ ⬥—⬥ long.

ENGAGE

Use ⬭ and ▬▬▬▬▬ to measure the length of these objects.

a pen

b your desk

Which do you find easier to use for each object?
Share your thinking with your partner.

LEARN Measure the same length using different objects

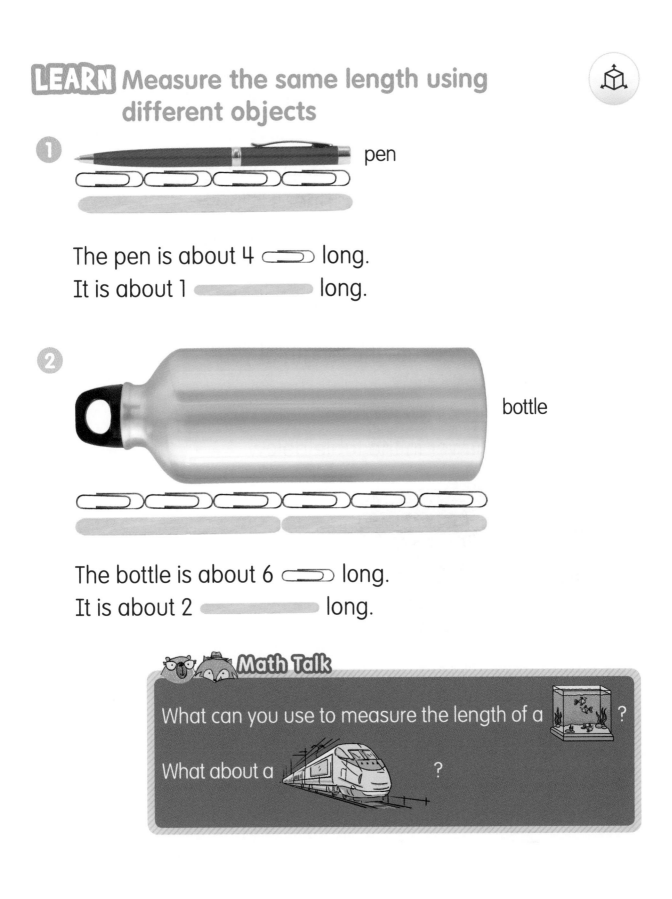

1 pen

The pen is about 4 🖇 long.

It is about 1 ⬭ long.

2 bottle

The bottle is about 6 🖇 long.

It is about 2 ⬭ long.

Math Talk

What can you use to measure the length of a 🐠 ?

What about a 🚄 ?

Hands-on Activity Using different objects to measure the same length

Work in pairs.

Your teacher will give you some 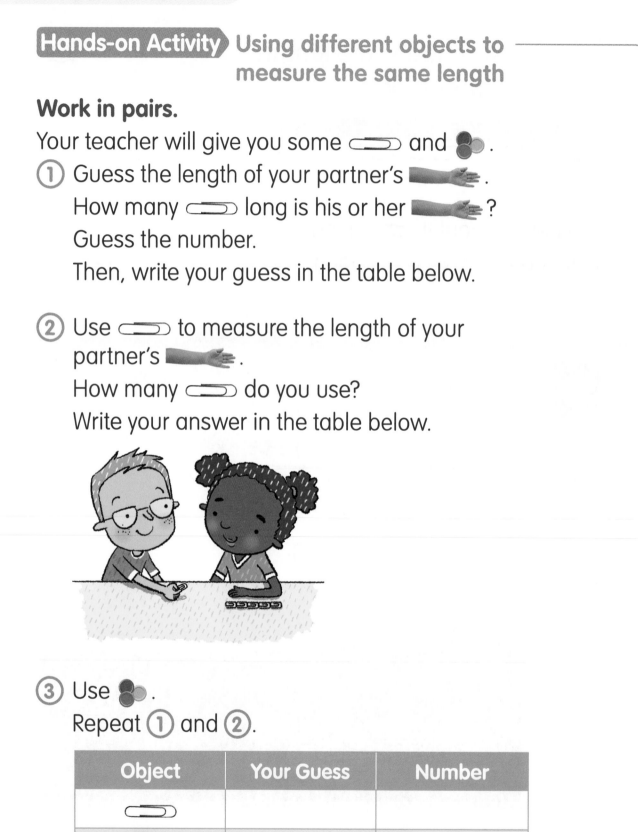 and ⬤ .

① Guess the length of your partner's .
How many long is his or her ?
Guess the number.
Then, write your guess in the table below.

② Use to measure the length of your partner's .
How many do you use?
Write your answer in the table below.

③ Use .
Repeat ① and ②.

Object	Your Guess	Number

④ Trace your partner's  on a piece of paper.

⑤ Guess the length of your partner's 👣.
How many 📎 long is his or her 👣?
Guess the number.
Then, write your guess in the table below.

⑥ Use 📎 to measure the length of your partner's 👣.
How many 📎 do you use?
Write your answer in the table below.

⑦ Use 🔵.
Repeat ⑤ and ⑥.

Object	Your Guess	Number
📎		
🔵		

⑧ Do you use more 📎 or 🔵 to measure each length?
Why is this so?
Share your thinking with your partner.

TRY Practice using different non-standard units to record the same length

Look at the pictures.
Then, fill in each blank.

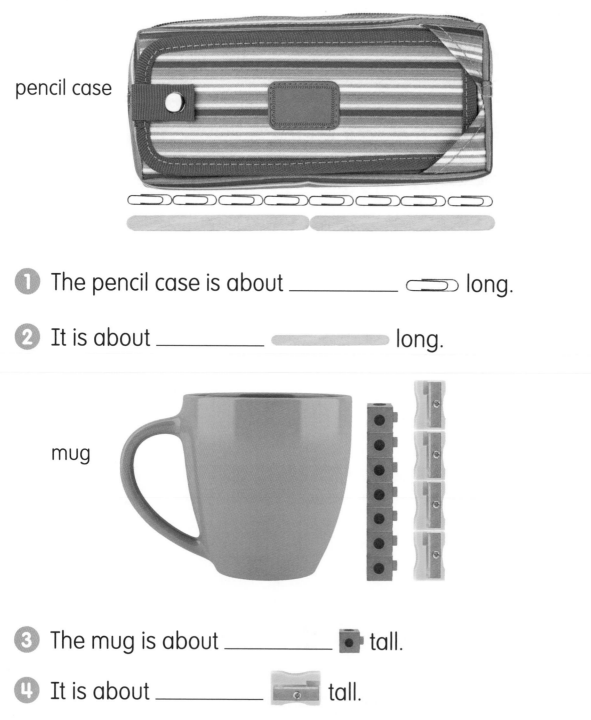

pencil case

1. The pencil case is about _____ ⬭ long.

2. It is about _____ ▬▬▬ long.

mug

3. The mug is about _____ ▪ tall.

4. It is about _____ ▱ tall.

Name: _____   Date: _____

INDEPENDENT PRACTICE

Look at the pictures.
Then, fill in each blank.

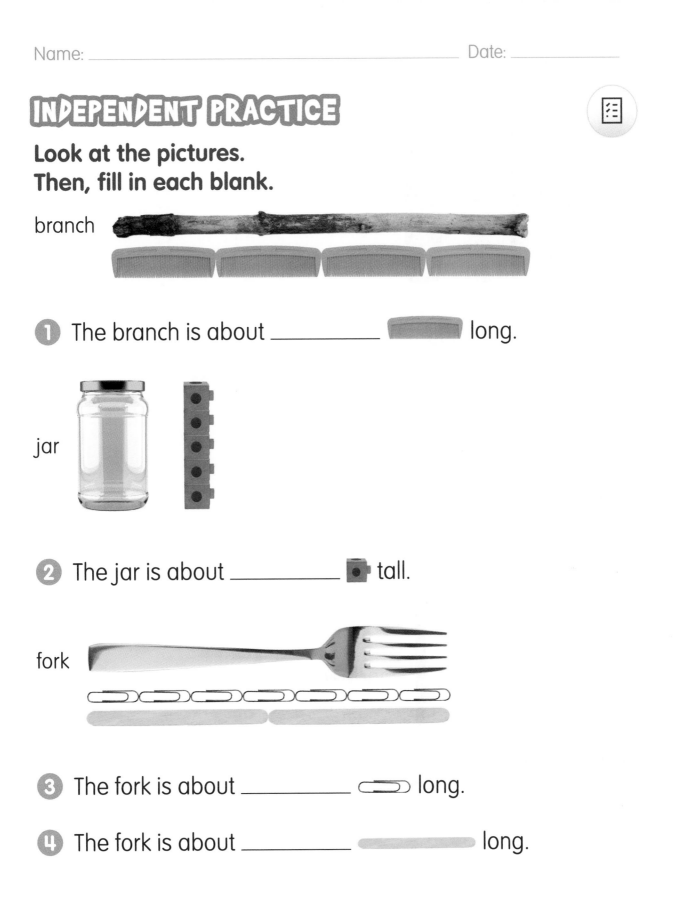

branch

1 The branch is about _____ long.

jar

2 The jar is about _____ tall.

fork

3 The fork is about _____ long.

4 The fork is about _____ long.

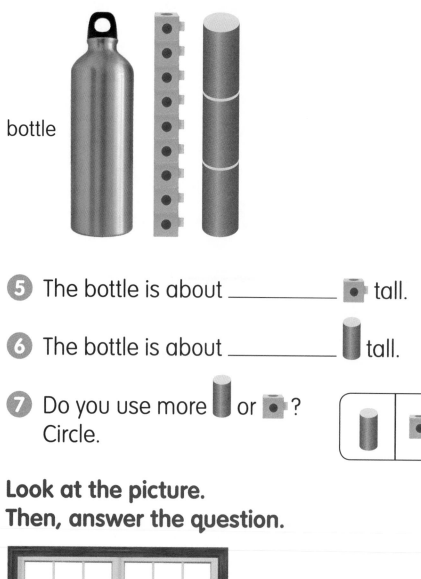

bottle

⑤ The bottle is about _____ tall.

⑥ The bottle is about _____ tall.

⑦ Do you use more or ? Circle.

Look at the picture.
Then, answer the question.

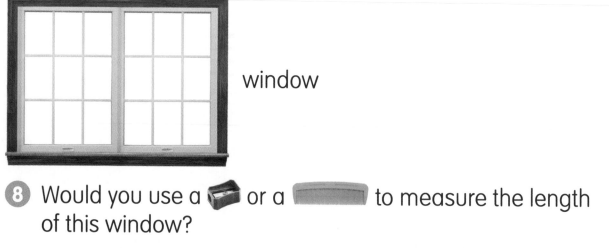

window

⑧ Would you use a or a to measure the length of this window?

_____

_____

_____

5 Measuring Length in Units

Learning Objective:
- Use the term "unit" to describe length.

New Vocabulary
unit

THINK

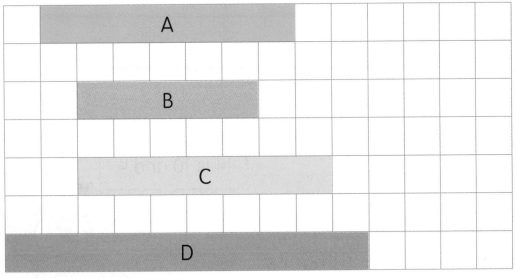

Each ☐ stands for 1 unit.

Which two strips are as long as each other?

ENGAGE

Use 🔵 to measure the length of each object.

a your math book

b your desk

c your stapler

How many 🔵 do you use for each object?

LEARN Measure length in units

Each ▬▬▬▬ stands for 1 unit.

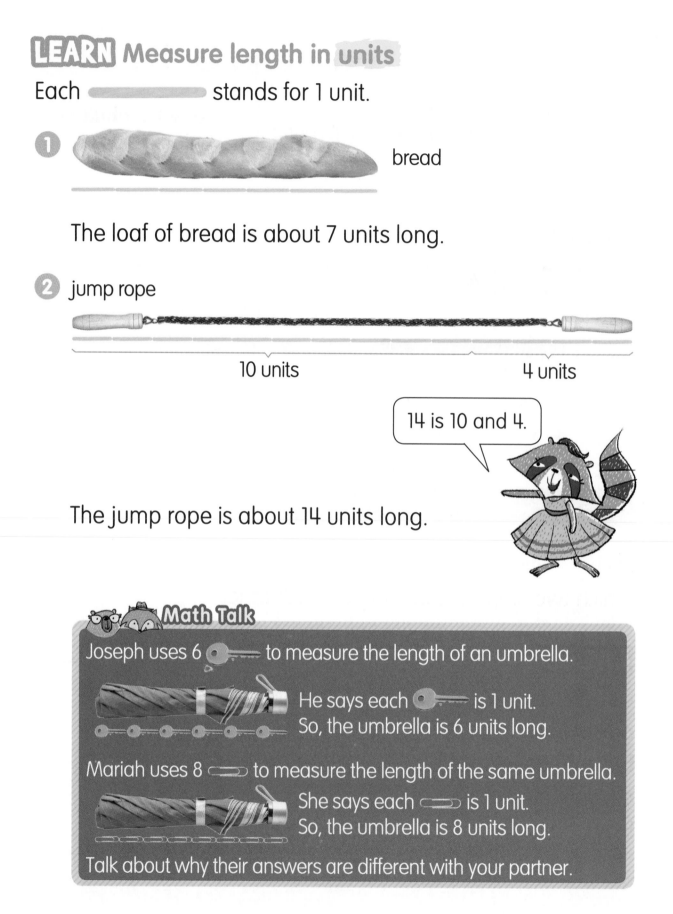

1 bread

The loaf of bread is about 7 units long.

2 jump rope

10 units   4 units

14 is 10 and 4.

The jump rope is about 14 units long.

Math Talk

Joseph uses 6 🔑 to measure the length of an umbrella.

He says each 🔑 is 1 unit.
So, the umbrella is 6 units long.

Mariah uses 8 ⬭ to measure the length of the same umbrella.

She says each ⬭ is 1 unit.
So, the umbrella is 8 units long.

Talk about why their answers are different with your partner.

① Use ⊂▭⊃ and 👣 to measure the lengths of these objects.

Object	Each ⊂▭⊃ stands for 1 unit	Each 👣 stands for 1 unit
Desk		
Whiteboard		
Cupboard		

② **Mathematical Habit 6** Use precise mathematical language

Talk about how you use ⊂▭⊃ and 👣 to measure length with your partner.

③ **Mathematical Habit 3** Construct viable arguments

Look at the two measurements for the desk.
Do you use more ⊂▭⊃ or 👣 to measure its length?
Is this true for the other objects you measured?
Share your thinking with your partner.

④ **Mathematical Habit 3** Construct viable arguments

Would you use ⊂▭⊃ or 👣 to measure the length of your bed?
Share your thinking with your partner.

TRY Practice recording length in units

Look at the picture.
Then, answer each question.
Each ☐ stands for 1 unit.

1. The towel rack is about _____ units long.

2. The screen is about _____ units tall.

3. The boy is about _____ units tall.

4. Is the brush longer than the mirror? _____

5. Is the towel rack shorter than the mirror? _____

6. Which is shorter, the brush or the towel rack? _____

   How much shorter? _____ units

INDEPENDENT PRACTICE

Look at each picture.
Then, answer each question.

1 Each 🔘 stands for 1 unit.

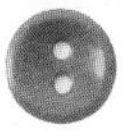

corn

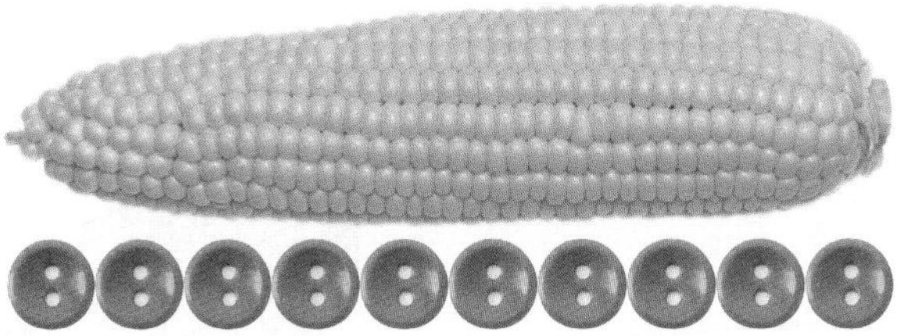

The corn is about _____ units long.

2 Each 🔘 stands for 1 unit.

spoon

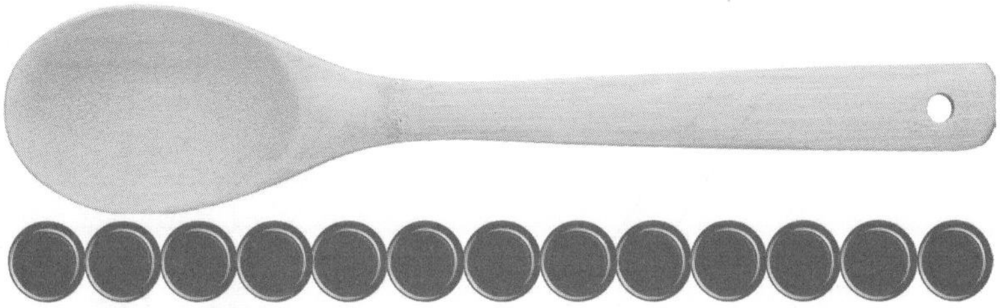

The spoon is about _____ units long.

3 Each ⬜ stands for 1 unit.

cactus

The cactus is about _____ units tall.

Use ⬭ **to measure.**
Each ⬭ **stands for 1 unit.**
Then, fill in each blank.

The picture shows Henry's house, his school, and the playground.

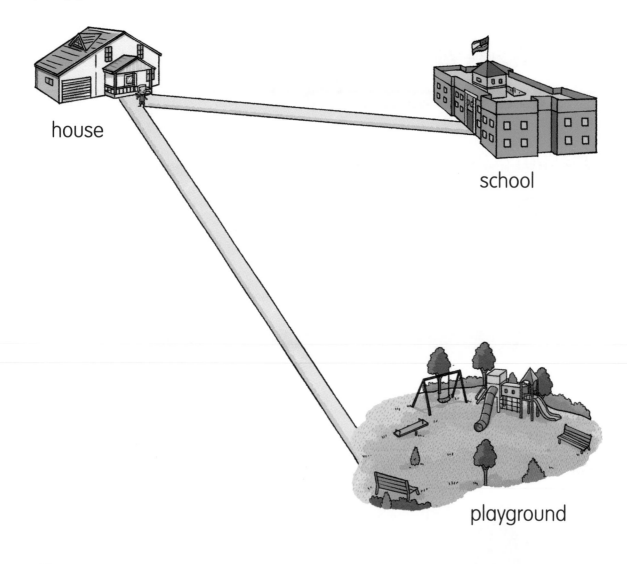

house

school

playground

④ The sidewalk from Henry's house to the school is about _____ units long.

⑤ The sidewalk from Henry's house to the playground is about _____ units long.

Fill in each blank.

Snails A, B, and C crawl along the lines.

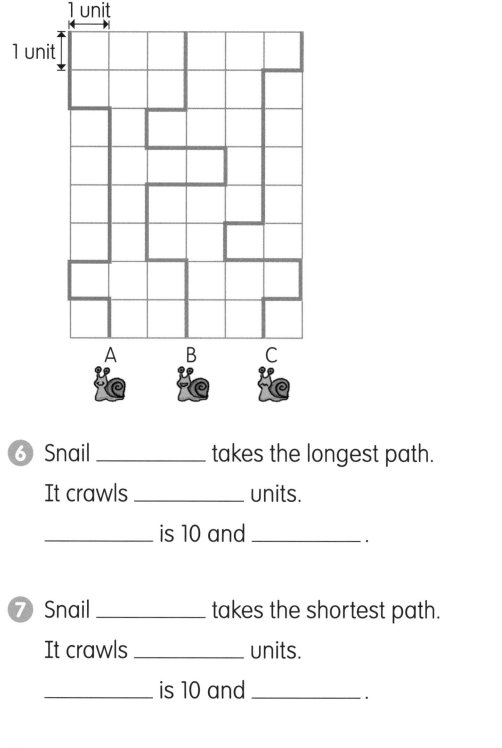

6 Snail _____ takes the longest path.

It crawls _____ units.

_____ is 10 and _____ .

7 Snail _____ takes the shortest path.

It crawls _____ units.

_____ is 10 and _____ .

8 Snail _____ crawls 13 units.

Answer each question.

Each ☐ **stands for 1 unit.**

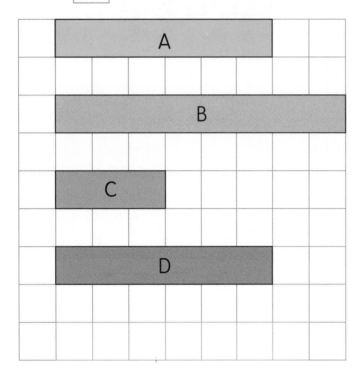

9 Which is the longest strip? _____

10 Which is the shortest strip? _____

11 a Which two strips have the same length?

_____ and _____

b How long is each of these strips? _____ units

12 What is the total length of strips A, B, and C?

_____ units

13 Draw a strip that is 7 units long below Strip D.
Label it **E**.

Name: _____ Date: _____

6 Comparing Weights

Lesson Objectives:
- Compare two weights using the terms "heavy," "heavier," "light," "lighter," and "as heavy as."
- Compare two weights indirectly by comparing each with a third weight.
- Compare more than two weights using the terms "lightest" and "heaviest."

New Vocabulary
heaviest
lightest

THINK

Brayden is heavier than Madeline.
Brayden is also heavier than Elena.
What can you tell about the weights of Madeline and Elena?
Share five possible things you can tell with your partner.

ENGAGE

Which object is heavier?

a   a book or a pencil

b   a stapler or a pencil case

c   an orange or an apple

How can you tell for sure?
Share your thinking with your partner.

© 2020 Marshall Cavendish Education Pte Ltd

① Guess which object is heavier.

box of paper clips

stapler

Write your guess in the table below.

Your Guess	It is

② Use  to check your answer.
Write your answer in the table above.

③ Repeat ① and ② for these objects.

a

eraser

pencil

Your Guess	It is

b

sharpener

crayon

Your Guess	It is

TRY Practice comparing two weights

Look at the picture.
Then, answer each question.

soft toy

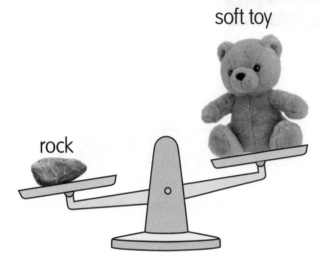

rock

1 The _____ is heavier.

2 The _____ is lighter.

3 Is a big object always heavier than a small object?

_____

A big object may be lighter
than a small object.

ENGAGE

Take a stapler, a glue stick, and an eraser.

a Place the stapler and the glue stick on a .
Which is heavier?

b Now, place the glue stick and the eraser on the .
Which is heavier?

c Can you tell which is the heaviest object?

LEARN Compare more than two weights

1

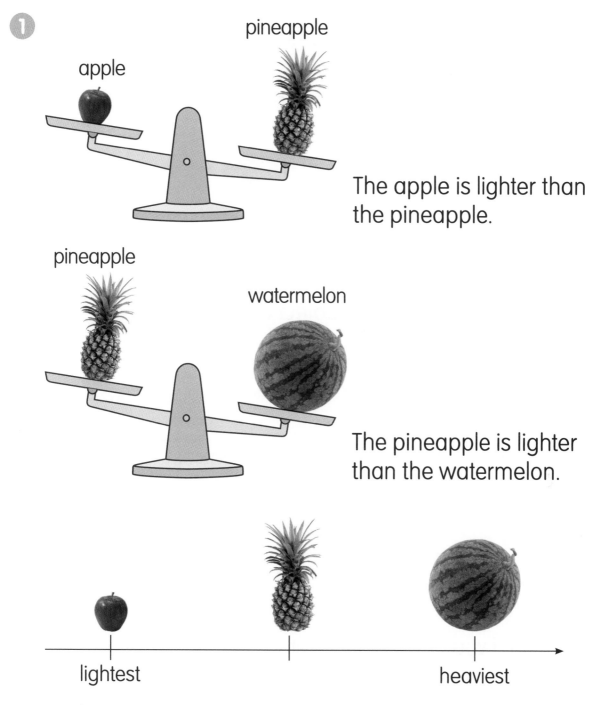

apple

pineapple

The apple is lighter than the pineapple.

pineapple

watermelon

The pineapple is lighter than the watermelon.

lightest

heaviest

So, the apple is lighter than the watermelon.

The apple is the lightest .
The watermelon is the heaviest .

Hands-on Activity Comparing more than two weights

Your teacher will give you a glue stick, a stapler, and some modeling clay.

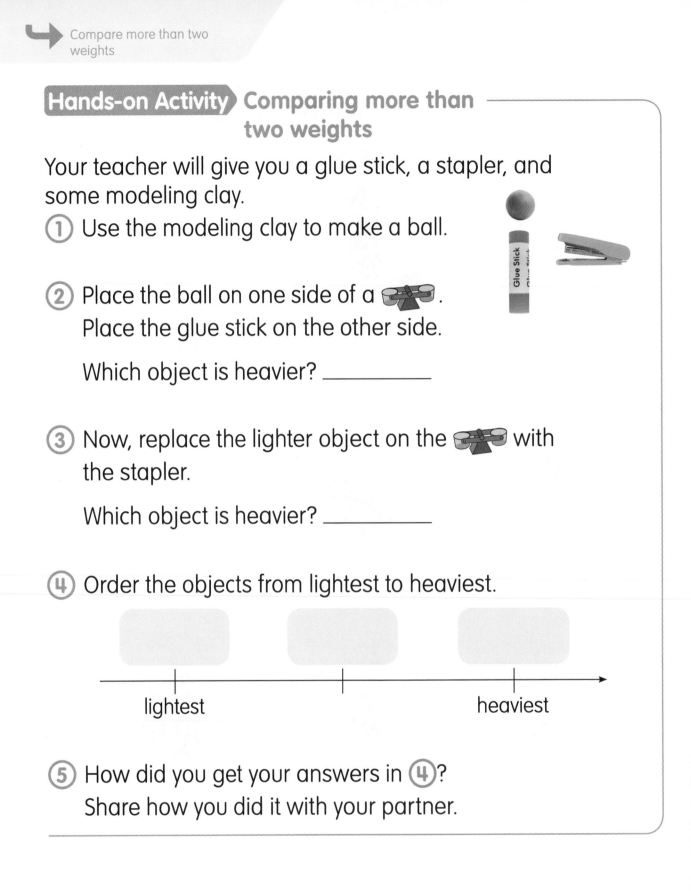

① Use the modeling clay to make a ball.

② Place the ball on one side of a ⚖. Place the glue stick on the other side.

Which object is heavier? _____

③ Now, replace the lighter object on the ⚖ with the stapler.

Which object is heavier? _____

④ Order the objects from lightest to heaviest.

lightest ———————————— heaviest

⑤ How did you get your answers in ④? Share how you did it with your partner.

TRY Practice comparing more than two weights

Look at the picture.
Then, fill in each blank.
Choose lighter or heavier.
Mai wants to find out which is the heaviest animal.

Scale A   Scale B

1. Mai looks at Scale A.
   She can tell that the rabbit is _____ than the cat.

2. Mai looks at Scale B.
   She can tell that the rabbit is _____ than the frog.

Fill in each blank.
Use your answers to ❶ and ❷ to help you.

3.

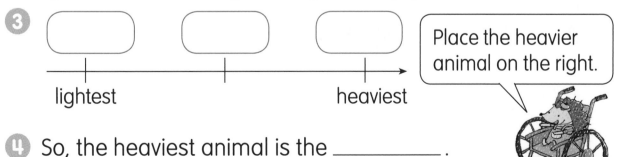

lightest   heaviest

Place the heavier animal on the right.

4. So, the heaviest animal is the _____.

Look at the picture.
Then, fill in each blank.
Choose lighter, heavier, lightest, or heaviest.

watch   comb   clock

5 The comb is _____ than the watch.

6 The clock is _____ than the watch.

7 So, the clock is _____ than the comb.

8 The _____ is the lightest.

9 The _____ is the heaviest.

Look at the picture.
Then, fill in each blank.

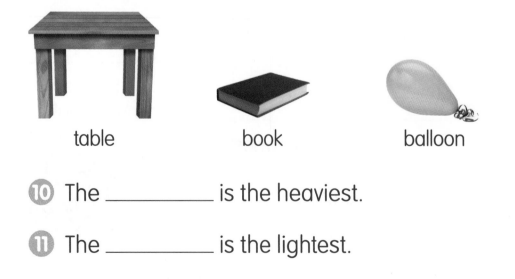

table   book   balloon

10 The _____ is the heaviest.

11 The _____ is the lightest.

Name: _____ Date: _____

INDEPENDENT PRACTICE

Look at the picture.
Then, fill in each blank.
Choose lighter, heavier, **or** as heavy as.

1 The book is _____ the football.

2 The doll is _____ than the book.

3 The football is _____ than the doll.

Look at the picture.
Then, fill in each blank.

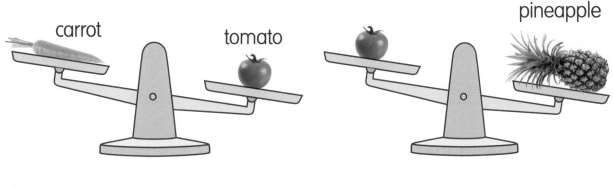

4 The _____ is lighter than the tomato.

5 The _____ is heavier than the tomato.

6 So, the carrot is _____ than the pineapple.

**Look at the picture.
Then, fill in each blank.**

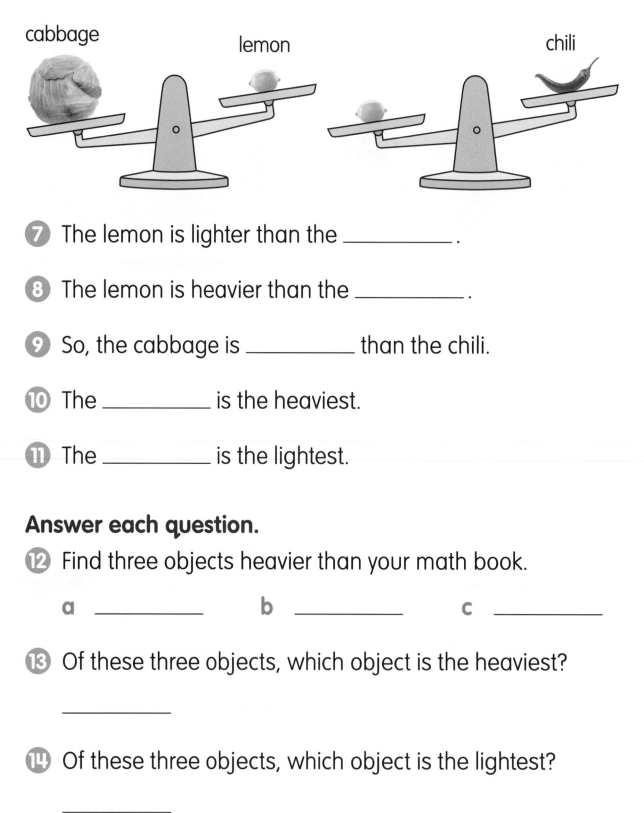

cabbage

lemon

chili

7 The lemon is lighter than the _____ .

8 The lemon is heavier than the _____ .

9 So, the cabbage is _____ than the chili.

10 The _____ is the heaviest.

11 The _____ is the lightest.

Answer each question.

12 Find three objects heavier than your math book.

a _____   b _____   c _____

13 Of these three objects, which object is the heaviest?

_____

14 Of these three objects, which object is the lightest?

_____

7 Measuring Weight

Learning Objectives:
- Measure weight using non-standard units.
- Compare weights using a non-standard object as a unit of measurement.

THINK

Andre is heavier than Anna.
Anna is lighter than Jaden.
Kennedy is heavier than Jaden.
Can you tell
a who is the lightest, and
b who is the heaviest?
Share your thinking with your partner.

ENGAGE

a Put your math book on one side of a ⚖.
Put one 🧊 at a time on the other side of the ⚖.
Stop when the ⚖ is balanced.
How many 🧊 do you use?

b Join two 🧊 to make a rectangular prism.
Replace the 🧊 on the ⚖ with rectangular prisms.
How many rectangular prisms do you need to balance the book?
Is your answer the same or different from **a**?
Why do you think so?

LEARN Measure weight using different objects

1

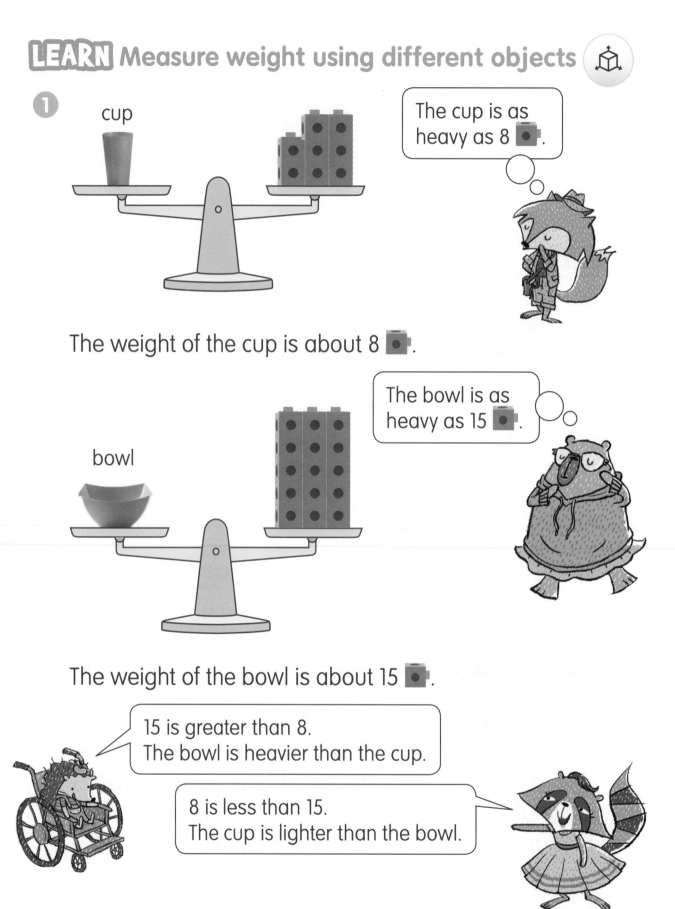

cup

The cup is as heavy as 8 🔲.

The weight of the cup is about 8 🔲.

bowl

The bowl is as heavy as 15 🔲.

The weight of the bowl is about 15 🔲.

15 is greater than 8.
The bowl is heavier than the cup.

8 is less than 15.
The cup is lighter than the bowl.

Activity 1　Using different objects to measure weight

① Use 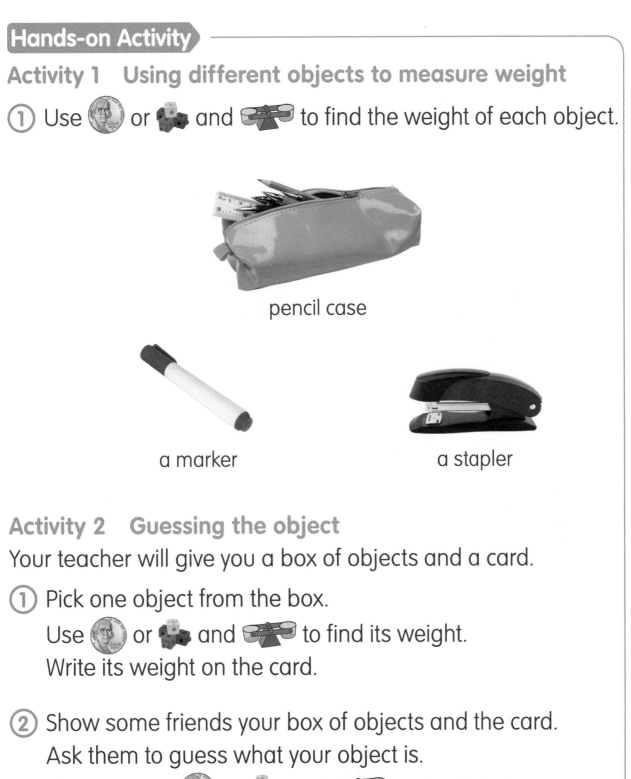 or and to find the weight of each object.

pencil case

a marker

a stapler

Activity 2　Guessing the object

Your teacher will give you a box of objects and a card.

① Pick one object from the box.
   Use or and to find its weight.
   Write its weight on the card.

② Show some friends your box of objects and the card.
   Ask them to guess what your object is.
   They can use or and to check their guesses.

TRY Practice using non-standard units to record and compare weights

Look at the picture.
Then, fill in each blank.

1 The weight of Bag A is about _____ ⚫.

2 Bag B is as heavy as _____ ⚫.

3 The weight of Bag C is about _____ ⚫.

4 Bag _____ is heavier than Bag _____.

5 Bag _____ is lighter than Bag _____.

6 Bag _____ is the lightest.

7 Bag _____ is the heaviest.

INDEPENDENT PRACTICE

Look at the picture.
Then, fill in each blank.

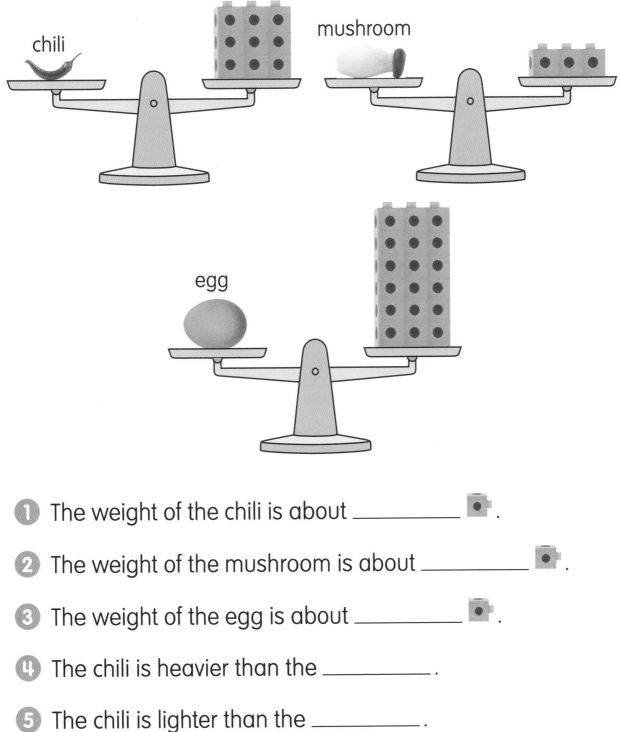

chili

mushroom

egg

1. The weight of the chili is about _____ .

2. The weight of the mushroom is about _____ .

3. The weight of the egg is about _____ .

4. The chili is heavier than the _____ .

5. The chili is lighter than the _____ .

6 The mushroom is _____ than the egg.

7 The _____ is the heaviest.

8 The _____ is the lightest.

9 Order the objects from lightest to heaviest.

_____, _____, _____
lightest   heaviest

Look at the picture.
Then, complete.

scissors

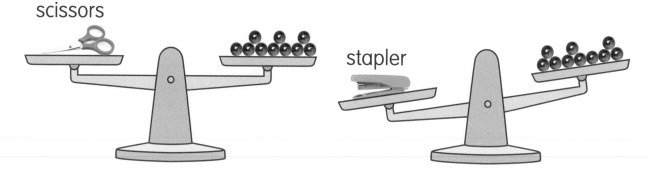

stapler

10 The weight of the scissors is about _____ ●.

11 _____ ● are heavier than the pair of scissors.

12 _____ ● are lighter than the stapler.

13 Which is heavier, the scissors or the stapler?

_____

There is more than one answer to **11** and **12**.

8 Measuring Weight in Units

Learning Objectives:
- Use the term "unit" to describe weight.
- Understand why there is a difference in measurement when different objects are used as 1 unit.

THINK

1 ▯ stands for 1 unit.

Diego can carry 10 units.

Carter can carry more units than Diego.

Riley can carry fewer units than Carter.

a Who is the strongest?

b Who is the weakest?

Talk about how you got your answers with your partner.

ENGAGE

sharpeners

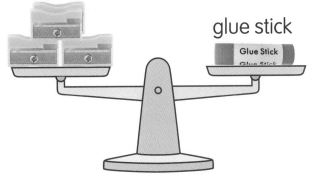

glue stick

a One glue stick has the same weight as

_____ sharpeners.

b How many sharpeners would two glue sticks weigh?
Share your thinking with your partner.

LEARN Measure weight in units

1 Each  stands for 1 unit.

strawberry

The weight of the strawberry is about 1 unit.

2 Each ⬛ stands for 1 unit.

strawberry

Why is the number of units different for the same strawberry?

The weight of the same strawberry is about 7 units.

Math Talk

Bailey measures the weight of her lunch box.
She uses 1 ⬛ as 1 unit.
The weight of her lunch box is about 18 units.
She then uses 1 ⚪ as 1 unit.
The weight of her lunch box is 6 units.
Which is lighter, 1 ⬛ or 1 ⚪ ?
Talk about why you think so with your partner.

① Use ⬭ as 1 unit.
Guess the weight of each object in Group 1.
Write your guesses in the table below.

Group 1

pencil   eraser   scissors

Object	Guess	Each ⬭ stands for 1 unit.	Each 🪙 stands for 1 unit.
Eraser	units		
Pencil	units		
Scissors	units		

② Use ⚖ and ⬭ to check your guesses.
Then, write your answers in the table above.

③ Next, use 🪙 as 1 unit.
Find the weight of the objects in Group 1.
Then, write your answers in the table above.

④ **Mathematical Habit** 3 Construct viable arguments
Talk about your findings with your partner.

⑤ Use ![coin] as 1 unit.
Guess the weight of each object in Group 2.
Write your guesses in the table below.

Group 2

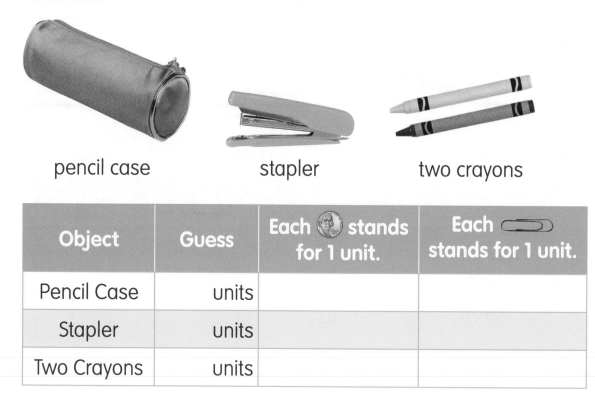

pencil case   stapler   two crayons

Object	Guess	Each ![coin] stands for 1 unit.	Each ![paperclip] stands for 1 unit.
Pencil Case	units		
Stapler	units		
Two Crayons	units		

⑥ Use ![scale] and ![coin] to check your guesses.
Then, write your answers in the table above.

⑦ Next, use ![paperclip] as 1 unit.
Find the weight of the objects in Group 2.
Then, write your answers in the table above.

⑧ **Mathematical Habit** 3 **Construct viable arguments**
Talk about your findings with your partner.

TRY Practice recording weight in units

Look at the picture.
Fill in each blank.
Each  **stands for 1 unit.**

1. The weight of Box A is about _____ units.

2. The weight of Box B is about _____ units.

3. The weight of Box C is about _____ units.

4. Box _____ is the heaviest.

5. Box _____ is the lightest.

6. Order the boxes from heaviest to lightest.

_____ , _____ , _____
heaviest   lightest

1 The Cooper family is sewing.

Talk about what you see in the picture with your partner.
Use these words to help you.

tall	long	short	heavy	light
taller	longer	shorter	heavier	lighter
tallest	longest	shortest	heaviest	lightest

2 Find three small objects in your classroom.
Order the objects from heaviest to lightest.
Use a ![balance] to help you.

Name: _____   Date: _____

INDEPENDENT PRACTICE

Look at the picture.
Then, fill in each blank.
Each ⚬ stands for 1 unit.

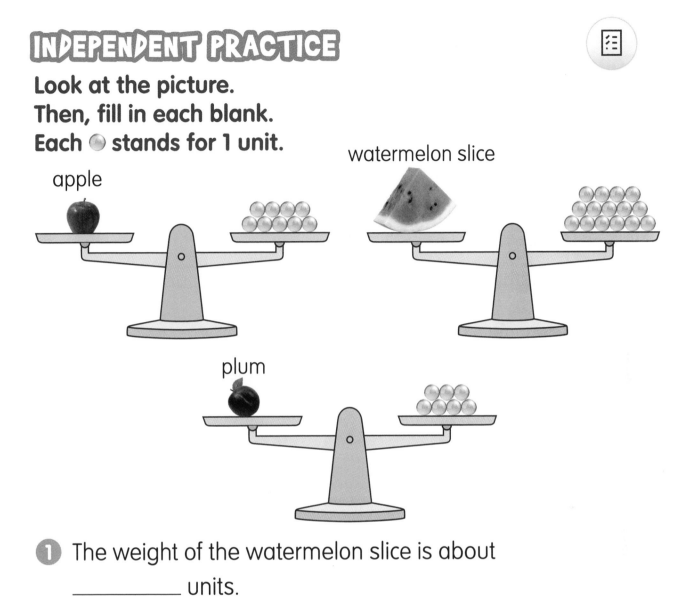

1. The weight of the watermelon slice is about _____ units.

2. The weight of the apple is about _____ units.

3. The weight of the plum is about _____ units.

4. The apple is heavier than the _____.

5. The apple is lighter than the _____.

6. The _____ is the lightest.

7. The _____ is the heaviest.

Look at the picture.
Complete.
Each 🔲 stands for 1 unit.

box

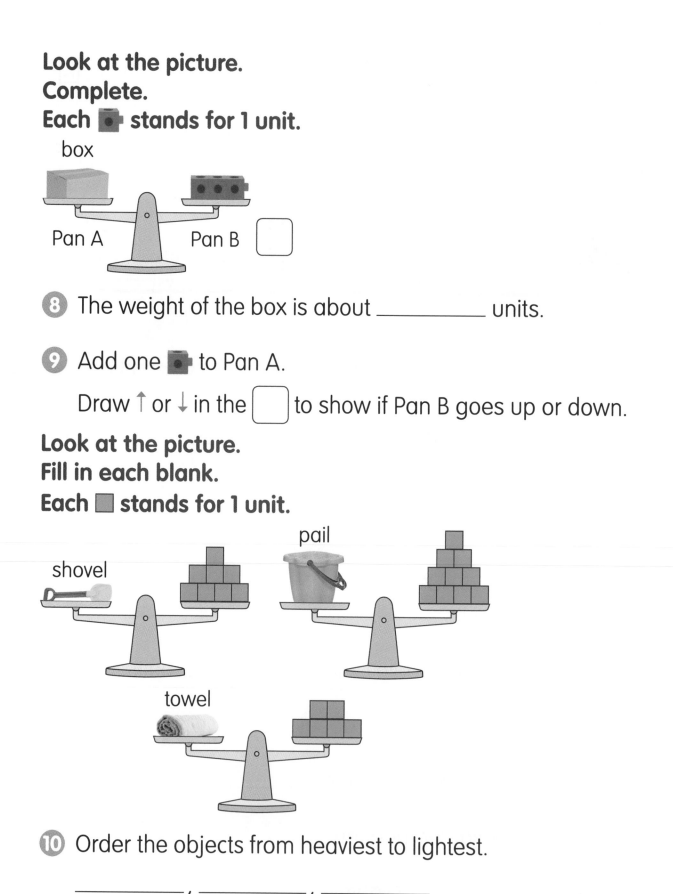

Pan A   Pan B ☐

8 The weight of the box is about _____ units.

9 Add one 🔲 to Pan A.

Draw ↑ or ↓ in the ☐ to show if Pan B goes up or down.

Look at the picture.
Fill in each blank.
Each ◼ stands for 1 unit.

pail

shovel

towel

10 Order the objects from heaviest to lightest.

_____ , _____ , _____
  heaviest   lightest

MATH JOURNAL

Mathematical Habit 2 Use mathematical reasoning

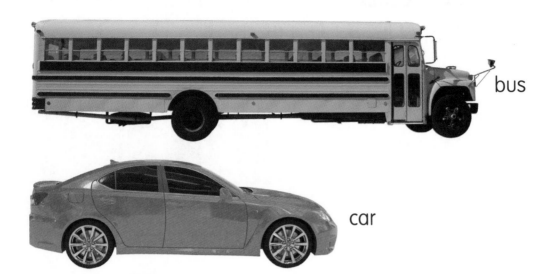

bus

car

motorbike

Which is the longest?
Which is the heaviest?
How can you tell?

Problem Solving with Heuristics

1 **Mathematical Habit 3** Construct viable arguments

Look at the loaf of bread and the book.

loaf of bread

book

There are more paper clips used than erasers.
Can you say that the book is longer than the loaf of bread?
Why?

2 **Mathematical Habit** **3** **Construct viable arguments**

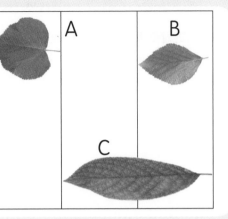

Set 1   Set 2

You want to find out how long each leaf is.
Which set of lines will you use?
Why?

Look at the pictures.
Then, answer each question.

3 **Mathematical Habit** **1** Persevere in solving problems

Which bag is heavier, A or B? _____

4 **Mathematical Habit** **1** Persevere in solving problems

Which bag is heavier, D or E? _____

5 **Mathematical Habit** **1** Persevere in solving problems

Order the bags from lightest to heaviest.

_____ , _____ , _____
   lightest   heaviest

CHAPTER WRAP-UP

 Take any three objects in your classroom. How can you tell which is longest and the heaviest?

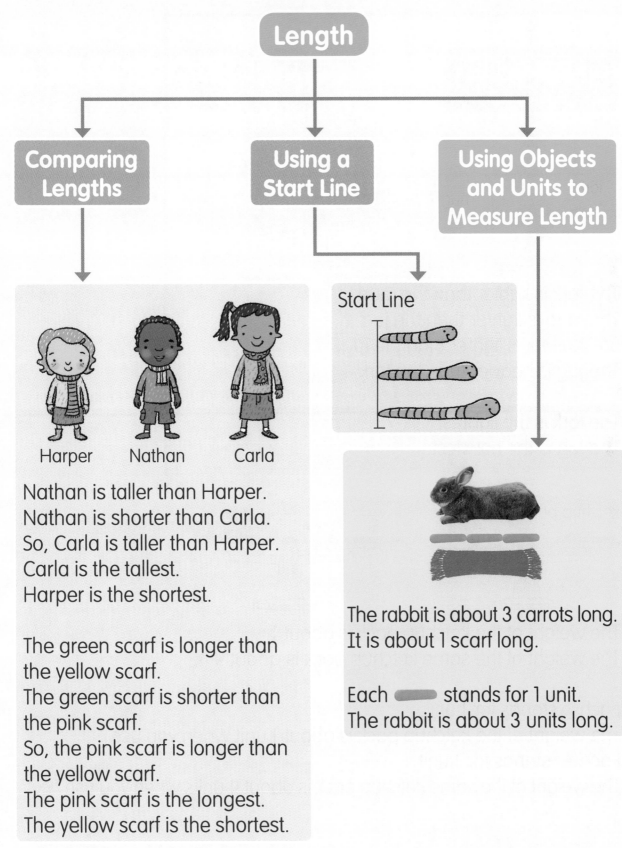

Length

Comparing Lengths

Harper   Nathan   Carla

Nathan is taller than Harper.
Nathan is shorter than Carla.
So, Carla is taller than Harper.
Carla is the tallest.
Harper is the shortest.

The green scarf is longer than the yellow scarf.
The green scarf is shorter than the pink scarf.
So, the pink scarf is longer than the yellow scarf.
The pink scarf is the longest.
The yellow scarf is the shortest.

Using a Start Line

Start Line

Using Objects and Units to Measure Length

The rabbit is about 3 carrots long.
It is about 1 scarf long.

Each ⬤ stands for 1 unit.
The rabbit is about 3 units long.

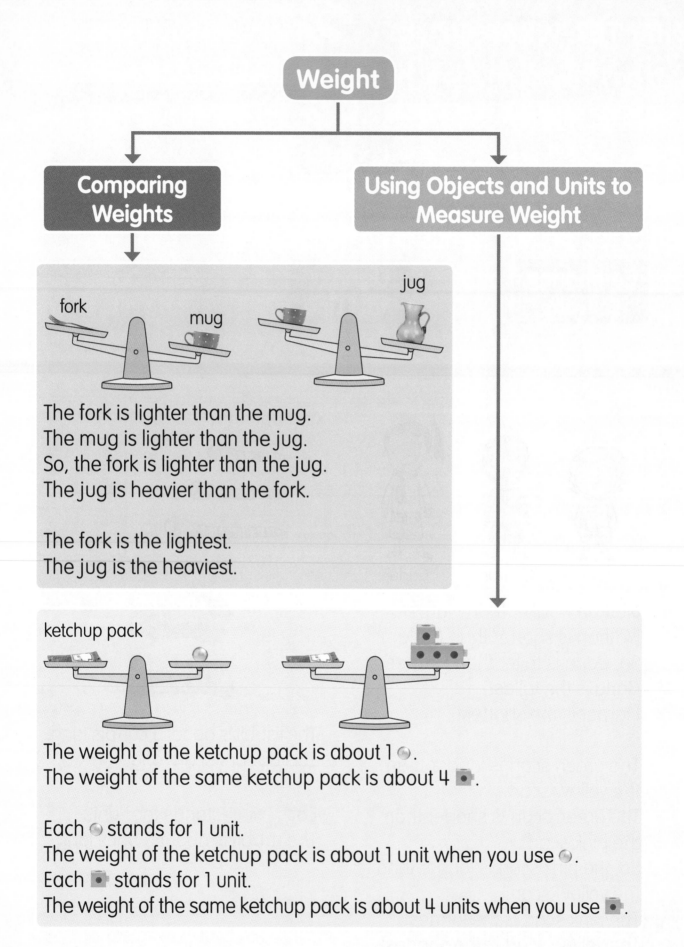

Weight

Comparing Weights

The fork is lighter than the mug.
The mug is lighter than the jug.
So, the fork is lighter than the jug.
The jug is heavier than the fork.

The fork is the lightest.
The jug is the heaviest.

Using Objects and Units to Measure Weight

The weight of the ketchup pack is about 1 ⊙.
The weight of the same ketchup pack is about 4 ⊡.

Each ⊙ stands for 1 unit.
The weight of the ketchup pack is about 1 unit when you use ⊙.
Each ⊡ stands for 1 unit.
The weight of the same ketchup pack is about 4 units when you use ⊡.

Name: _____   Date: _____

**Look the picture.
Then, fill in each blank.**

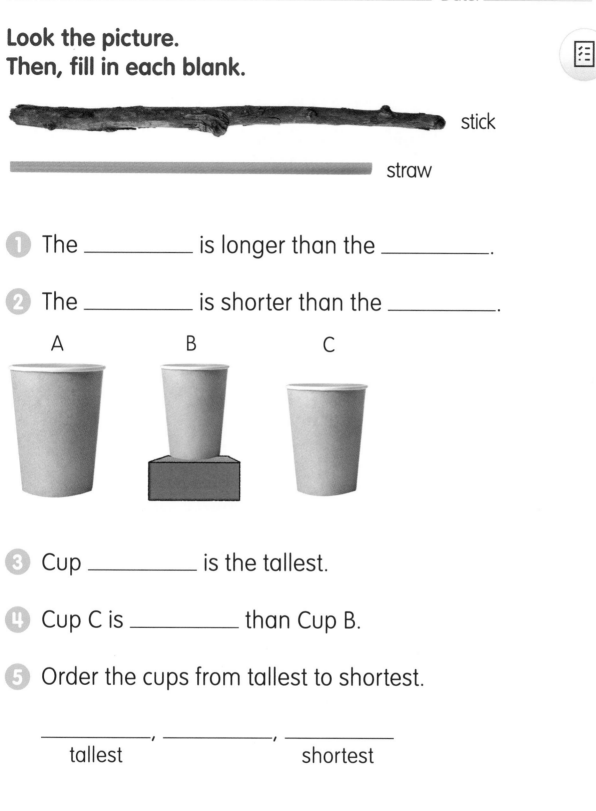

stick

straw

1 The _____ is longer than the _____.

2 The _____ is shorter than the _____.

A   B   C

3 Cup _____ is the tallest.

4 Cup C is _____ than Cup B.

5 Order the cups from tallest to shortest.

_____, _____, _____
   tallest   shortest

Look at the picture.
Then, answer each question.

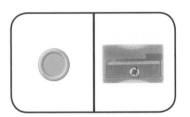

6 Do you use more ⬤ or 🔲 ?
Circle.

7 How many more? _____

Look at the pictures.
Then, fill in each blank.
Each ⬯ stands for 1 unit.

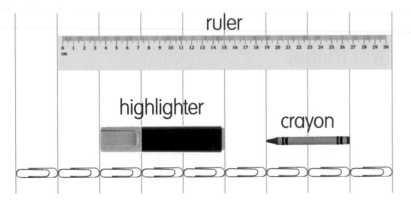

8 The highlighter is about _____ units long.

9 The _____ is the longest.

10 The ruler is _____ units longer than the crayon.

**Look at the picture.
Then, fill in each blank.**

vase

flower

11 The _____ is heavier than the _____.

12 The _____ is lighter than the _____.

**Look at the picture.
Then, fill in each blank.**

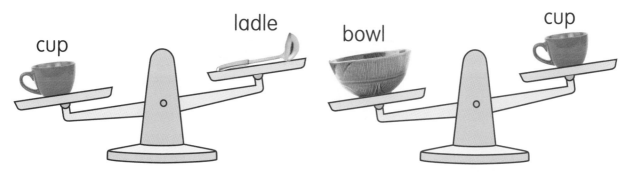

13 The ladle is _____ than the cup.

14 The bowl is _____ than the cup.

15 So, the bowl is _____ than the ladle.

16 The _____ is the heaviest.

Look at the pictures.
Fill in each blank.
Each ▢ **stands for 1 unit.**

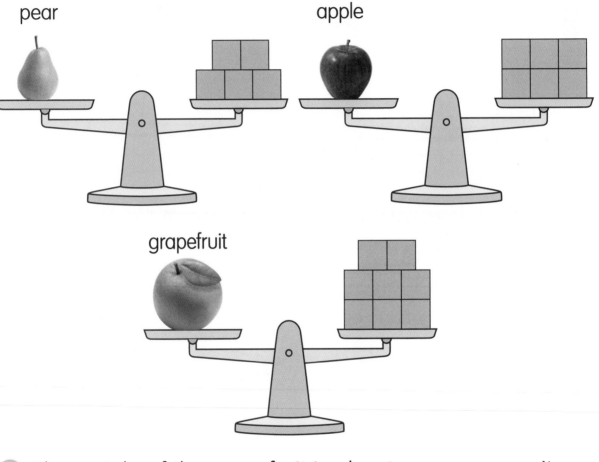

pear   apple

grapefruit

17) The weight of the grapefruit is about _____ units.

18) The weight of the pear is about _____ units.

19) The apple is _____ than the pear.

20) The grapefruit is the _____.

21) The pear is the _____.

Look at the pictures.
Then, solve.

22 **a** Max uses 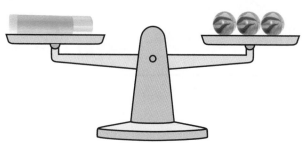 to measure the weight of a glue stick.
Each 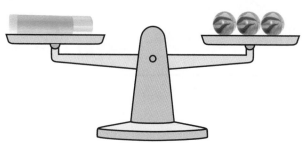 stands for 1 unit.

glue stick

The weight of the glue stick is _____ units.

b Clara then uses 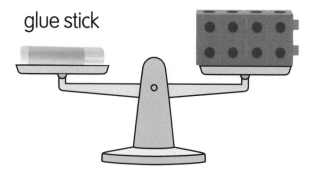 to measure the weight of the same glue stick.
Each 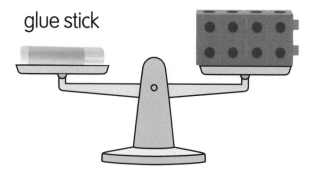 stands for 1 unit.

glue stick

The weight of the glue stick is _____ units.

c Why are the answers in **a** and **b** different?
Write what you think.

_____

_____

Assessment Prep

Answer each question.

23 Which sentences describe the picture?
Color the boxes.

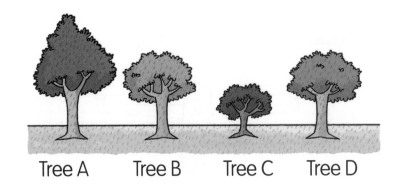

Tree A   Tree B   Tree C   Tree D

Tree A is taller than Tree C.	Tree C is the shortest.
Tree A is as tall as Tree D.	Tree B is taller than Tree C but shorter than Tree A.

24 Which sentences describe the picture?
Color the boxes.

The weight of the lemon is 5 ▬.
The lemon is heavier than the peach.
The peach weighs 4 ▬ more than the lemon.
6 ▬ is heavier than 1 lemon.

Name: _____   Date: _____

Gardening

1 Victor compares the heights of the trees in his yard.

Tree A   Tree B   Tree C

a   Tree _____ is taller than Tree _____.

b   Tree _____ is shorter than Tree _____.

c   Tree _____ is the tallest.

2 Victoria cuts the grass in her garden.
She wants to find out how long a grass blade is.

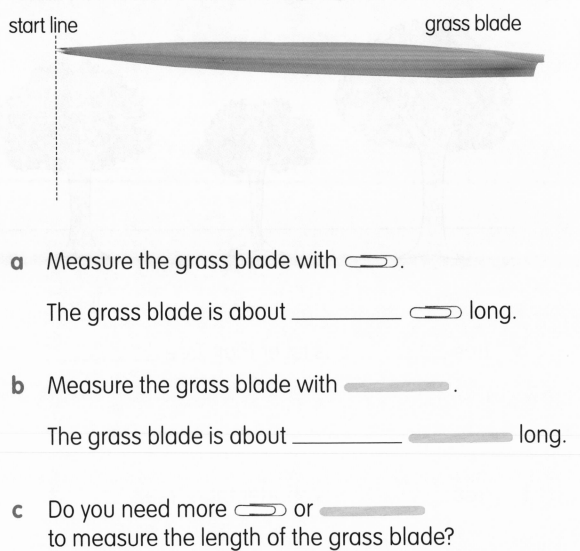

start line   grass blade

a Measure the grass blade with ⬭.

The grass blade is about _____ ⬭ long.

b Measure the grass blade with ▬▬▬.

The grass blade is about _____ ▬▬▬ long.

c Do you need more ⬭ or ▬▬▬
to measure the length of the grass blade?

_____

3

Parker wants to know which pot of plants is heavier. He places the pots on a seesaw to find out.

Pot A   Pot B

a   Pot A is _____ (heavier / lighter) than Pot B.

b   Write how you know.

4 Each stands for 1 unit.

Pot A

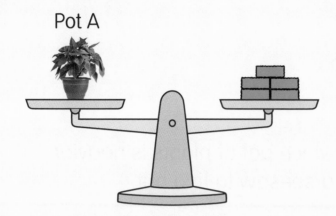

Pot B

a   The weight of Pot A is _____ units.

b   The weight of Pot B is _____ units.

c   Pot _____ is heavier than Pot _____.

5 Each 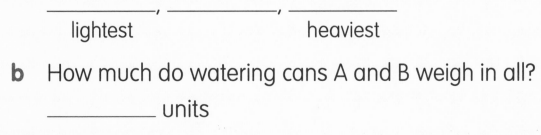 stands for 1 unit.

watering can A

watering can B

watering can C

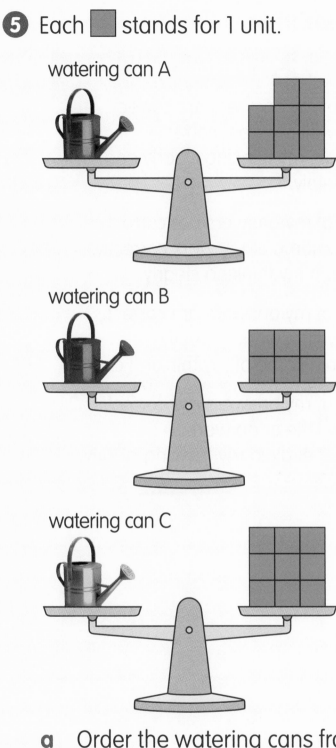

a Order the watering cans from lightest to heaviest.

_____, _____, _____
  lightest   heaviest

b How much do watering cans A and B weigh in all?

_____ units

Rubric

Point(s)	Level	My Performance
7–8	4	• Most of my answers are correct. • I show all my work correctly. • I explain my thinking clearly and completely.
5–6.5	3	• Some of my answers are correct. • I show some of my work correctly. • I explain my thinking clearly.
3–4.5	2	• A few of my answers are correct. • I show little work correctly. • I explain some of my thinking clearly.
0–2.5	1	• A few of my answers are correct. • I show little or no work. • I do not explain my thinking clearly.

Teacher's Comments

Chapter 10 Numbers to 120

How many animals and flowers are there? How can I count?

How can you compare and order numbers more than 40?

Name: _____   Date: _____

Counting to 40

| 20 twenty | 21 | 22 | 23 | 24 | 25 | 26 | 27 | 28 | 29 | 30 thirty |

| 30 thirty | 31 | 32 | 33 | 34 | 35 | 36 | 37 | 38 | 39 | 40 forty |

▶ **Quick Check**

Count on.
Then, fill in each blank.

1 21, 22, 23, _____, _____, _____

2 35, 36, 37, _____, _____, _____

Using place value

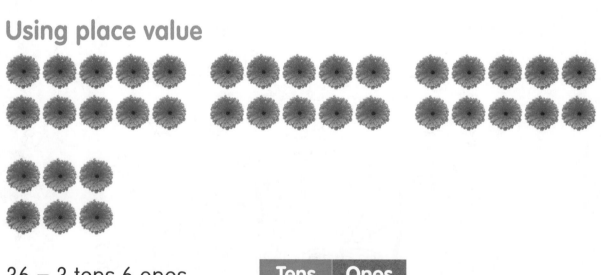

36 = 3 tens 6 ones
36 = 30 + 6

Tens	Ones
3	6

▶ **Quick Check**

Write each missing number.

3

Tens	Ones

34 =

4 2 tens 4 ones = _____

5 _____ tens 2 ones = 32

6 20 + _____ = 25

7 _____ + 8 = 38

Comparing and ordering numbers

Compare 29, 39, and 32.

Step 1 Compare the tens.
3 tens are greater than 2 tens.
So, 29 is the least number.
In 32 and 39, the tens are the same.

Tens	Ones
2	9
3	9
3	2

Step 2 Next, compare the ones.
9 ones are greater than 2 ones.
So, 39 is greater than 32.
39 is the greatest number.

Order the numbers from greatest to least.

39
greatest

32

29
least

▶ **Quick Check**

**Compare and order the numbers.
Then, fill in each blank.**

40   31   37

8 The greatest number is _____.

9 The least number is _____.

10 Order the numbers from least to greatest.

_____ , _____ , _____
least   greatest

Number patterns

23, 25, 27, 29, 31, 33, …
The numbers are arranged in a pattern.
Each number is 2 more than the number before it.
The next number is 2 more than 33.
It is 35.

▶ **Quick Check**

Find the missing numbers in each number pattern.

11 24, 26, 28, 30, _____ , _____ , 36

12 40, _____ , _____ , 37, 36, 35, 34

1 Counting to 120

Learning Objectives:
- Count on from 40 to 120.
- Read and write 41 to 120 in numbers and words.

New Vocabulary

fifty	sixty
seventy	eighty
ninety	one hundred

one hundred ten
one hundred twenty

THINK

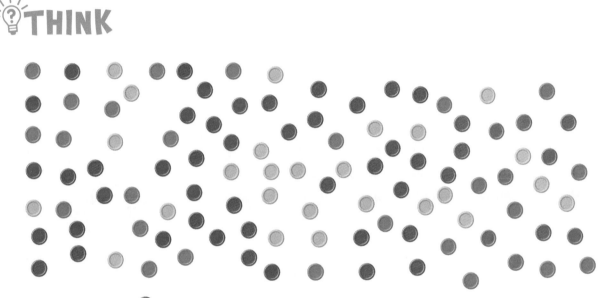

How many are there?
Can you find out without counting one at a time?
Talk about the different ways you can use with your partner.

ENGAGE

a Use to fill four .
How many do you have?

b Choose some more .
How many do you have now?

c Share another way to count with your partner.

LEARN Count on from 40

1 Count the sticks.

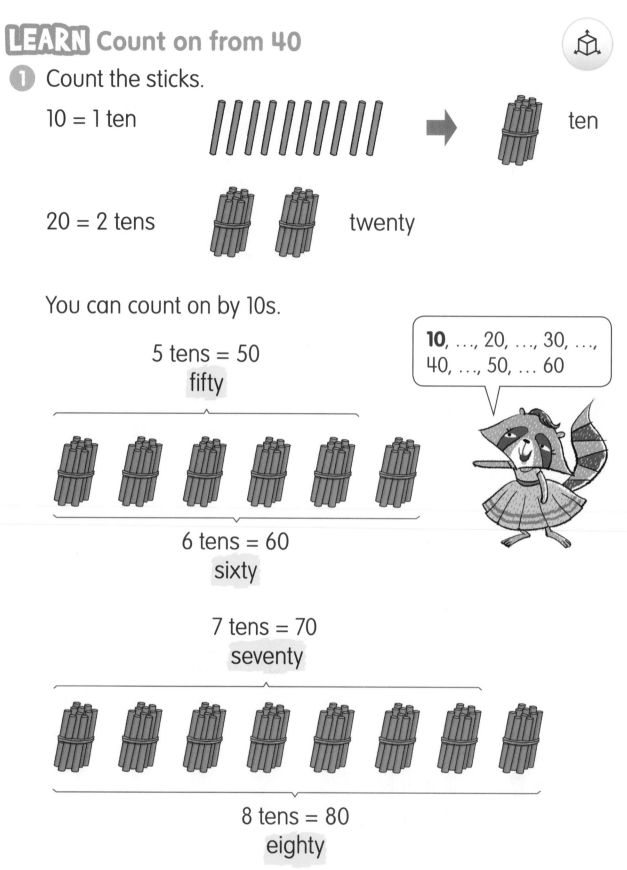

10 = 1 ten

ten

20 = 2 tens

twenty

You can count on by 10s.

5 tens = 50
fifty

10, …, 20, …, 30, …,
40, …, 50, … 60

6 tens = 60
sixty

7 tens = 70
seventy

8 tens = 80
eighty

9 tens = 90
ninety

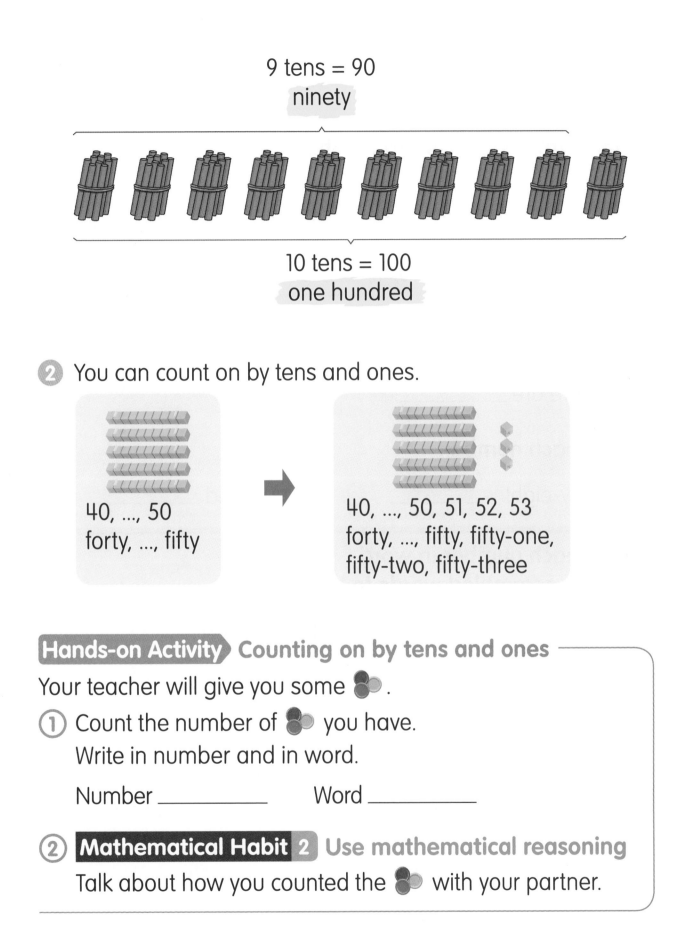

10 tens = 100
one hundred

2️⃣ You can count on by tens and ones.

40, ..., 50
forty, ..., fifty

40, ..., 50, 51, 52, 53
forty, ..., fifty, fifty-one,
fifty-two, fifty-three

Hands-on Activity Counting on by tens and ones

Your teacher will give you some 🔵.

① Count the number of 🔵 you have.
Write in number and in word.

Number _____   Word _____

② **Mathematical Habit 2** Use mathematical reasoning

Talk about how you counted the 🔵 with your partner.

TRY Practice counting on from 40

Count on by tens and ones.
Then, write each missing number.

1

> ten, …, twenty, …, thirty, …,
> forty, …, seventy-one, …

10, …, 20, …, 30, …, 40, …, _____, …,

_____, …, _____, 71, _____,

_____, _____, _____.

There are _____ 🧊.

Write each number.

2 forty-eight _____   3 one hundred _____

Write each number in word.
Use the scrambled words to help you.

4 50 yfitf _____   5 91 ntieny-noe _____

ENGAGE

Place a handful of 🔵 on the table.

a Ask your partner to guess the number.

b Work together to find the number without counting each one.

What way did you use?

LEARN Guess the number of objects

1 How many 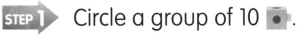 do you think there are?

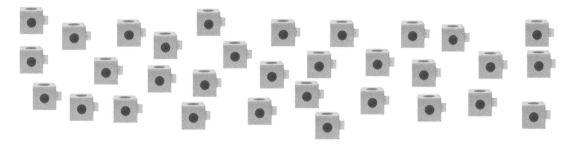

STEP 1 Circle a group of 10 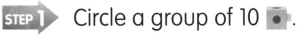.

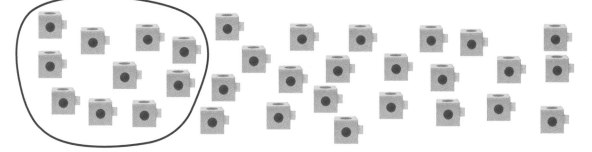

STEP 2 Look at the rest of the 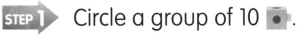.
About how many groups of 10 are there?
Can you tell without counting?

There are about 3 groups of 10 altogether.
10 + 10 + 10 = 30
There are about 30 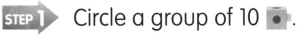.

There are about 30 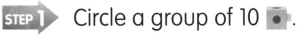.
Count the 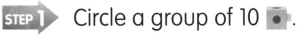.

1, 2, 3, 4, …, 10, …, 20, …,
30, 31, 32
There are 32 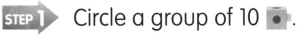 in all.

There are 32 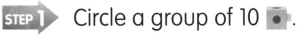.

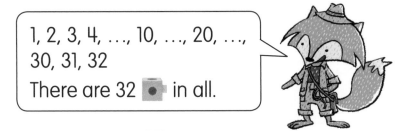

Hands-on Activity Guessing and counting

Work in pairs.
Your teacher will give you a string.

① Take some  and spread them on your desk.

② Ask your partner to ring the string around 10 🔘.

③ **Mathematical Habit 7 Make use of structure**
Ask your partner to guess how many 🔘 there are.

④ Count the number of 🔘.
Check if your partner guessed correctly.

⑤ Trade places.
Repeat ① to ④.

TRY Practice guessing the number of objects

Guess the number of 🧊.
Then, circle groups of 10 and count on.

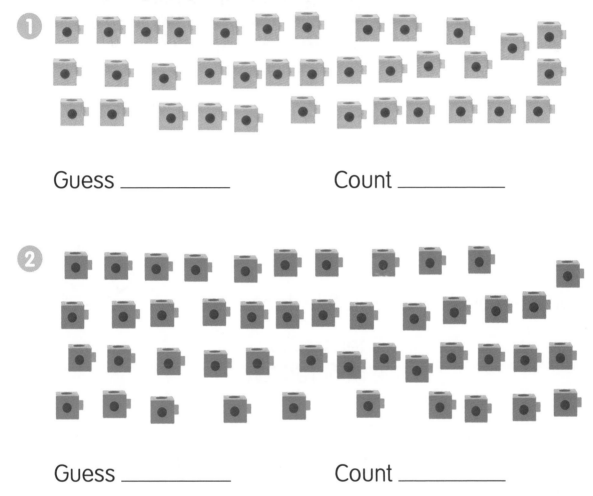

1

Guess _____   Count _____

2

Guess _____   Count _____

ENGAGE

Count 10 ▱▱▱▱▱▱▱.
What number do you have?
Now, count on 3 more.
What number do you have now?
Share how you count with your partner.

1 You can count on from 100 by ones.

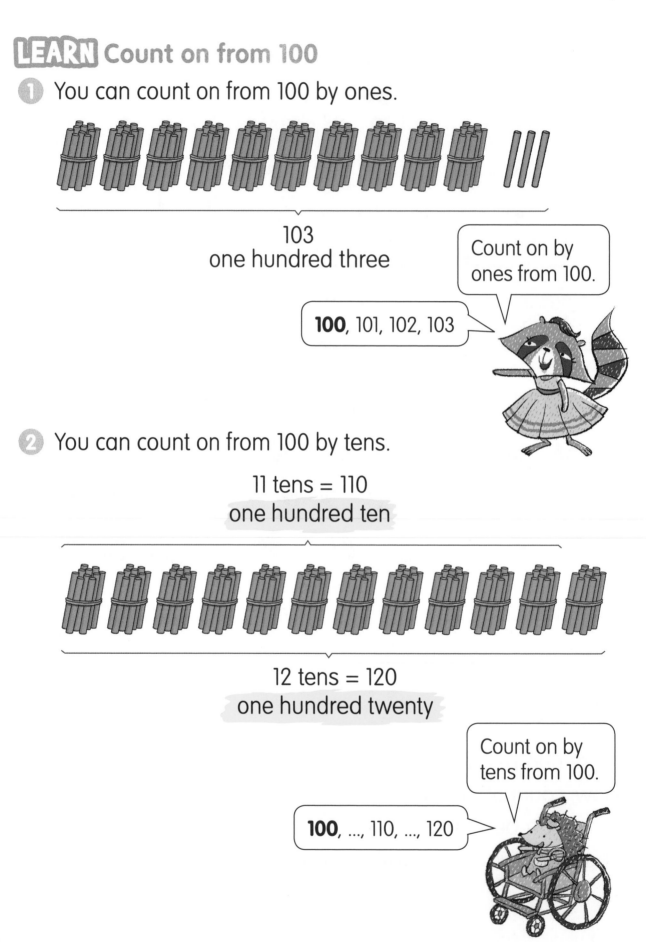

103
one hundred three

Count on by ones from 100.

100, 101, 102, 103

2 You can count on from 100 by tens.

11 tens = 110
one hundred ten

12 tens = 120
one hundred twenty

Count on by tens from 100.

100, ..., 110, ..., 120

3 You can count on from 100 by tens and ones.

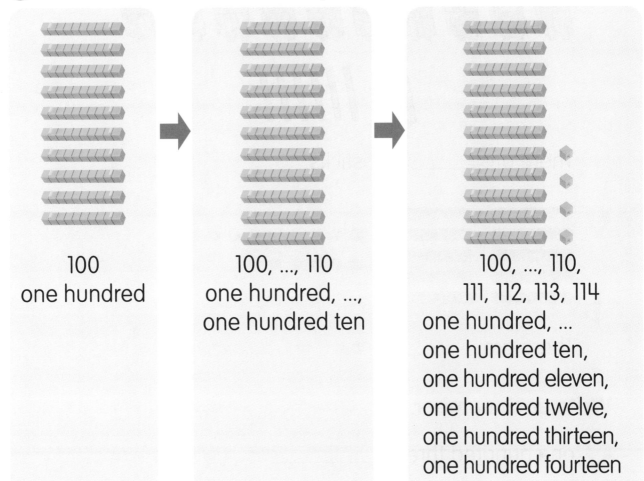

100
one hundred

→

100, ..., 110
one hundred, ...,
one hundred ten

→

100, ..., 110,
111, 112, 113, 114
one hundred, ...
one hundred ten,
one hundred eleven,
one hundred twelve,
one hundred thirteen,
one hundred fourteen

TRY Practice counting on from 100

Count on by tens and ones.
Then, write each missing number.

1

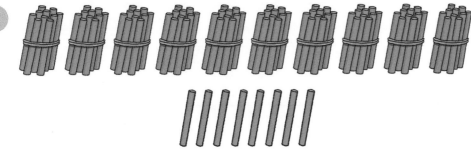

There are _____ sticks.

2

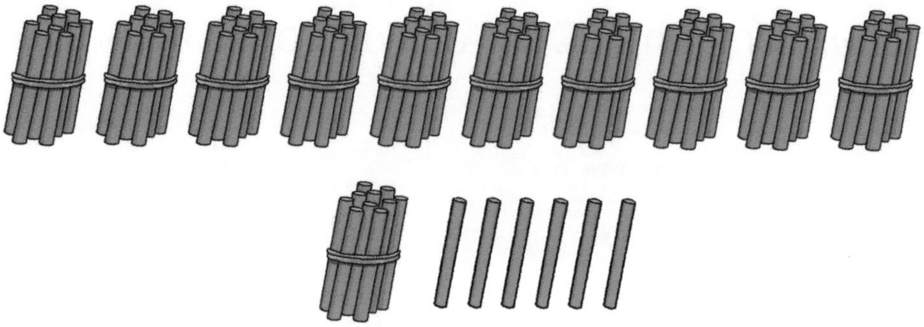

There are _____ sticks.

3

There are _____ 🔲.

Write each number.

4 one hundred three _____

5 one hundred fourteen _____

Write each number in word.

6 106 _____

7 117 _____

8 112 _____

INDEPENDENT PRACTICE

Count on by tens and ones.
Then, fill in each blank.

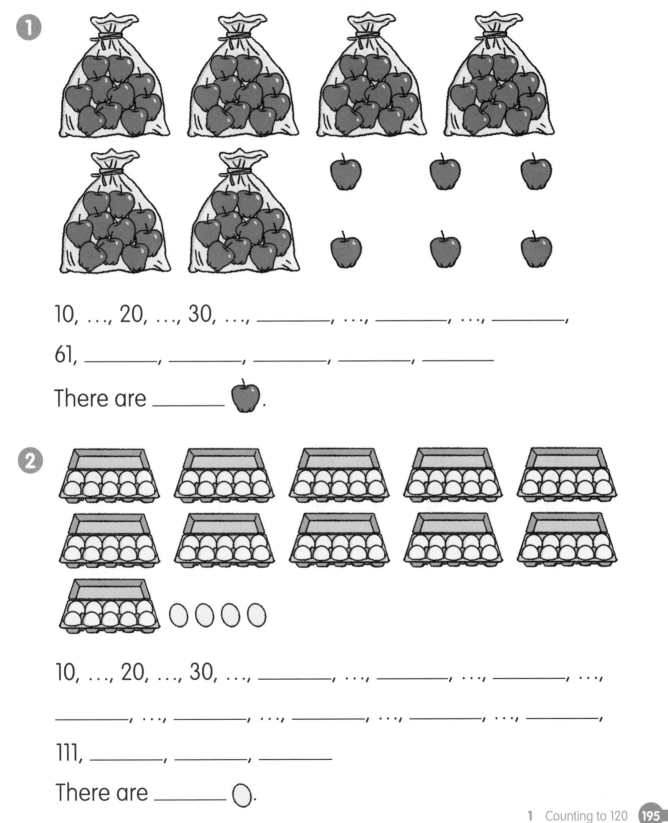

1

10, …, 20, …, 30, …, _____, …, _____, …, _____,

61, _____, _____, _____, _____, _____

There are _____ 🍎.

2

10, …, 20, …, 30, …, _____, …, _____, …, _____, …,

_____, …, _____, …, _____, …, _____, …, _____,

111, _____, _____, _____

There are _____ ⬭.

Count the flowers by tens and ones.
Then, draw lines to match the numbers.

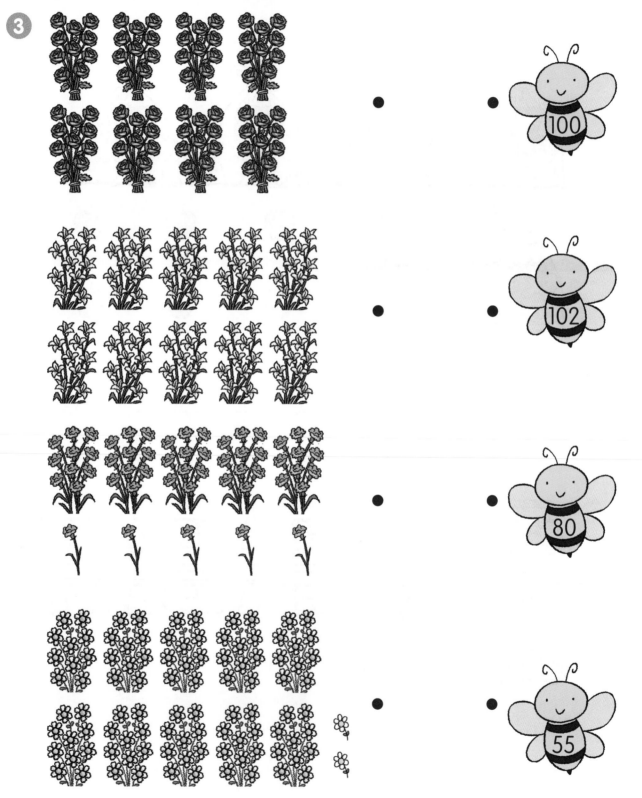

3

Guess the number of each type of insect.
Then, circle in groups of 10 and count on.

④

Guess _____   Count _____

⑤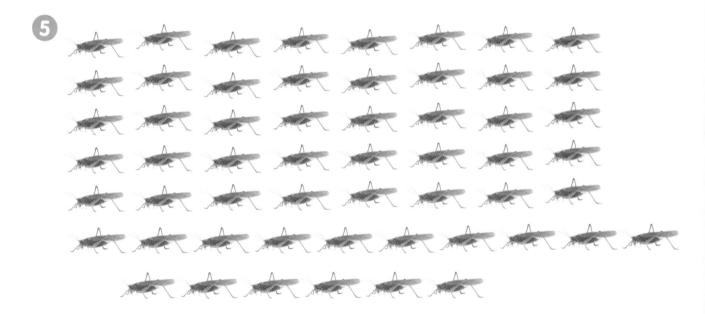

Guess _____   Count _____

6

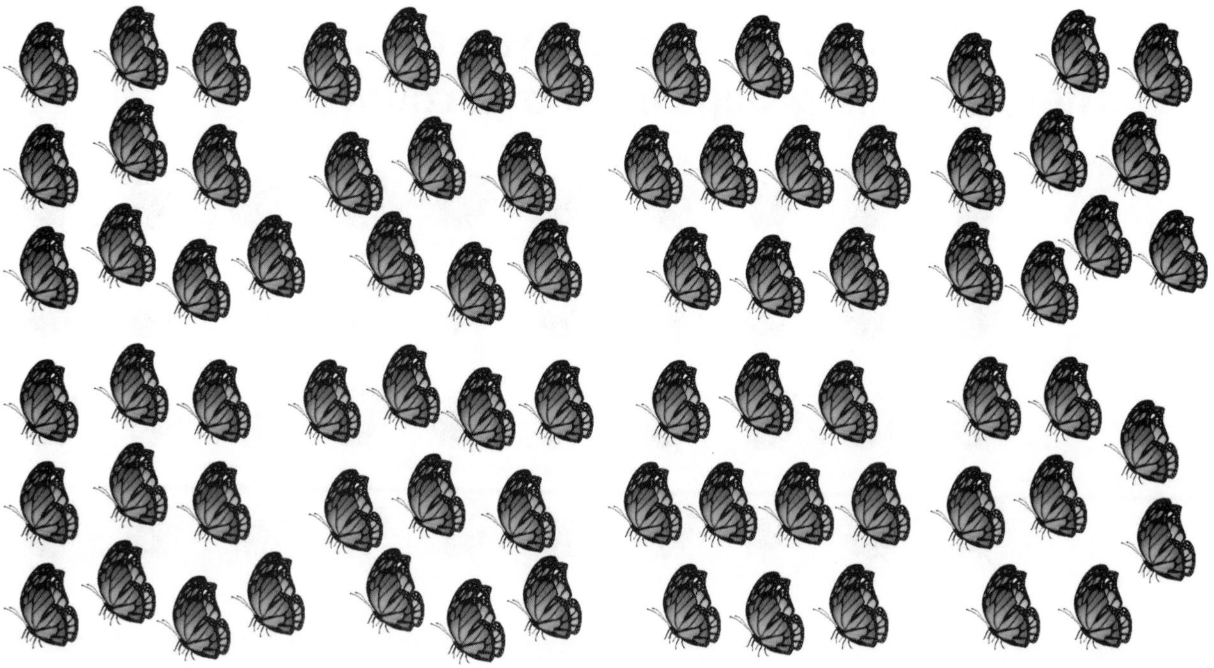

Guess _____   Count _____

Write each number.

7 fifty-nine _____

8 sixty-eight _____

9 one hundred twelve _____

Write each number in word.

10 75 _____

11 62 _____

12 120 _____

2 Place Value

Learning Objectives:
- Use a place-value chart to show numbers to 100.
- Use tens and ones to show numbers to 100.
- Decompose 2-digit numbers in different ways.

THINK

1 Fill in the blank.

$76 =$

Tens	Ones
5	

2 Show two different ways to complete the following. The number of tens must be less than 5.

$89 =$

Tens	Ones

$=$

Tens	Ones

ENGAGE

Use ▦ to show 45 and 54 on two place-value charts.
Talk about the differences you see with your partner.

LEARN Use place value to show numbers to 100

1

90 and 8 make 98.
So, $90 + 8 = 98$.

90   8

$98 = 9$ tens 8 ones
$98 = 90 + 8$

Tens	Ones
9	8

2 You can use tens and ones to show a number in different ways.

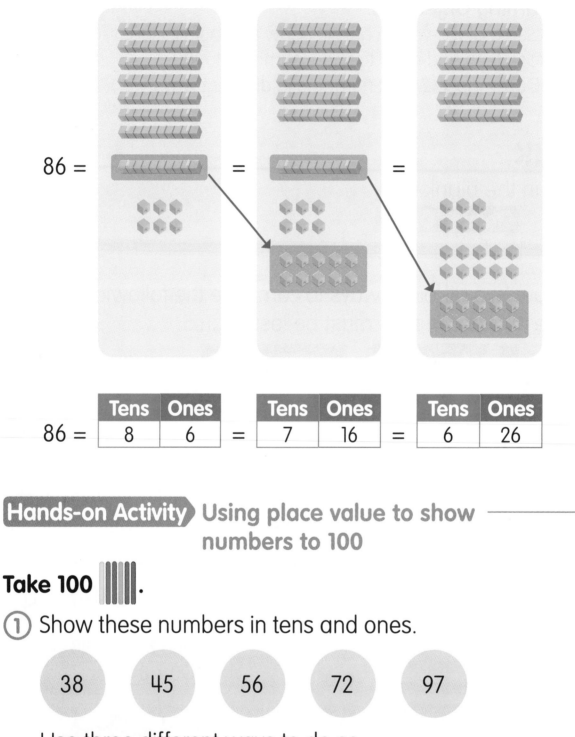

	Tens	Ones		Tens	Ones		Tens	Ones
86 =	8	6	=	7	16	=	6	26

Hands-on Activity Using place value to show numbers to 100

Take 100 .

① Show these numbers in tens and ones.

(38)   (45)   (56)   (72)   (97)

Use three different ways to do so.
You can bundle each group of 10 together.

TRY Practice using place value to show numbers to 100

Fill in each blank.

1.

80 and 7 make _____.

So, 80 + 7 = _____.

87 = _____ tens _____ ones

Tens	Ones

Which 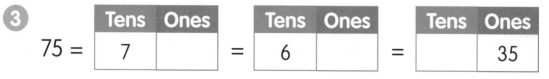 shows 62?
Make a ✔ if they do.

2.

Write each missing number.

3.

Tens	Ones
7	

75 =

Tens	Ones
6	

=

Tens	Ones
	35

=

SHOW THE NUMBER!

45

forty five

What you need:

Players: 4
What you need: [image], Word cards

What to do:

1. Player 1 says a number and uses the correct word cards to show the number.

2. The other players use [image] to show the number.

   The first player to show the correct answer gets 1 point.

3. Trade places.
   Repeat 1 and 2.

Who is the winner?

The player with the most points after nine rounds wins!

INDEPENDENT PRACTICE

Write each missing number.

1

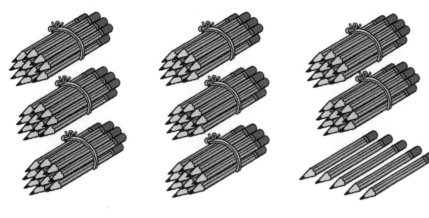

85 = _____ tens _____ ones

80 + 5 = _____

Tens	Ones

Which ▢ **shows 80?**
Make a ✔ if they do.
Make an ✗ if they do not.

2

Which ▨ shows 99?

Make a ✔ if they do.

Make an X if they do not.

Then, draw ▭ for tens and □ for ones to show the correct answer.

3

Use tens and ones to write 74 in three different ways.

4

$74 =$

Tens	Ones

$=$

Tens	Ones

$=$

Tens	Ones

3 Comparing, Ordering, and Number Patterns

Learning Objectives:
- Use a strategy to compare numbers to 100.
- Order numbers to 100.
- Find the missing numbers in a number pattern.

THINK

There are five cards.
Each card has a number.
All five numbers make a number pattern.
Two numbers are covered up.
What do you think the numbers are likely to be?
Show three different number choices.

ENGAGE

| 50 | 51 | 52 | 53 | 54 | 55 | 56 | 57 | 58 | 59 | 60 |

1 Point at a number.
   a Count on to find 2 more than the number.
   b Count back to find 2 less than the number.

2 Count on from 60 to find 2 more than 60.

3 Count back from 50 to find 2 less than 50.

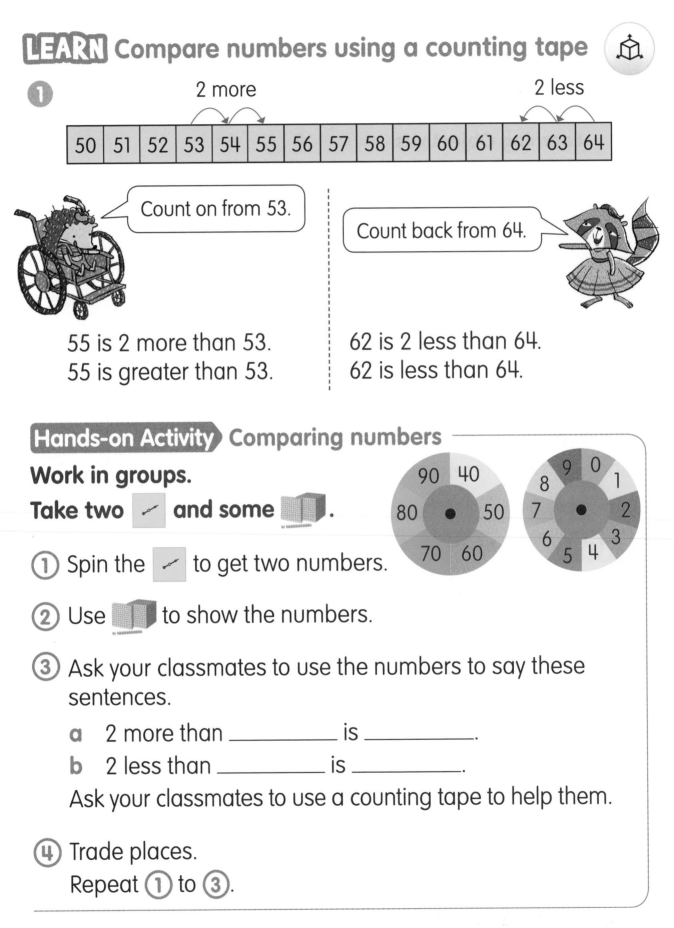

① 2 more 2 less

| 50 | 51 | 52 | 53 | 54 | 55 | 56 | 57 | 58 | 59 | 60 | 61 | 62 | 63 | 64 |

Count on from 53.

Count back from 64.

55 is 2 more than 53.
55 is greater than 53.

62 is 2 less than 64.
62 is less than 64.

Hands-on Activity Comparing numbers

Work in groups.
Take two ✏ **and some** ▮.

① Spin the ✏ to get two numbers.

② Use ▮ to show the numbers.

③ Ask your classmates to use the numbers to say these sentences.

   a   2 more than _____ is _____.
   b   2 less than _____ is _____.
   Ask your classmates to use a counting tape to help them.

④ Trade places.
   Repeat ① to ③.

Fill in each blank.
Use the counting tape to help you.

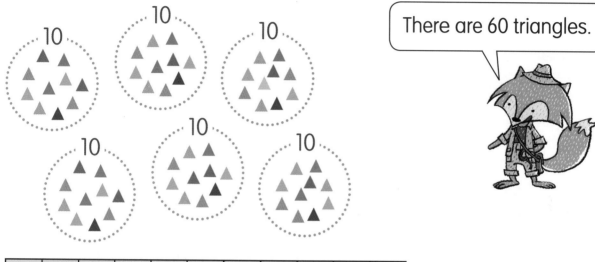

There are 60 triangles.

| 55 | 56 | 57 | 58 | 59 | 60 | 61 | 62 | 63 | 64 | 65 |

1 3 more than 60 is _____.

2 3 less than 60 is _____.

ENGAGE

a Use 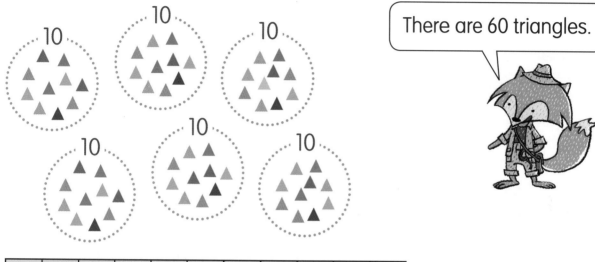 to show 65 on a place-value chart.

b Replace the tens to get a number that is less.
Show two different ways.
Write the two numbers.

c Replace the tens to get a greater number.
Show two different ways.
Write the two numbers.

LEARN Compare numbers with different tens

1 Compare 60 and 59.

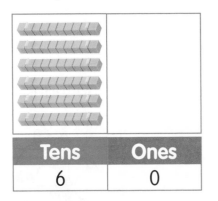

Tens	Ones
6	0

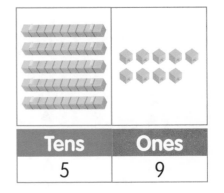

Tens	Ones
5	9

Compare the tens.
They are different.
6 tens are greater than 5 tens.
So, 60 is greater than 59.
You can write 60 > 59.

">" means greater than.

TRY Practice comparing numbers with different tens

**Compare the numbers.
Then, fill in each blank.**

72 **56**

Are the tens equal?

1 7 tens are greater than _____ tens.

So, _____ is greater than _____.

2 _____ > _____

ENGAGE

a Use 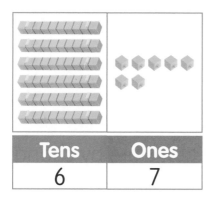 to show 57 on a place-value chart.

b Replace the ones to get a number that is less.
Show two different ways.
Write the two numbers.

c Replace the ones to get a greater number.
Show three different ways.
Write the three numbers.

LEARN Compare numbers with equal tens

1 Compare 67 and 69.

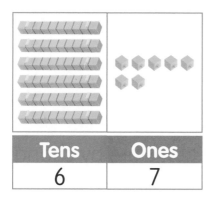

Tens	Ones
6	7

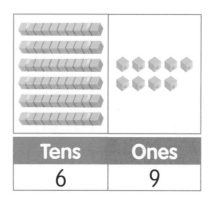

Tens	Ones
6	9

Compare the tens.
The tens are the same.

So, compare the ones.
7 ones are less than 9 ones.
So, 67 is less than 69.
You can write 67 < 69.

"<" means less than.

TRY Practice comparing numbers with equal tens

Compare the numbers.
Fill in each blank.

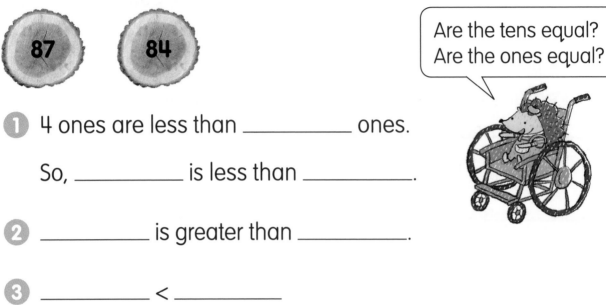

87   **84**

Are the tens equal?
Are the ones equal?

1 4 ones are less than _____ ones.

So, _____ is less than _____.

2 _____ is greater than _____.

3 _____ < _____

ENGAGE

a Write a number between 50 and 60.

b Ask your partner to write two more numbers by changing the tens.

c Order these numbers from least to greatest.

Use  to help you.

LEARN Compare and order three numbers

1 Compare 68, 83, and 95.

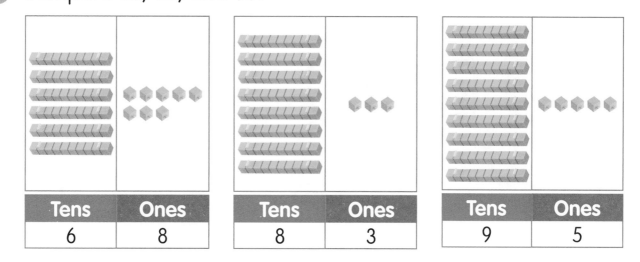

Tens	Ones
6	8

Tens	Ones
8	3

Tens	Ones
9	5

Compare the tens.
8 tens are greater than 6 tens.
9 tens are greater than 8 tens.
So, 9 tens is the greatest.
95 is the greatest.
68 is the least.

Order the numbers from greatest to least.

greatest   least

Order the numbers from least to greatest.

least   greatest

TRY Practice comparing and ordering three numbers

Compare and order the numbers.
Then, fill in each blank.

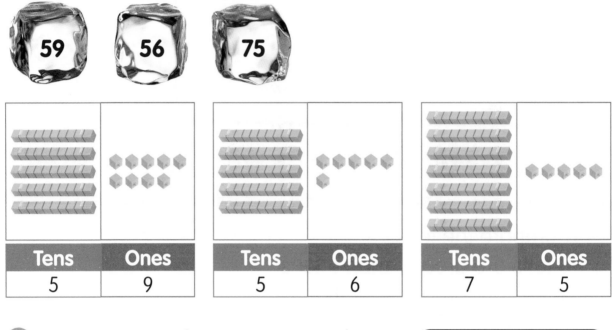

Tens	Ones
5	9

Tens	Ones
5	6

Tens	Ones
7	5

1 _____ is the greatest number.

2 _____ is the least number.

> Compare the tens.
> Then, compare the ones.

3 Order the numbers from greatest to least.

_____, _____, _____
  greatest   least

4 Order the numbers from least to greatest.

_____, _____, _____
  least   greatest

Order the numbers from least to greatest.

5

84   48   100

_____, _____, _____
least   greatest

How many tens
does 100 have?

Mathematical Habit **3** Construct viable arguments

Rafael arranges his numbers in this way to compare them.

7 6

5 9

8 0

Talk about how his way works with your partner.
Then, use Rafael's way to compare 48, 90, and 72.

ENGAGE

 Look at the numbers.
50, 52, _____, _____, 58, 60
Do you notice a pattern?
Write each missing number.

2 Make another number pattern for your partner to solve.

LEARN Find missing numbers in a number pattern

1. The numbers on the counting tape make a pattern. Some numbers are missing.

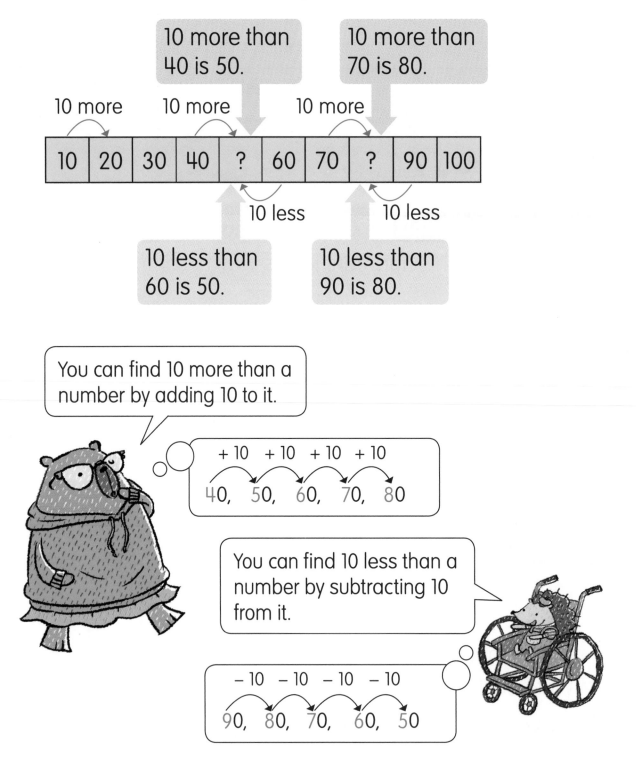

10 more than 40 is 50.

10 more than 70 is 80.

10 more   10 more   10 more

| 10 | 20 | 30 | 40 | ? | 60 | 70 | ? | 90 | 100 |

10 less   10 less

10 less than 60 is 50.

10 less than 90 is 80.

You can find 10 more than a number by adding 10 to it.

+10 +10 +10 +10
40, 50, 60, 70, 80

You can find 10 less than a number by subtracting 10 from it.

−10 −10 −10 −10
90, 80, 70, 60, 50

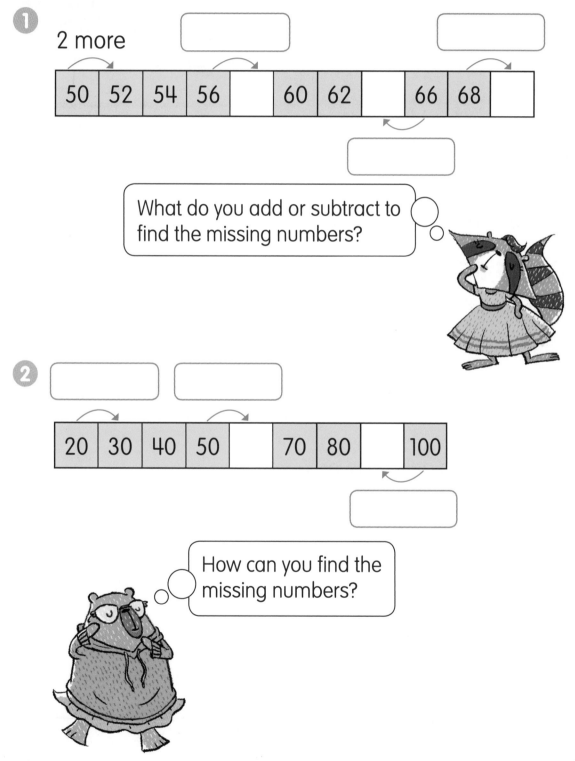

TRY Practice finding missing numbers in a number pattern

The numbers are arranged in a pattern.
Fill in each box.

1

2 more

| 50 | 52 | 54 | 56 | | 60 | 62 | | 66 | 68 | |

What do you add or subtract to find the missing numbers?

2

| 20 | 30 | 40 | 50 | | 70 | 80 | | 100 |

How can you find the missing numbers?

WHAT IS MY NUMBER?

Yes

Is the number greater than 70?

What you need:

Players: 4
What you need: Pencil, Paper

What to do:

1. Player 1 thinks of a number between 50 and 100.

2. Player 1 writes the number down.
   Then, he or she covers it up.

3. Each player takes turns to ask a question to find the number.
   Player 1 can only answer **Yes** or **No**.
   The first player to guess the number correctly gets one point.

4. Trade places.
   Repeat 1 to 3.

Who is the winner?

The player with the most points after four rounds wins!

INDEPENDENT PRACTICE

Compare 49 and 53.
Then, fill in each blank.
Use the counting tape to help you.

48	49	50	51	52	53	54

1 _____ is less than _____.

2 _____ is 4 less than _____.

3 _____ is greater than _____.

4 _____ is 4 more than _____.

Fill in each blank.
Use the counting tape to help you.

87	88	89	90	91	92	93	94	95	96

5 2 more than 93 is _____.

6 3 less than 93 is _____.

7 _____ is 2 more than 87.

8 _____ is 2 less than 91.

Fill in each blank with >, <, or =.

9 88 ◯ 99

10 76 ◯ 6 tens 7 ones

11 55 ◯ 4 tens 15 ones

12 38 ◯ 2 tens 19 ones

Compare the numbers.
Then, fill in each blank.

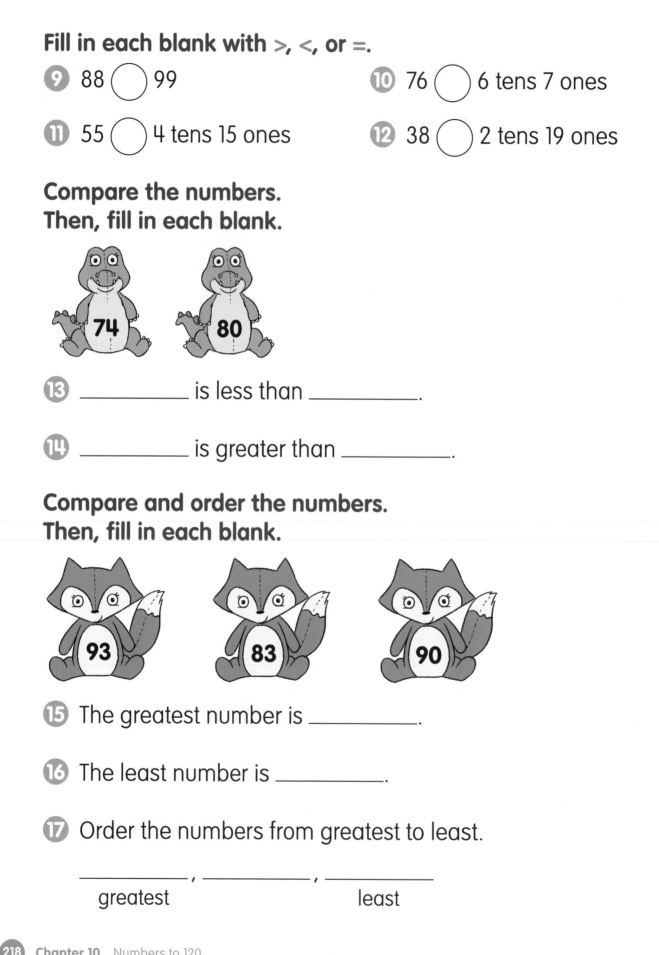

74   80

13 _____ is less than _____.

14 _____ is greater than _____.

Compare and order the numbers.
Then, fill in each blank.

93   83   90

15 The greatest number is _____.

16 The least number is _____.

17 Order the numbers from greatest to least.

_____, _____, _____
greatest   least

Order the numbers from least to greatest.

18

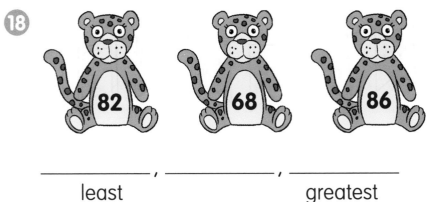

_____ , _____ , _____

least   greatest

The numbers are arranged in a pattern.
Write what the rule is.
Then, write the missing numbers in each number pattern.

19

I find _____ more than a number by adding

_____ to that number.

I find _____ less than a number by subtracting

_____ from that number.

20

I find _____ less than a number by subtracting

_____ from that number.

I find _____ more than a number by adding

_____ to that number.

Look at each number pattern.
Write the missing numbers in each number pattern.

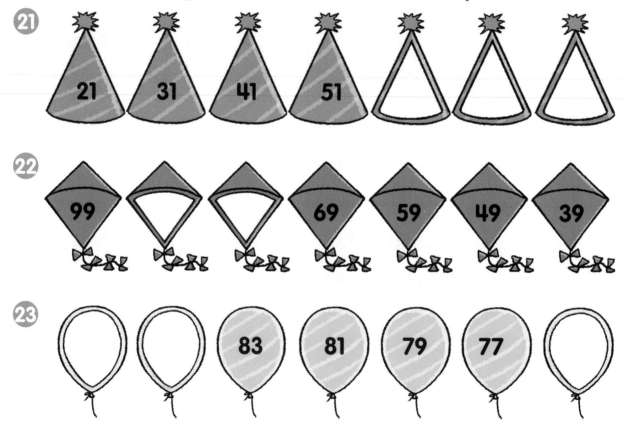

21 21 31 41 51

22 99 69 59 49 39

23 83 81 79 77

Mathematical Habit 2 Use mathematical reasoning

Which set of numbers is not in order from least to greatest?
Write down why you think so.

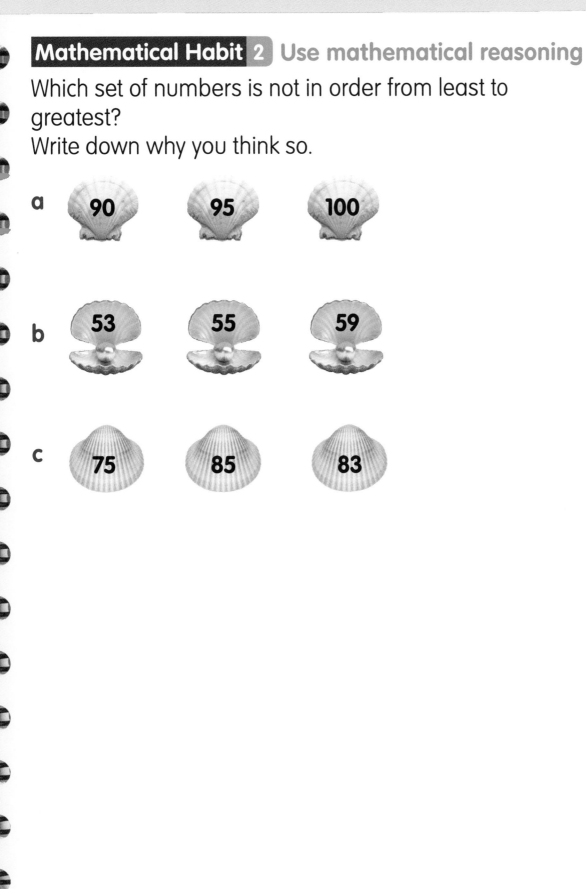

a   90   95   100

b   53   55   59

c   75   85   83

Problem Solving with Heuristics

1 **Mathematical Habit** 8 **Look for patterns**

Make two different number patterns.
Explain the rule for each number pattern.

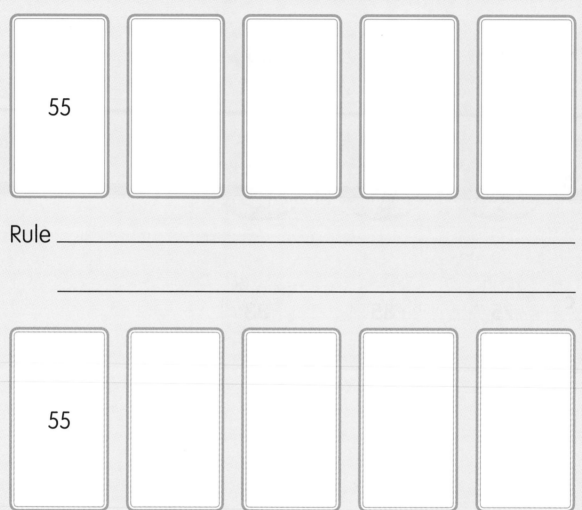

55

Rule _____

_____

55

Rule _____

_____

2 **Mathematical Habit 1** Persevere in solving problems

I am thinking of a number between 40 and 90.
When I subtract one digit from the other, I get 3.
What are all the possible numbers?

Make a list.

You can subtract the digit in the tens place from the digit in the ones place.

You can also subtract the digit in the ones place from the digit in the tens place.

CHAPTER WRAP-UP

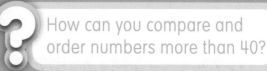

Numbers to 120

- Counting to 120
- Place Value
- Comparing and Ordering Numbers
- Number Patterns

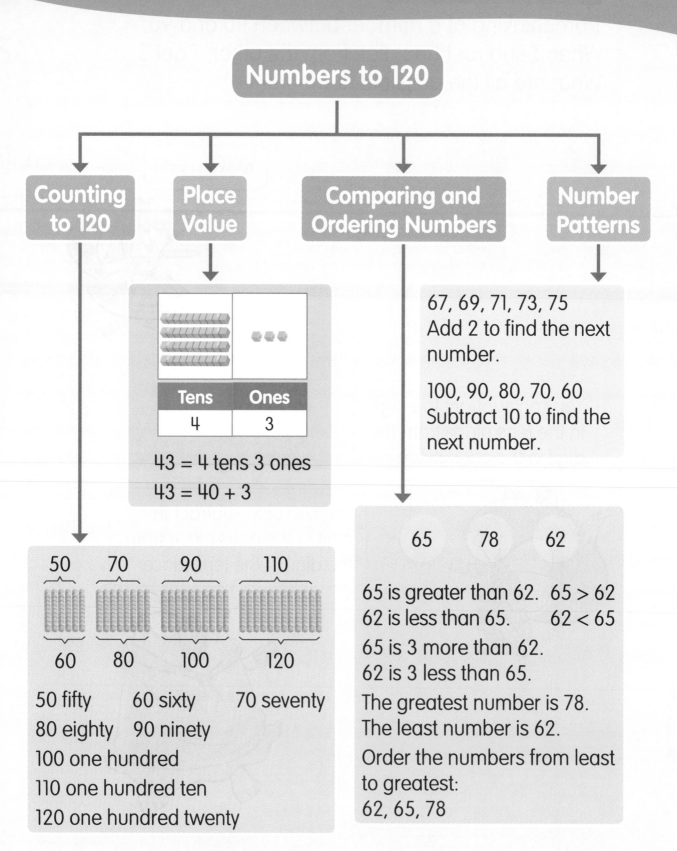

Place Value

Tens	Ones
4	3

43 = 4 tens 3 ones

43 = 40 + 3

Number Patterns

67, 69, 71, 73, 75
Add 2 to find the next number.

100, 90, 80, 70, 60
Subtract 10 to find the next number.

Counting to 120

50 — 60
70 — 80
90 — 100
110 — 120

50 fifty   60 sixty   70 seventy

80 eighty   90 ninety

100 one hundred

110 one hundred ten

120 one hundred twenty

Comparing and Ordering Numbers

65   78   62

65 is greater than 62.   65 > 62
62 is less than 65.   62 < 65

65 is 3 more than 62.
62 is 3 less than 65.

The greatest number is 78.
The least number is 62.

Order the numbers from least to greatest:
62, 65, 78

Name: _____ Date: _____

Count.
Then, fill in each blank.

1 10, …, 20, …, 30, …, 40, …, _____, …, _____, …,

_____, …, _____,…, _____,…,

_____,…, _____, 111, _____, _____,

_____, _____

There are _____ straws.

2 Write the number of straws in word.

_____

Count.
Write each missing number.

3 _____ = _____ tens _____ ones

_____ = _____ + _____

Tens	Ones

Which 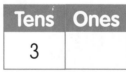 shows 75?

Make a ✓ if they do.

Make a ✗ if they do not.

Then, draw ☐☐☐☐ for tens and ☐ for ones to show the correct answer.

④

Write each missing number.

⑤

Tens	Ones
5	

58 = ☐ =

Tens	Ones
3	

=

Tens	Ones
	18

Use tens and ones to write **90** in three different ways.

⑥

Tens	Ones

90 = ☐ =

Tens	Ones

=

Tens	Ones

Draw [   ] **for tens and** □ **for ones to show 93.**
Show four different ways.

7

a	b
c	d

Fill in each blank.
Use the counting tape to help you.

| 57 | 58 | 59 | 60 | 61 | 62 | 63 | 64 | 65 | 66 | 67 | 68 | 69 | 70 |

8 _____ is 4 less than 66.

9 _____ is 4 more than 60.

10 57 is 3 less than _____.

11 3 more than 59 is _____.

12 58 is _____ less than 62.

13 65 is _____ more than 61.

Compare the numbers.
Then, fill in each blank.

14

78   90

_____ is greater than _____.

_____ > _____

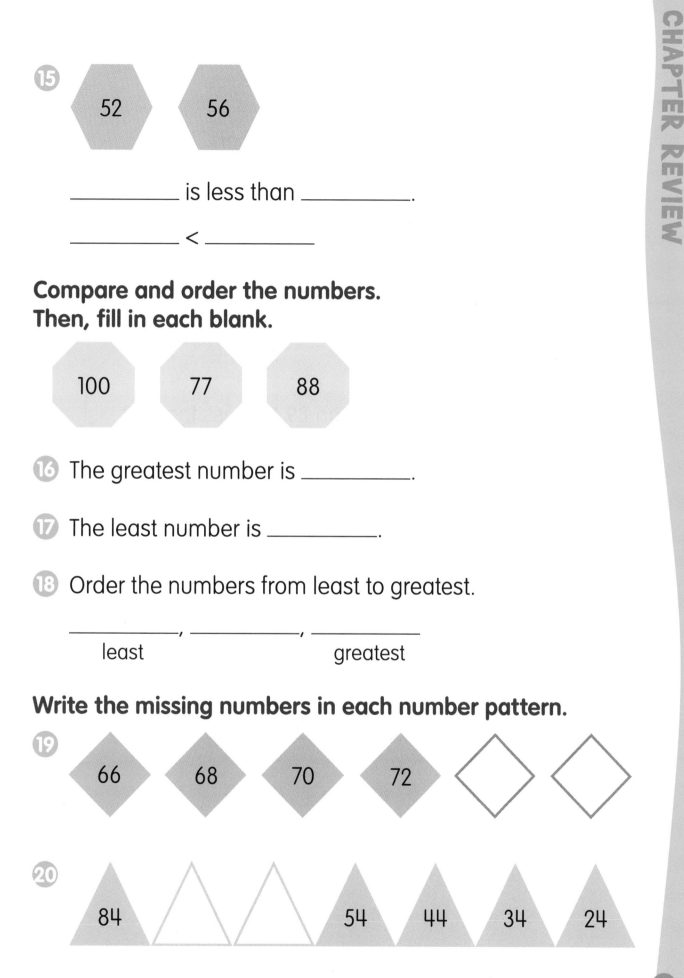

15   52   56

_____ is less than _____.

_____ < _____

**Compare and order the numbers.
Then, fill in each blank.**

100   77   88

16 The greatest number is _____.

17 The least number is _____.

18 Order the numbers from least to greatest.

_____, _____, _____
   least   greatest

Write the missing numbers in each number pattern.

19 66   68   70   72

20 84   __   __   54   44   34   24

Assessment Prep

Answer each question.

㉑ Which sentences describe the numbers?
Color the ⬚.

89   99   98

99 is greater than 89 but less than 98.

98 is greater than 89 but less than 99.

Order the numbers from greatest to least: 89, 98, 99

Order the numbers from least to greatest: 89, 99, 98

㉒ Which sentence describes the number pattern?

43   53   63   73   83

Ⓐ 10 more than 53 is 43.

Ⓑ 83 is 10 less than 73.

Ⓒ I add 10 to get the number before 43.

Ⓓ I subtract 10 to get the number before 43.

Name: _____ Date: _____

A Day in Nature

1 How many flowers are there?
Count on by tens and ones.
Write each missing number.

a There are _____ tens _____ ones.

b There are _____ flowers in all.

2 Look at the numbers.
Fill in each blank.

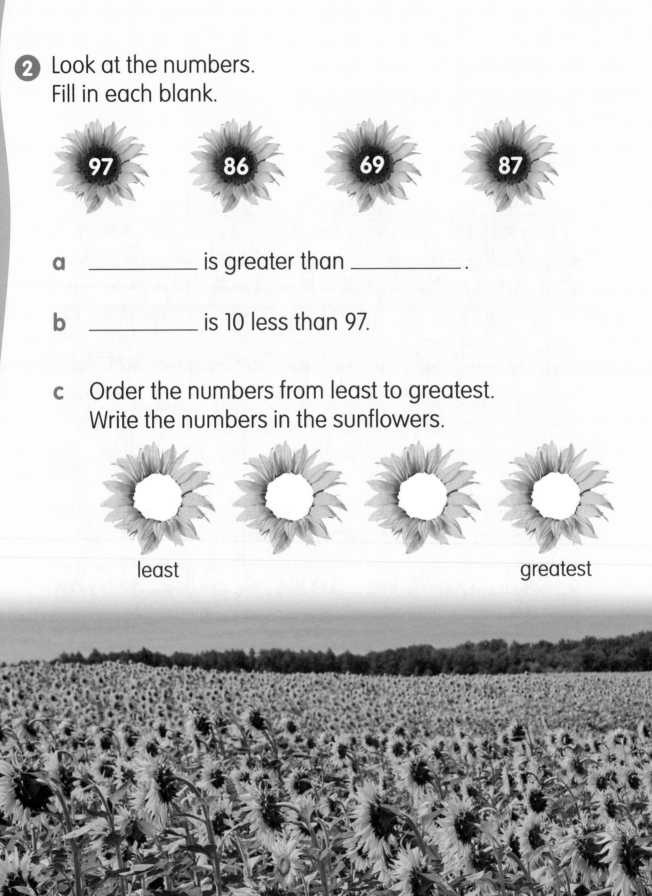

97　86　69　87

a _____ is greater than _____ .

b _____ is 10 less than 97.

c Order the numbers from least to greatest.
Write the numbers in the sunflowers.

least　　　　　　　　　　　　　　　　　greatest

3

a   Show 86 and 69 on place-value charts.
Draw ▭ for tens and □ for ones.

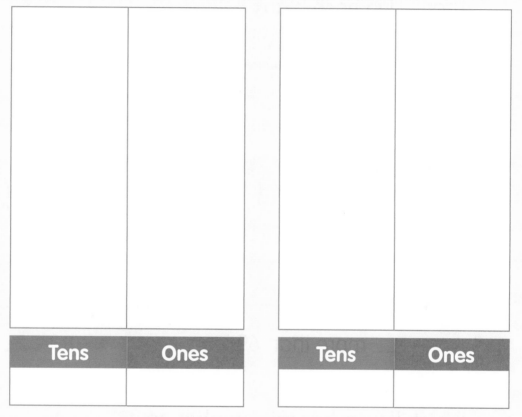

Tens	Ones

Tens	Ones

b   _____ is less than _____ .

c   Fill in the blank with >, <, or =.

86 ◯ 69

4 The numbers on the flowers below make a pattern.

a What is the rule?

Add _____ to get the next number.

b Use this rule to find each missing number.
Then, fill in each blank.

____ less than 67 is ____.

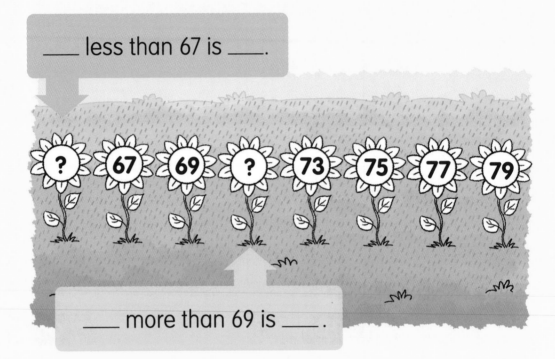

____ more than 69 is ____.

c Which flower has this number on it?
Read the clues to find out.

Clues
The number is greater than 67.
It has a 7 in the ones place.

Color the flower with this number.

Rubric

Point(s)	Level	My Performance
7–8	4	• Most of my answers are correct. • I show all my work correctly. • I explain my thinking clearly and completely.
5–6.5	3	• Some of my answers are correct. • I show some of my work correctly. • I explain my thinking clearly.
3–4.5	2	• A few of my answers are correct. • I show little work correctly. • I explain some of my thinking clearly.
0–2.5	1	• A few of my answers are correct. • I show little or no work. • I do not explain my thinking clearly.

Teacher's Comments

STEAM

Mallard Park

Is there a pond near where you live?
Mallards [MAAL-urds] probably swim there.
They build their nests nearby.
Each nest holds about ten eggs.

Task

Make a mallard park.
Your teacher will put up a large sheet of
drawing paper.
Draw a large park with a pond.
Call it Mallard Park.

Work in pairs.

1. Draw a nest on a sheet of drawing paper.
   Cut it out.

2. Cut out ten eggs from some gray or light
   brown paper.

3. Glue the eggs to your nest.

4. Tape your nest to the park.

5. Count all the eggs in the park.

6. Write a number story about the eggs.
   Share your story with the class.

7. Listen as your teacher reads the
   story *Make Way for Ducklings*.

8. Compare your park to where
   the ducklings live in the story.

Addition and Subtraction Within 100

How can you use what you know about regrouping to add and subtract?

Name: _____ Date: _____

Adding within 40

23 + 17 = ?

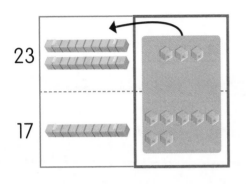

23

17

Step 1
Add the ones.

	Tens	Ones
	1	
	2	3
+	1	7
		0

3 ones + 7 ones = 10 ones

Regroup the ones.
10 ones = 1 ten

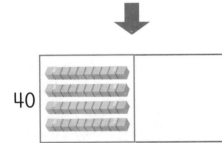

Step 2
Add the tens.

	Tens	Ones
	1	
	2	3
+	1	7
	4	0

1 ten + 2 tens + 1 ten = 4 tens

40

So, 23 + 17 = 40.

▶ **Quick Check**

Add.

① 24 + 5 = _____

Tens	Ones
2	4
+	5
☐	☐

② 21 + 15 = _____

Tens	Ones
2	1
+ 1	5
☐	☐

③ 15 + 8 = _____

Tens	Ones
☐	☐
+ ☐	☐
☐	☐

④ 9 + 18 = _____

Tens	Ones
☐	☐
+ ☐	☐
☐	☐

⑤ 16 + 24 = _____

Tens	Ones
☐	☐
+ ☐	☐
☐	☐

⑥ 14 + 19 = _____

Tens	Ones
☐	☐
+ ☐	☐
☐	☐

Subtracting within 40

36 – 19 = ?

You cannot take away 9 ones from 6 ones.
So, you need to regroup.

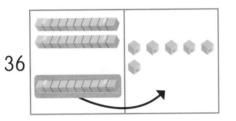

36

Step 1

Regroup the tens and ones.

Regroup the tens in 36.

36 = 3 tens 6 ones

　　= 2 tens 16 ones

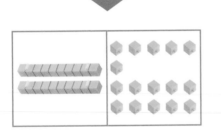

	Tens	Ones
	2	16
	~~3~~	~~6~~
–	1	9

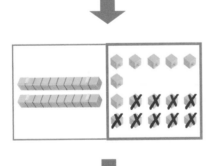

Step 2

Subtract the ones.

	Tens	Ones
	2	16
	~~3~~	~~6~~
–	1	9
		7

16 ones – 9 ones = 7 ones

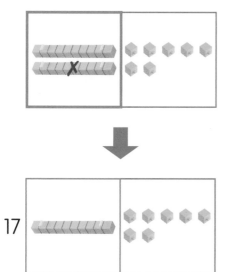

17

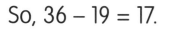

So, 36 – 19 = 17.

Step 3

Subtract the tens.

Tens	Ones
2	16
3̶	6̶
– 1	9
1	7

2 tens – 1 ten = 1 ten

Check

```
  1 7
+ 1 9
  3 6
```

▶ **Quick Check**

Subtract.
Show how to check your answer.

7 27 – 6 = _____

Tens	Ones
2	7
–	6
☐	☐

Check

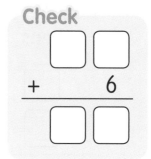

8 28 – 12 = _____

Tens	Ones
2	8
– 1	2
☐	☐

Check

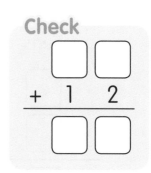

9 32 − 9 = _____

Tens   Ones

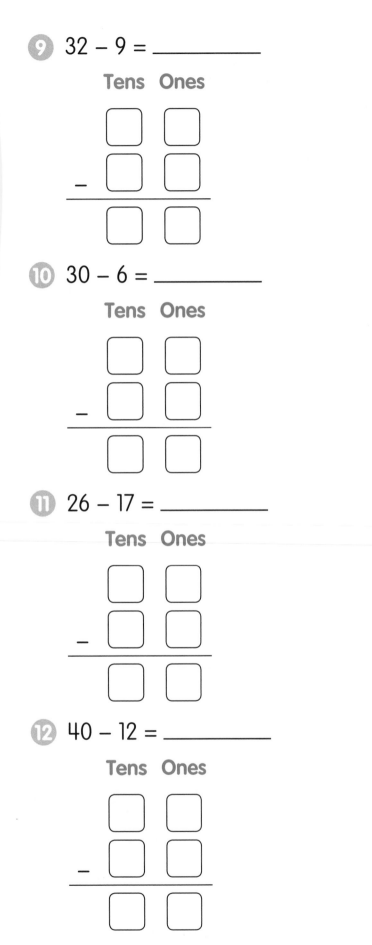

Check

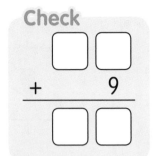

10 30 − 6 = _____

Tens   Ones

Check

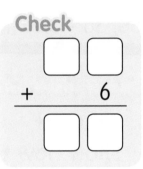

11 26 − 17 = _____

Tens   Ones

Check

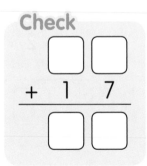

12 40 − 12 = _____

Tens   Ones

Check

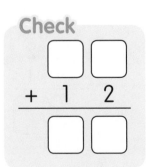

1 Addition Without Regrouping

Learning Objectives:
- Add ones to a 2-digit number without regrouping.
- Add tens to a 2-digit number.
- Add ones and tens to a 2-digit number without regrouping.

THINK

$42 +$ _____ $= 98$

Use two different ways to find the answer.

Talk about how you find the answer with your partner.

ENGAGE

Use 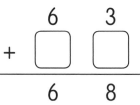 to show the following problem.

```
Tens  Ones

  6     3
+ ☐     ☐
 _____
  6     8
```

Then, find each missing number.

Use 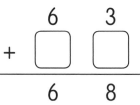 to help you.

LEARN Add ones to a 2-digit number without regrouping

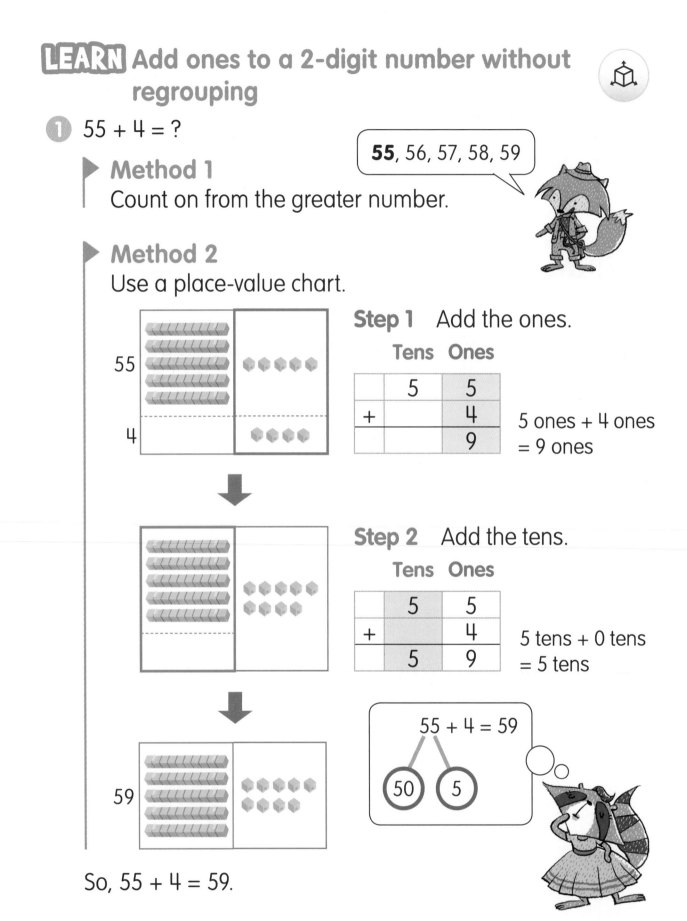

1. 55 + 4 = ?

▶ **Method 1**
Count on from the greater number.

55, 56, 57, 58, 59

▶ **Method 2**
Use a place-value chart.

55

4

Step 1 Add the ones.

Tens	Ones
5	5
+	4
	9

5 ones + 4 ones = 9 ones

Step 2 Add the tens.

Tens	Ones
5	5
+	4
5	9

5 tens + 0 tens = 5 tens

59

55 + 4 = 59

50   5

So, 55 + 4 = 59.

TRY Practice adding ones to a 2-digit number without regrouping

Add.

1 62 + 3 = ?

> **Method 1**
> Count on from the greater number.

62, _____, _____, _____

> **Method 2**
> Use a place-value chart.

First, add the ones.
Then, add the tens.

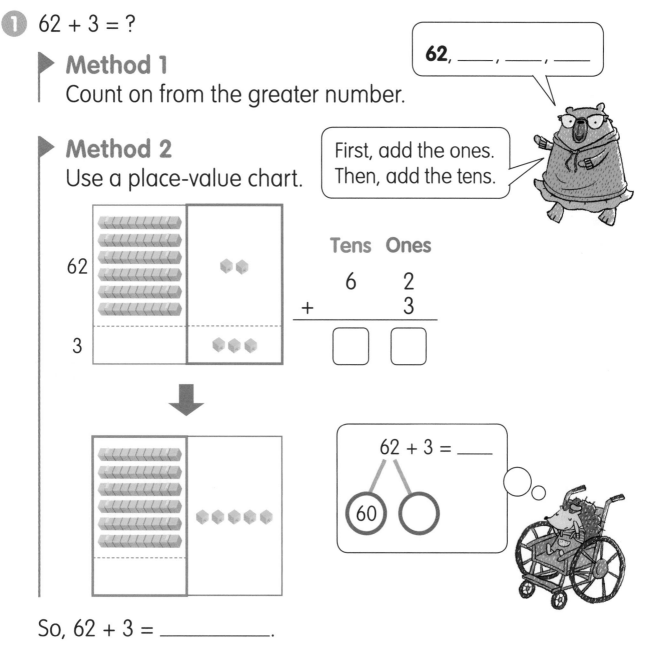

Tens	Ones
6	2
+	3
☐	☐

62 + 3 = ____

60

So, 62 + 3 = _____.

2 83 + 4 = _____

ENGAGE

1 Show your work on a place-value chart.

   a Find 2 + 6.

   b Find 2 ones + 6 ones.

   c Find 2 tens + 6 tens.

2 Find 74 + 15 mentally.

Talk about how you get your answers in **1** and **2** with your partner.

LEARN Add tens to a 2-digit number

1 50 + 30 = ?

▶ **Method 1**

Count on by tens from 50.

50, …, 60, …, 70, …, 80

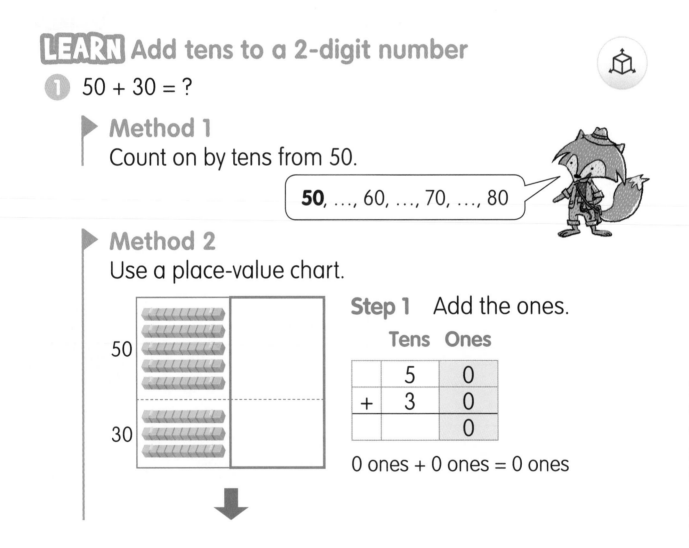

▶ **Method 2**

Use a place-value chart.

Step 1 Add the ones.

Tens	Ones
5	0
+ 3	0
	0

0 ones + 0 ones = 0 ones

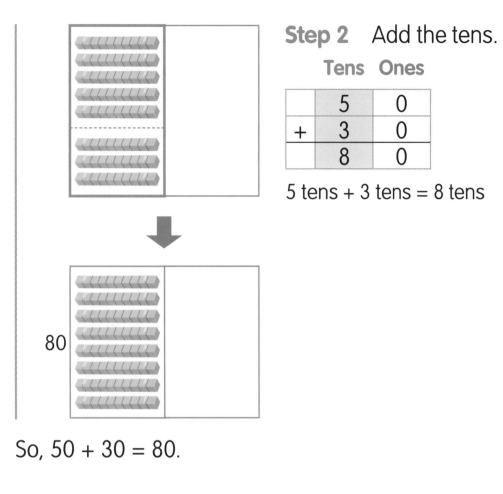

Step 2   Add the tens.

	Tens	Ones
	5	0
+	3	0
	8	0

5 tens + 3 tens = 8 tens

80

So, 50 + 30 = 80.

2 46 + 30 = ?

46, …, 56, …, 66, …, 76

▶ **Method 1**
Count on by tens from 46.

▶ **Method 2**
Use a place-value chart.

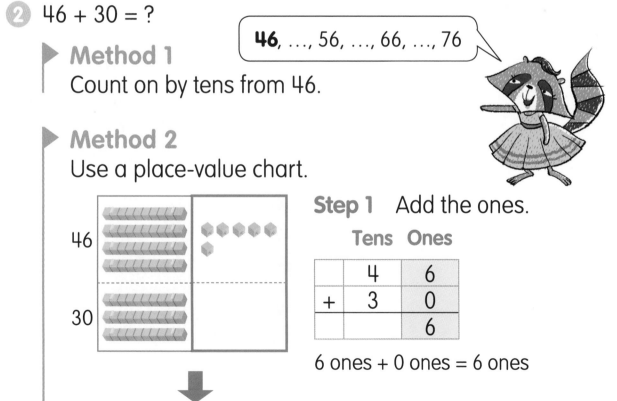

46

30

Step 1   Add the ones.

	Tens	Ones
	4	6
+	3	0
		6

6 ones + 0 ones = 6 ones

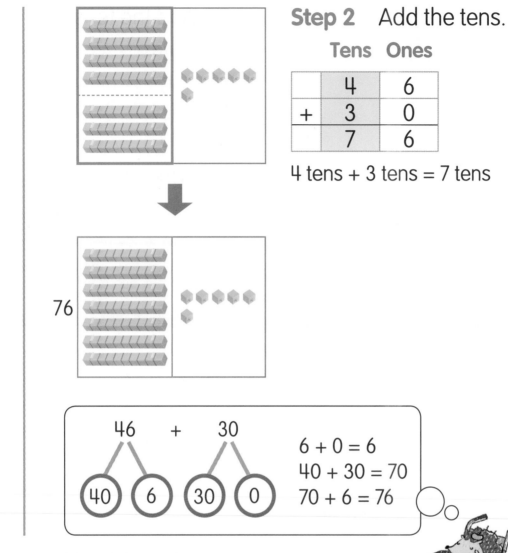

Step 2 Add the tens.

	Tens	Ones
	4	6
+	3	0
	7	6

4 tens + 3 tens = 7 tens

76

46 + 30

40 6 30 0

6 + 0 = 6
40 + 30 = 70
70 + 6 = 76

So, 46 + 30 = 76.

Math Talk

Victor adds 20 to 45.
He says the answer is 74.
Is Victor correct?
Share your thinking with your partner.

TRY Practice adding tens to a 2-digit number

Add.

1 50 + 40 = ?

▶ **Method 1**
Count on by tens from 50.

50, …, ____, …, ____, …, ____, …, ____

▶ **Method 2**
Use a place-value chart.

First, add the ones.
Then, add the tens.

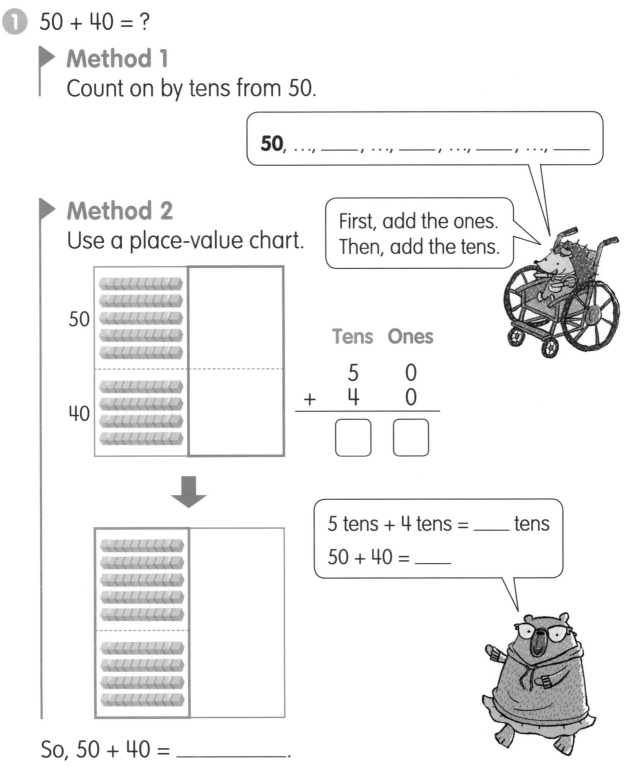

Tens	Ones
5	0
+ 4	0
□	□

5 tens + 4 tens = ____ tens
50 + 40 = ____

So, 50 + 40 = _____.

2 58 + 20 = ?

▶ **Method 1**
Count on by tens from 58.

58, …, ____, …, ____

▶ **Method 2**
Use a place-value chart.

First, add the ones.
Then, add the tens.

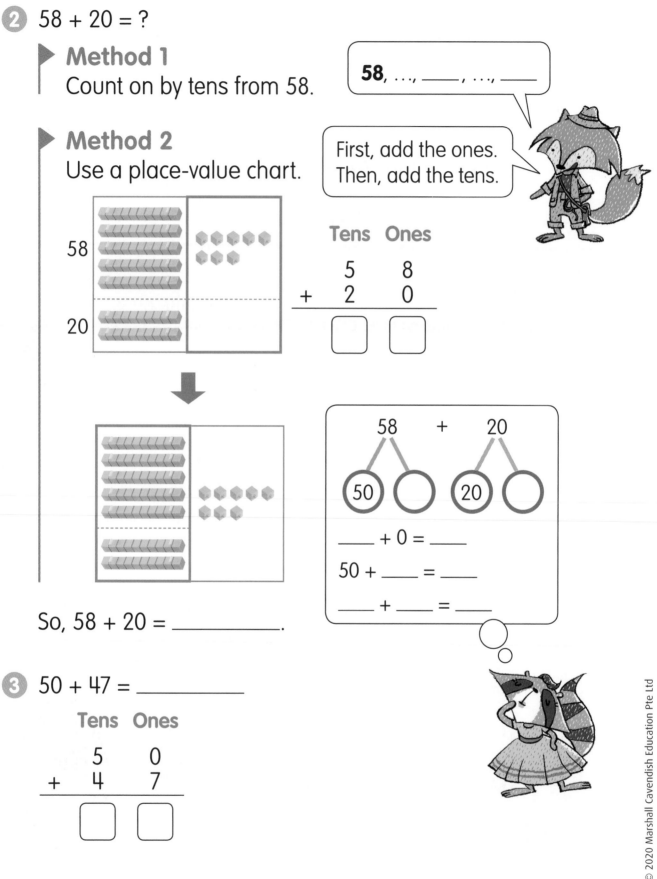

	Tens	Ones
	5	8
+	2	0
	☐	☐

58 + 20

50 ◯ 20 ◯

____ + 0 = ____

50 + ____ = ____

____ + ____ = ____

So, 58 + 20 = _____.

3 50 + 47 = _____

	Tens	Ones
	5	0
+	4	7
	☐	☐

Use  to show this problem.

Tens Ones

```
    3    5
  + ☐    ☐
  ─────────
    7    9
```

Then, find each missing number.
Use to help you.

LEARN Add ones and tens to a 2-digit number without regrouping

1 42 + 56 = ?

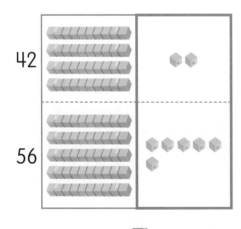

Step 1 Add the ones.

Tens Ones

	Tens	Ones
	4	2
+	5	6
		8

2 ones + 6 ones = 8 ones

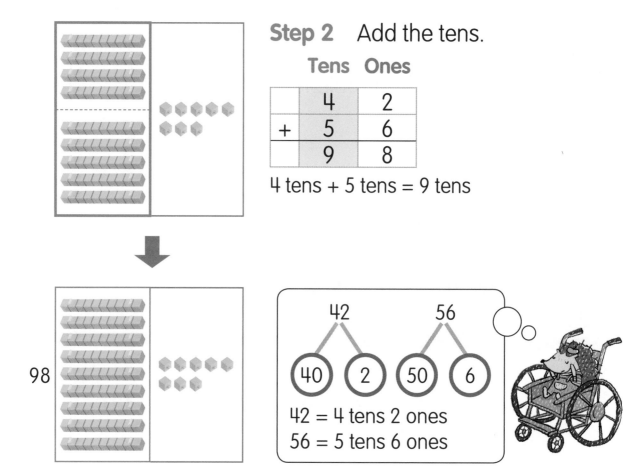

Step 2   Add the tens.

	Tens	Ones
	4	2
+	5	6
	9	8

4 tens + 5 tens = 9 tens

98

42   56

40   2   50   6

42 = 4 tens 2 ones
56 = 5 tens 6 ones

So, 42 + 56 = 98.

Math Talk

Aubrey added 31 and 53.

Tens	Ones
3	1
+ 5	3
8	9

What mistake did Aubrey make?
What steps should she use to find
the answer?

Hands-on Activity Adding two 2-digit numbers without regrouping

Work in groups.

Take a 🎲 and some ▦ .

① Roll the 🎲 .
Write the number in the tens place of the place-value chart.

Tens	Ones

② Roll the 🎲 again.
Write the number in the ones place of the place-value chart.

③ Add this number to 22 and solve.

④ Ask your partner to use ▦ to check the answer.

Tens Ones

```
      2   2
  +  [ ] [ ]
  ─────────
     [ ] [ ]
```

⑤ Trade places.
Repeat ① to ④ for these numbers.

a   Tens Ones
```
      1   3
  +  [ ] [ ]
  ─────────
     [ ] [ ]
```

b   Tens Ones
```
      2   0
  +  [ ] [ ]
  ─────────
     [ ] [ ]
```

c   Tens Ones
```
      3   1
  +  [ ] [ ]
  ─────────
     [ ] [ ]
```

TRY Practice adding ones and tens to a 2-digit number without regrouping

Add.

1 53 + 36 = ?

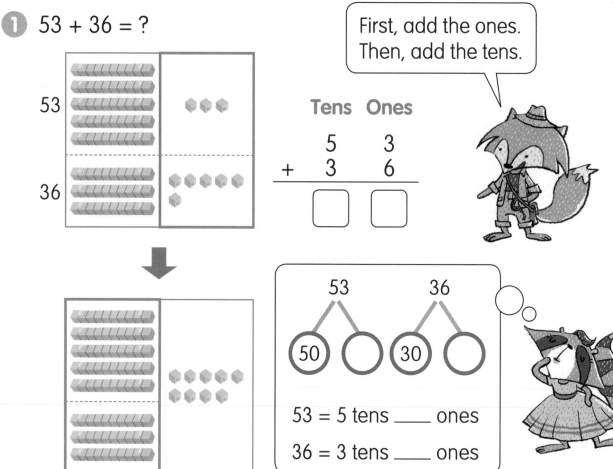

First, add the ones.
Then, add the tens.

Tens Ones

```
    5   3
+   3   6
  ___  ___
 |   | |   |
```

53
36

53
50 ◯   36
30 ◯

53 = 5 tens _____ ones
36 = 3 tens _____ ones

So, 53 + 36 = _____.

2 45 + 32 = _____

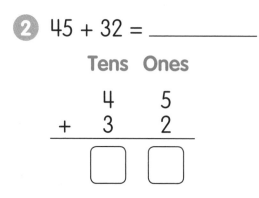

Tens Ones

```
    4   5
+   3   2
  ___  ___
 |   | |   |
```

3 22 + 67 = _____

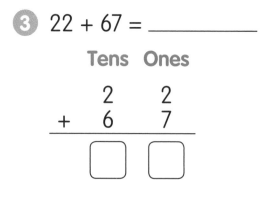

Tens Ones

```
    2   2
+   6   7
  ___  ___
 |   | |   |
```

INDEPENDENT PRACTICE

Add.
Count on from the greater number.

1 52 + 4 = _____

52, 53, 54, 55, _____

2 94 + 3 = _____

94, _____, _____, _____

3 61 + 4 = _____

61, _____, _____, _____, _____

4 53 + 40 = _____

53, …, _____, …, _____, …, _____,
…, _____

Write each missing number.

5 42 + 6 = _____

Tens	Ones
4	2
+	6
☐	☐

42 + 6 = ___

40

6 81 + 7 = _____

Tens	Ones
8	1
+	7
☐	☐

81 + 7 = ___

80

7 36 + 60 = _____

Tens	Ones
3	6
+	6	0
☐	☐

36   +   60

30   0

____ + 0 = ____

30 + ____ = ____

____ + ____ = ____

Add.
Then, draw lines to match the same answers.

8

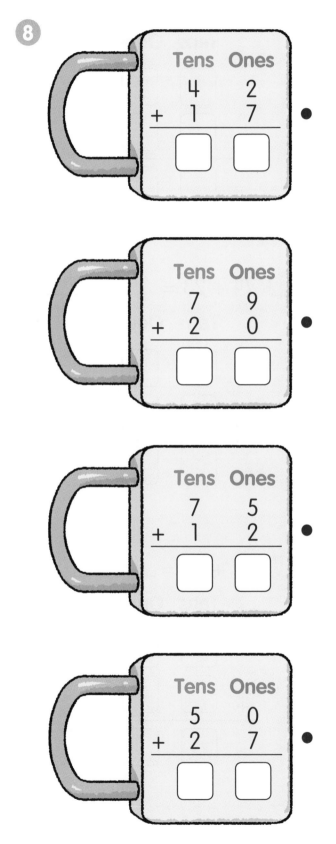

Tens	Ones
4	2
+ 1	7
☐	☐

Tens	Ones
7	9
+ 2	0
☐	☐

Tens	Ones
7	5
+ 1	2
☐	☐

Tens	Ones
5	0
+ 2	7
☐	☐

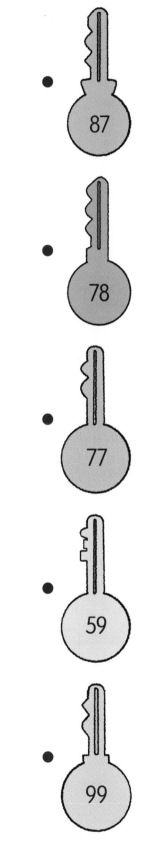

87

78

77

59

99

Add.

9 42 + 32 = _____

Tens	Ones
☐	☐
+ ☐	☐
☐	☐

10 53 + 35 = _____

Tens	Ones
☐	☐
+ ☐	☐
☐	☐

11 64 + 31 = _____

Tens	Ones
☐	☐
+ ☐	☐
☐	☐

12 74 + 23 = _____

Tens	Ones
☐	☐
+ ☐	☐
☐	☐

13 44 + 55 = _____

Tens	Ones
☐	☐
+ ☐	☐
☐	☐

14 29 + 60 = _____

Tens	Ones
☐	☐
+ ☐	☐
☐	☐

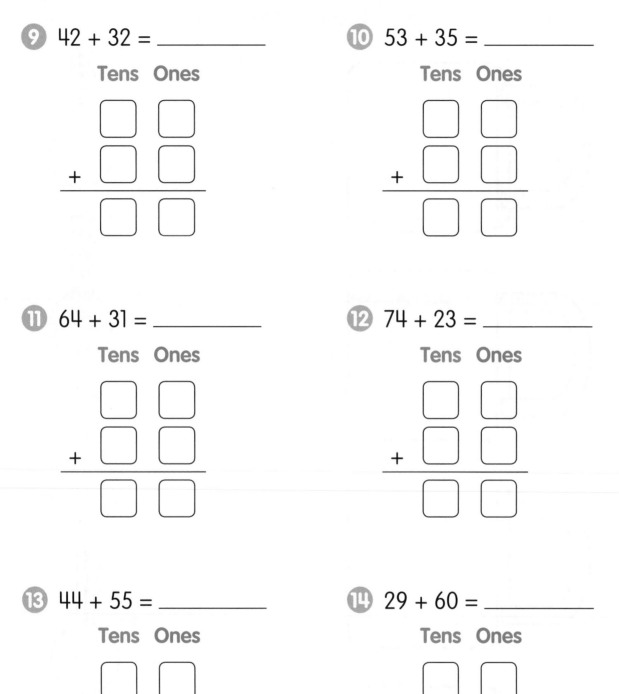

2 Addition With Regrouping

Learning Objectives:
- Add ones to a 2-digit number with regrouping.
- Add ones and tens to a 2-digit number with regrouping.

THINK

16 + _____ = 65

Use two different ways to find the answer.

Talk about how you find the answer with your partner.

ENGAGE

a   Add 58 and 2 mentally.
What way did you use?

b   Add 58 and 7.
What way did you use this time?
Did you use the same way as **a** to add?
Why or why not?
Share your thinking with your partner.

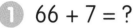

LEARN Add ones to a 2-digit number with regrouping

1 66 + 7 = ?

66 = 6 tens 6 ones

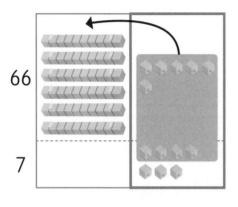

66

7

Step 1 Add the ones.

Tens	Ones
1	
6	6
+	7
	3

6 ones + 7 ones = 13 ones

Regroup the ones.
13 ones = 1 ten 3 ones

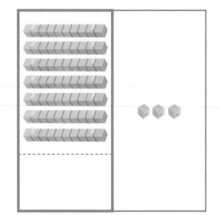

Step 2 Add the tens.

Tens	Ones
1	
6	6
+	7
7	3

1 ten + 6 tens + 0 tens = 7 tens

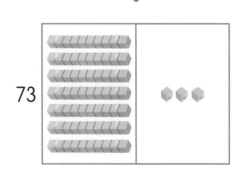

73

So, 66 + 7 = 73.

TRY Practice adding ones to a 2-digit number with regrouping

Add and regroup.

1 62 + 9 = ?

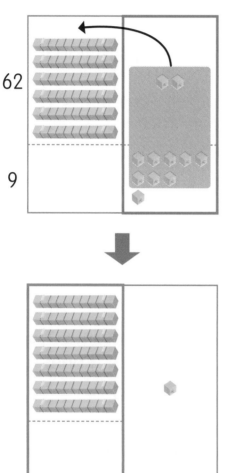

First, add the ones.
Regroup the ones into a 10 and ones.
Then, add the tens.

Tens	Ones
6	2
+	9
☐	☐

So, 62 + 9 = _____.

2 56 + 8 = _____

Tens	Ones
5	6
+	8
☐	☐

3 73 + 7 = _____

Tens	Ones
7	3
+	7
☐	☐

ENGAGE

Use to help you add.

Show your work on a place-value chart.

a Add 30 and 20.   **b** Add 4 and 8.

c Add 34 and 28.

How can you use the in **a** and **b** to help you?

LEARN Add ones and tens to a 2-digit number with regrouping

> $33 = 3$ tens 3 ones
> $18 = 1$ ten 8 ones

1 $33 + 18 = ?$

Step 1 Add the ones.

Tens	Ones
1	
3	3
+ 1	8
	1

3 ones + 8 ones = 11 ones

Regroup the ones.
11 ones = 1 ten 1 one

Step 2 Add the tens.

Tens	Ones
1	
3	3
+ 1	8
5	1

1 ten + 3 tens + 1 ten = 5 tens

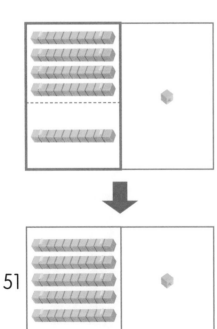

So, $33 + 18 = 51$.

Hands-on Activity Adding two 2-digit numbers with regrouping

Work in groups.

Take a , a , and some .

① Roll the .
Write the number in the tens place of the place-value chart.

Tens	Ones

② Roll the .
Write the number in the ones place of the place-value chart.

③ Add this number to 19 and solve.

④ Ask your partner to use to check the answer.

```
    Tens  Ones
     1     9
  +  ☐     ☐
  ─────────────
     ☐     ☐
```

⑤ Trade places.
Repeat ① to ④ for these numbers.

a
```
   Tens  Ones
    2     8
 +  ☐     ☐
 ───────────
    ☐     ☐
```

b
```
   Tens  Ones
    2     9
 +  ☐     ☐
 ───────────
    ☐     ☐
```

c
```
   Tens  Ones
    1     8
 +  ☐     ☐
 ───────────
    ☐     ☐
```

TRY Practice adding ones and tens to a 2-digit number with regrouping

Add and regroup.

1 57 + 19 = ?

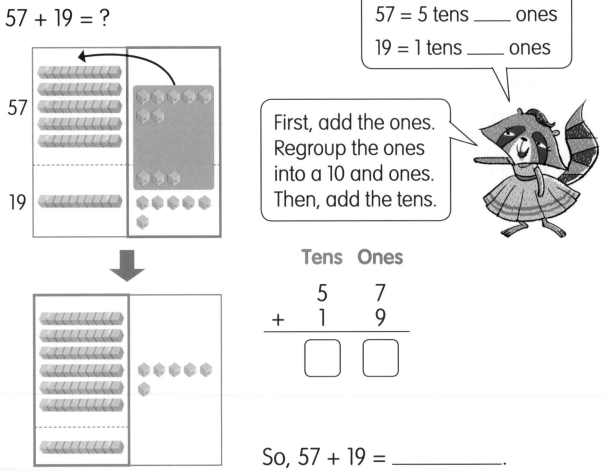

57 = 5 tens _____ ones

19 = 1 tens _____ ones

First, add the ones. Regroup the ones into a 10 and ones. Then, add the tens.

Tens Ones

```
      5   7
  +   1   9
    ┌───┐ ┌───┐
    │   │ │   │
    └───┘ └───┘
```

So, 57 + 19 = _____.

MATH SHARING

Mathematical Habit 3 Construct viable arguments

Lucia uses this way to add 54 and 37.

54
50 4

37
30 7

STEP 1   4 + 7 = 11

STEP 2   50 + 30 = 80

STEP 3   11 + 80 = 91

Talk about how this way works with your partner.
Then, use this way to add 45 and 17.

INDEPENDENT PRACTICE

Only nine astronauts can make a space launch.
Add.
Then, match your answers to the astronauts below
to find who can make the launch.
Then, color these astronauts.

1

Tens	Ones
7	5
+	8

☐ ☐

Tens	Ones
	8
+ 8	7

☐ ☐

Tens	Ones
2	9
+ 4	2

☐ ☐

Tens	Ones
2	9
+ 2	4

☐ ☐

Tens	Ones
2	6
+ 3	5

☐ ☐

Tens	Ones
4	4
+ 3	8

☐ ☐

Tens	Ones
4	2
+ 3	9

☐ ☐

Tens	Ones
4	6
+ 4	7

☐ ☐

Tens	Ones
5	7
+ 3	5

☐ ☐

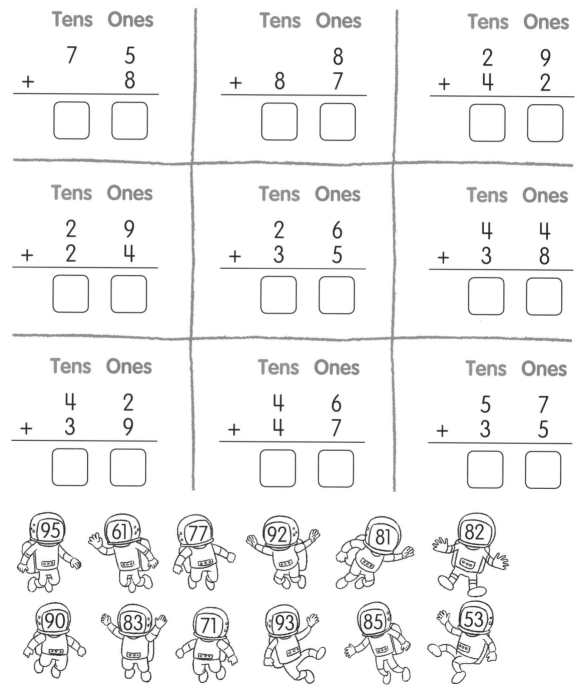

95 61 77 92 81 82

90 83 71 93 85 53

Add and regroup.

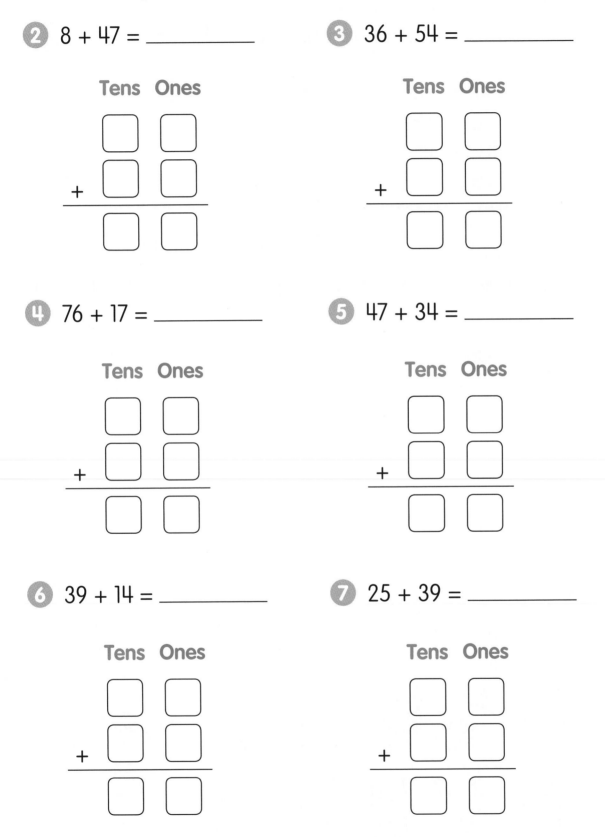

2   8 + 47 = _____

    Tens Ones

+

3   36 + 54 = _____

    Tens Ones

+

4   76 + 17 = _____

    Tens Ones

+

5   47 + 34 = _____

    Tens Ones

+

6   39 + 14 = _____

    Tens Ones

+

7   25 + 39 = _____

    Tens Ones

+

3 Subtraction Without Regrouping

Learning Objectives:
- Subtract ones from a 2-digit number without regrouping.
- Subtract tens from a 2-digit number.
- Subtract ones and tens from a 2-digit number without regrouping.

THINK

Zoe has 58 beads.
She gives away some beads.
She has 35 beads left.
How many beads does Zoe give away?
Use two different ways to find the answer.
Write a number sentence to show each way.
Talk about how you find the answer with your partner.

ENGAGE

Use [ ] to show 55.
What can you do with your [ ] to get 51.
Write a number sentence to show this.

LEARN Subtract ones from a 2-digit number without regrouping

1. 48 − 3 = ?

▶ **Method 1**
Count back from 48.

48, 47, 46, 45

▶ **Method 2**
Use a place-value chart.

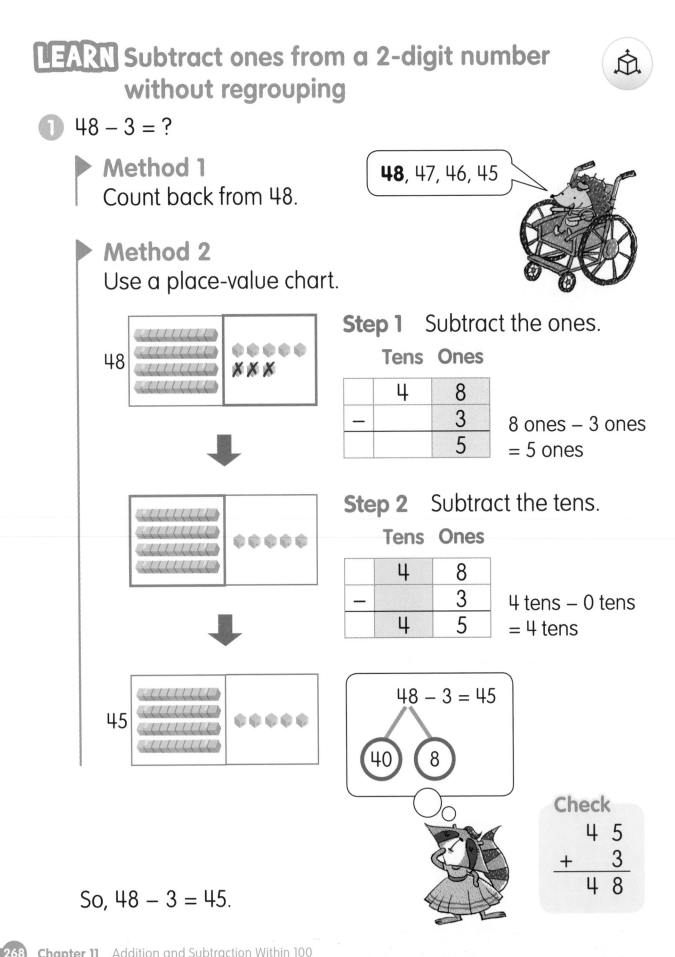

48

Step 1 Subtract the ones.

Tens	Ones
4	8
−	3
	5

8 ones − 3 ones
= 5 ones

Step 2 Subtract the tens.

Tens	Ones
4	8
−	3
4	5

4 tens − 0 tens
= 4 tens

45

48 − 3 = 45

40   8

Check

```
   4 5
 +   3
   4 8
```

So, 48 − 3 = 45.

© 2020 Marshall Cavendish Education Pte Ltd

TRY Practice subtracting ones from a 2-digit number without regrouping

Subtract.

1. 68 – 4 = ?

▶ **Method 1**
Count back from 68.

68, _____, _____, _____, _____

▶ **Method 2**
Use a place-value chart.

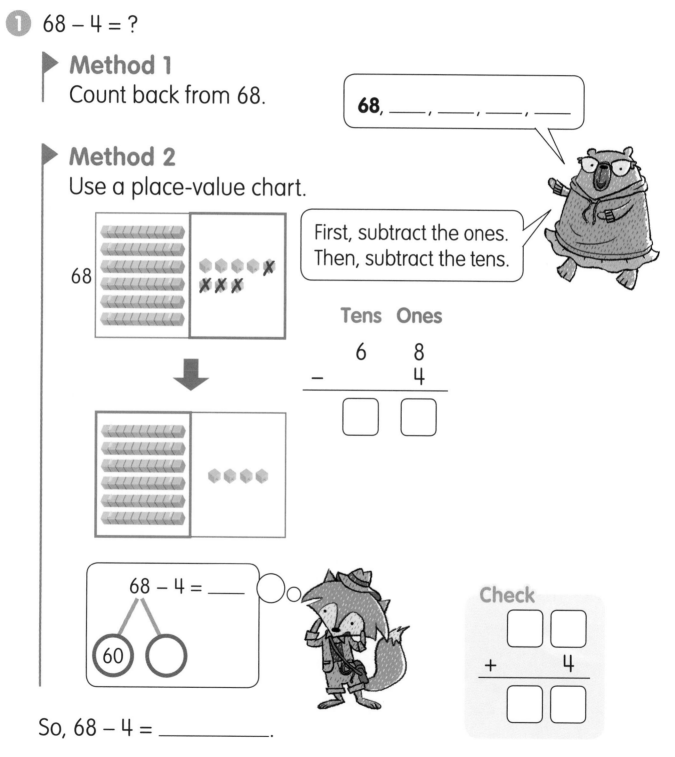

68

First, subtract the ones.
Then, subtract the tens.

Tens	Ones
6	8
–	4
☐	☐

68 – 4 = _____

60

So, 68 – 4 = _____.

Check

☐	☐
+	4
☐	☐

2 56 − 3 = _____

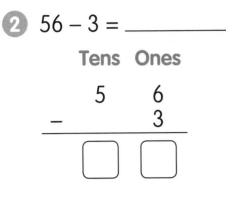

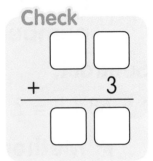
Check

3 98 − 7 = _____

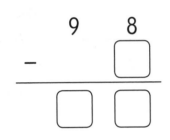

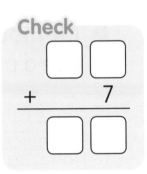
Check

ENGAGE

1 Show your work on a place-value chart.
   a Find 8 − 3.
   b Find 8 ones − 3 ones.
   c Find 8 tens − 3 tens.

2 Find 94 − 23 mentally.

Talk about how you get your answers in **1** and **2** with your partner.

LEARN Subtract tens from a 2-digit number

① 70 – 40 = ?

▶ **Method 1**
Count back by tens from 70.

> **70**, …, 60, …, 50, …, 40, …, 30

▶ **Method 2**
Use a place-value chart.

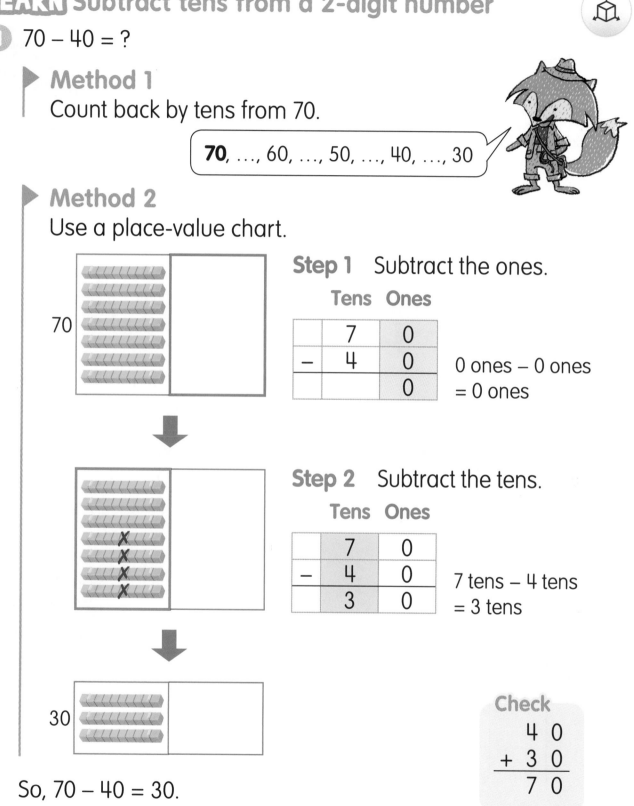

Step 1   Subtract the ones.

Tens	Ones
7	0
– 4	0
	0

0 ones – 0 ones
= 0 ones

Step 2   Subtract the tens.

Tens	Ones
7	0
– 4	0
3	0

7 tens – 4 tens
= 3 tens

Check

```
   4 0
 + 3 0
 ─────
   7 0
```

So, 70 – 40 = 30.

2 55 – 30 = ?

▶ **Method 1**
Count back by tens from 55.

55, …, 45, …, 35, …, 25

▶ **Method 2**
Use a place-value chart.

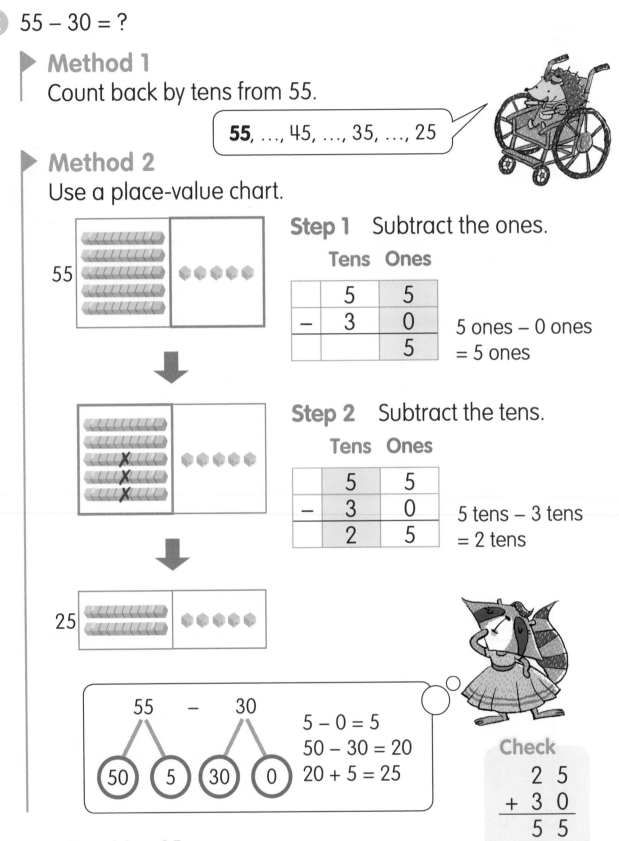

Step 1 Subtract the ones.

	Tens	Ones
	5	5
–	3	0
		5

5 ones – 0 ones
= 5 ones

Step 2 Subtract the tens.

	Tens	Ones
	5	5
–	3	0
	2	5

5 tens – 3 tens
= 2 tens

55 – 30
50   5   30   0

5 – 0 = 5
50 – 30 = 20
20 + 5 = 25

Check

```
  2 5
+ 3 0
─────
  5 5
```

So, 55 – 30 = 25.

TRY Practice subtracting tens from a 2-digit number

Subtract.

1 60 − 40 = ?

▶ **Method 1**
Count back by tens from 60.

> **60**, …, ____, …, ____, …,
> ____, …, ____

▶ **Method 2**
Use a place-value chart.

> First, subtract the ones.
> Then, subtract the tens.

60

Tens	Ones
6	0
− 4	0
☐	☐

> 6 tens − 4 tens = ____ tens
> So, 60 − 40 = ____.

Check

☐	☐	
+	4	0
☐	☐	

So, 60 − 40 = _____.

2 72 − 40 = ?

▶ **Method 1**
Count back by tens from 72.

72, ..., _____, ..., _____, ...,

_____, ..., _____

▶ **Method 2**
Use a place-value chart.

First, subtract the ones.
Then, subtract the tens.

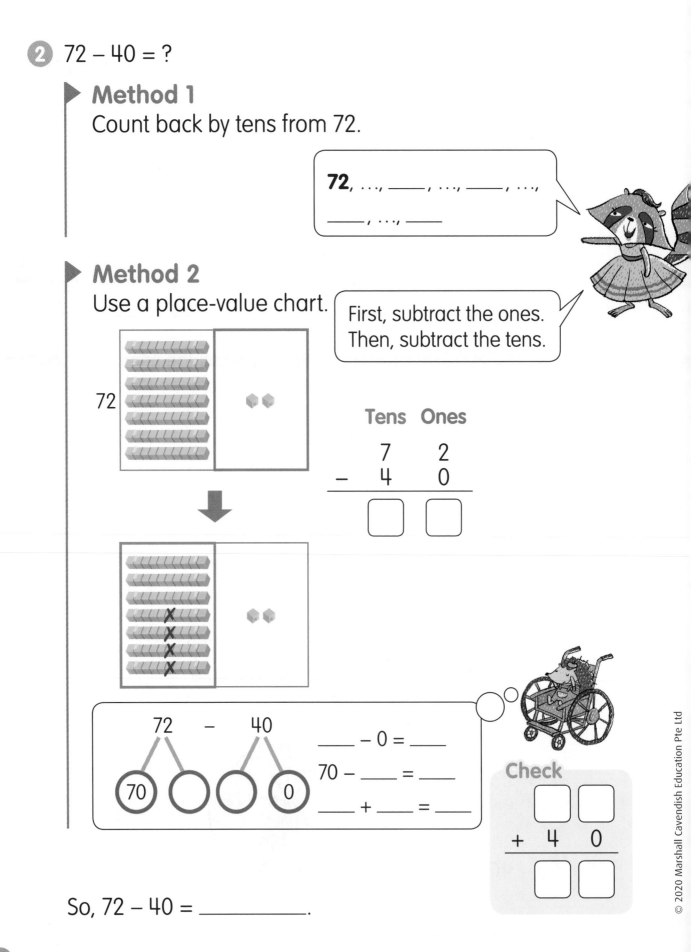

72

	Tens	Ones
	7	2
−	4	0
	☐	☐

72 − 40

70 ○ ○ 0

_____ − 0 = _____

70 − _____ = _____

_____ + _____ = _____

Check

	Tens	Ones
	☐	☐
+	4	0
	☐	☐

So, 72 − 40 = _____.

© 2020 Marshall Cavendish Education Pte Ltd

③ 90 − 40 = _____

Tens	Ones
9	0
− 4	0
☐	☐

Check

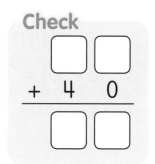

```
      ☐   ☐
  +   4   0
      ☐   ☐
```

④ 87 − 60 = _____

Tens	Ones
8	7
− 6	0
☐	☐

Check

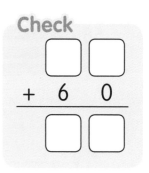

```
      ☐   ☐
  +   6   0
      ☐   ☐
```

⑤ 89 − 80 = _____

Tens	Ones
8	9
− 8	0
☐	☐

Check

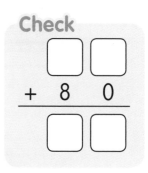

```
      ☐   ☐
  +   8   0
      ☐   ☐
```

ENGAGE

Use 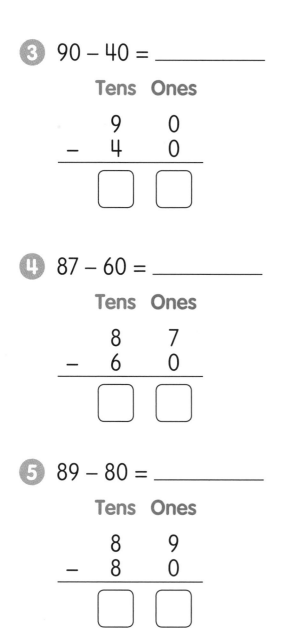 and a place-value chart to help you.

Show 59 on the place-value chart.

What is 33 less than 59?

Use two different ways to find the answer.

Then, talk about what ways you use with your partner.

LEARN Subtract ones and tens from a 2-digit number without regrouping

1 58 – 24 = ?

58 = 5 tens 8 ones
24 = 2 tens 4 ones

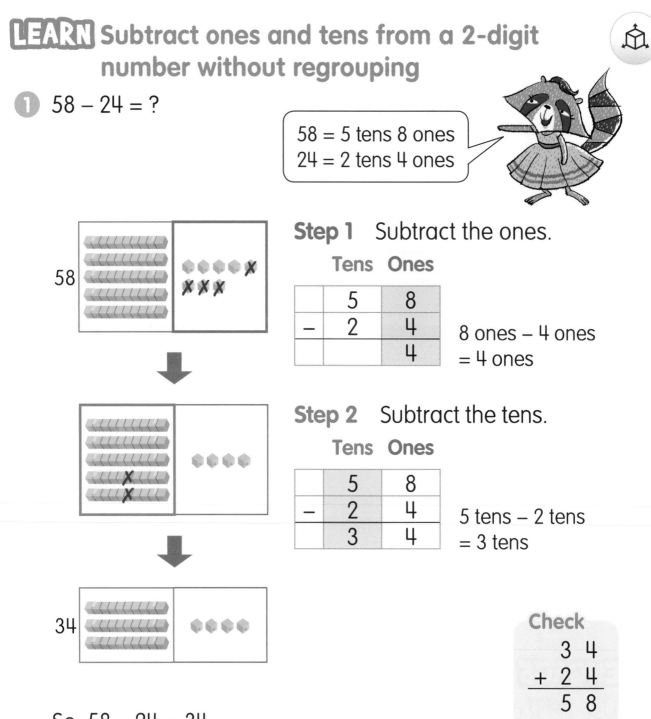

Step 1 Subtract the ones.

Tens	Ones
5	8
– 2	4
	4

8 ones – 4 ones
= 4 ones

Step 2 Subtract the tens.

Tens	Ones
5	8
– 2	4
3	4

5 tens – 2 tens
= 3 tens

So, 58 – 24 = 34.

Check

```
  3 4
+ 2 4
-----
  5 8
```

Work in groups.

Take a ✏ **, a** 🎲 **, and some** 📚 **.**

① Spin to get a number.
Write the number in the tens place
of the place-value chart.

Tens	Ones

② Roll the 🎲.
Write the number in the ones place of the
place-value chart.

③ Subtract this number from 98 and solve.

④ Ask your partner to use 📚 to check
the answer.

Tens Ones

```
     9   8
 -  [ ] [ ]
    ───────
    [ ] [ ]
```

⑤ Trade places.
Repeat ① to ④.

a Tens Ones

```
     9   6
 -  [ ] [ ]
    ───────
    [ ] [ ]
```

b Tens Ones

```
     8   9
 -  [ ] [ ]
    ───────
    [ ] [ ]
```

c Tens Ones

```
     8   7
 -  [ ] [ ]
    ───────
    [ ] [ ]
```

TRY Practice subtracting ones and tens from a 2-digit number without regrouping

Subtract.

1 69 − 33 = ?

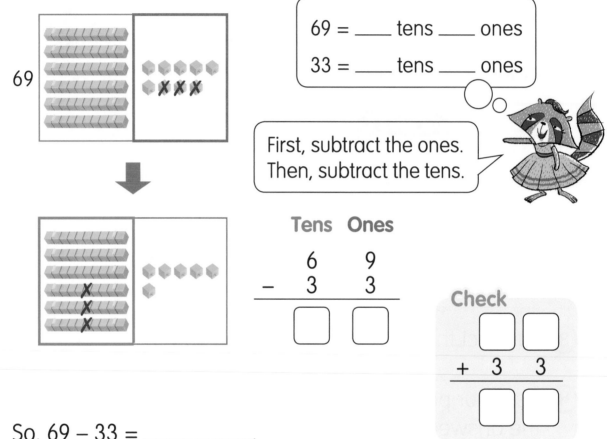

69 = _____ tens _____ ones

33 = _____ tens _____ ones

First, subtract the ones.
Then, subtract the tens.

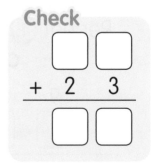

	Tens	Ones
	6	9
−	3	3
	☐	☐

Check

	Tens	Ones
	☐	☐
+	3	3
	☐	☐

So, 69 − 33 = _____.

2 76 − 23 = _____

	Tens	Ones
	7	6
−	2	3
	☐	☐

Check

	Tens	Ones
	☐	☐
+	2	3
	☐	☐

INDEPENDENT PRACTICE

Subtract.
Count back from the greater number.

1 77 – 3 = _____

77, 76, 75, _____

2 59 – 3 = _____

59, _____, _____, _____

3 88 – 4 = _____

88, _____, _____, _____, _____

4 80 – 40 = _____

80, …, _____, …, _____, …, _____,
…, _____

Write each missing number.

5 $67 - 6 =$ _____

Tens	Ones
6	7
−	6
☐	☐

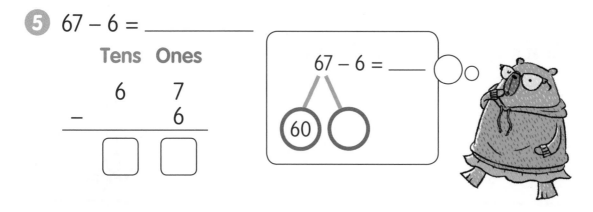

$67 - 6 =$ ____

60 ◯

6 $88 - 8 =$ _____

Tens	Ones
8	8
−	8
☐	☐

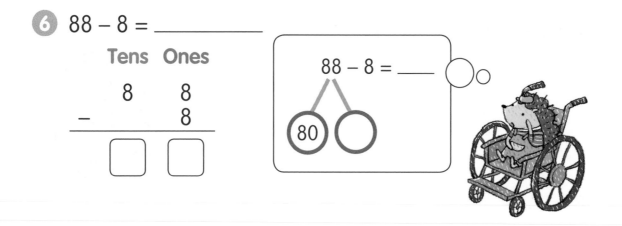

$88 - 8 =$ ____

80 ◯

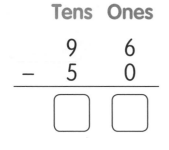

7 $96 - 50 =$ _____

Tens	Ones
9	6
− 5	0
☐	☐

96 − 50

90 ◯   ◯ 0

____ − 0 = ____

90 − ____ = ____

____ + ____ = ____

The koala is hungry.
It can only eat six leaves at a time.
The number on each leaf must be greater than 50.
Which six leaves will it eat?
Subtract to find out.
Then, color the six leaves that match your answers.

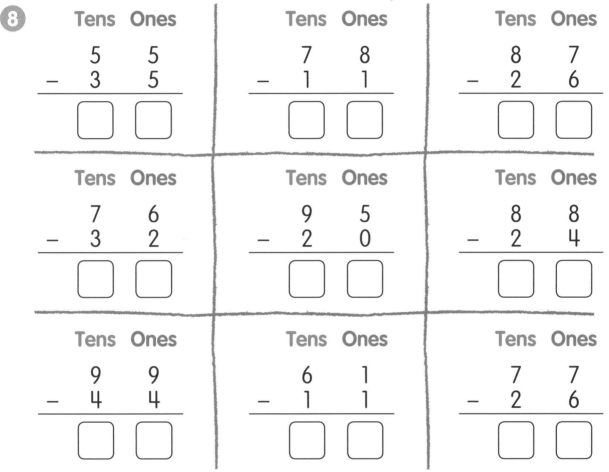

8

Tens	Ones
5	5
– 3	5
☐	☐

Tens	Ones
7	8
– 1	1
☐	☐

Tens	Ones
8	7
– 2	6
☐	☐

Tens	Ones
7	6
– 3	2
☐	☐

Tens	Ones
9	5
– 2	0
☐	☐

Tens	Ones
8	8
– 2	4
☐	☐

Tens	Ones
9	9
– 4	4
☐	☐

Tens	Ones
6	1
– 1	1
☐	☐

Tens	Ones
7	7
– 2	6
☐	☐

Subtract.

9 79 – 7 = _____

Tens Ones

$\begin{array}{cc} \square & \square \\ -\ \square & \square \\ \hline \square & \square \end{array}$

10 90 – 70 = _____

Tens Ones

$\begin{array}{cc} \square & \square \\ -\ \square & \square \\ \hline \square & \square \end{array}$

11 75 – 35 = _____

Tens Ones

$\begin{array}{cc} \square & \square \\ -\ \square & \square \\ \hline \square & \square \end{array}$

12 87 – 44 = _____

Tens Ones

$\begin{array}{cc} \square & \square \\ -\ \square & \square \\ \hline \square & \square \end{array}$

13 98 – 42 = _____

Tens Ones

$\begin{array}{cc} \square & \square \\ -\ \square & \square \\ \hline \square & \square \end{array}$

14 67 – 12 = _____

Tens Ones

$\begin{array}{cc} \square & \square \\ -\ \square & \square \\ \hline \square & \square \end{array}$

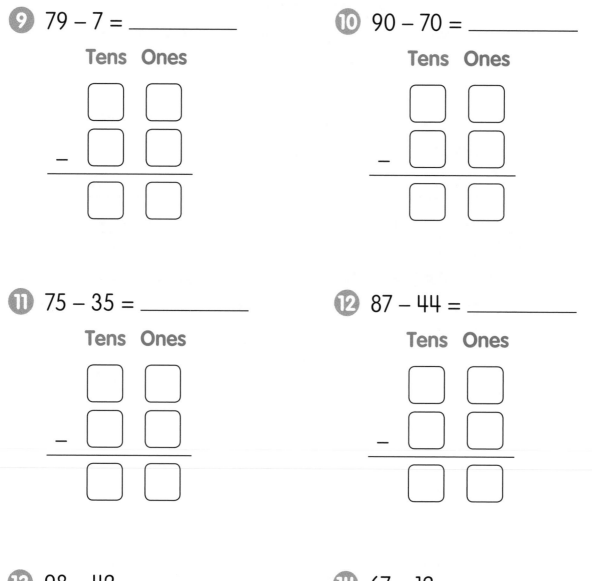

4 Subtraction With Regrouping

Learning Objectives:
- Subtract ones from a 2-digit number with regrouping.
- Subtract ones and tens from a 2-digit number with regrouping.

THINK

Morgan has 64 toy animals.
She has 28 more toy animals than William.
How many toy animals does William have?
Use two different ways to find the answer.
Write a number sentence to show each way.
Then, talk about how you find the answer with your partner.

ENGAGE

Use ![cube] to make 64.
Take away 7 ![cube].
How did you do it?
How many ![rod] and ![cube] do you have left?

$64 - 7 = ?$

Subtract ones from a 2-digit number with regrouping

1 52 – 9 = ?

You cannot take away 9 ones from 2 ones. So, you need to regroup.

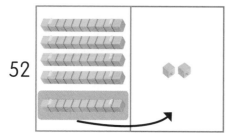

52

Step 1 Regroup the tens and ones.

Regroup the tens in 52.

52 = 5 tens 2 ones
   = 4 tens 12 ones

Tens	Ones
4 5̶	12 2̶
–	9

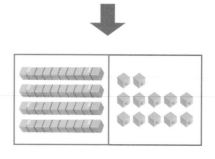

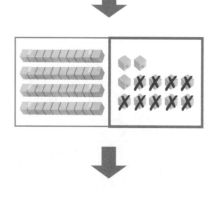

Step 2 Subtract the ones.

Tens	Ones
4 5̶	12 2̶
–	9
	3

12 ones – 9 ones = 3 ones

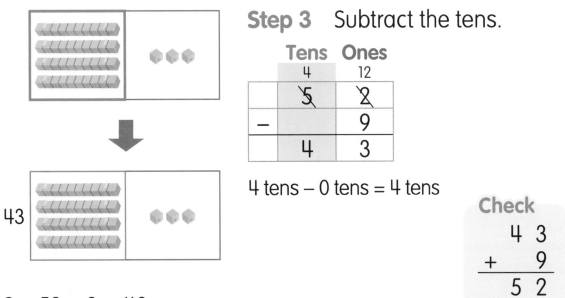

Step 3   Subtract the tens.

	Tens	Ones
	4	12
	~~5~~	~~2~~
−		9
	4	3

4 tens − 0 tens = 4 tens

Check

```
    4  3
 +     9
 ─────────
    5  2
```

So, 52 − 9 = 43.

TRY Practice subtracting ones from a 2-digit number with regrouping

Regroup.
Then, fill in each blank.

1. 63 = 6 tens _____ ones

   = 5 tens _____ ones

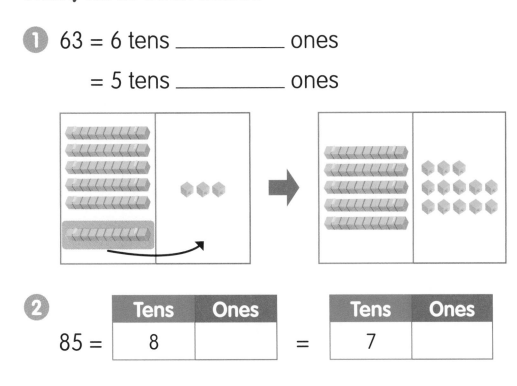

2.

Tens	Ones
8	

85 =   =

Tens	Ones
7	

Regroup and subtract.

3 55 − 7 = ?

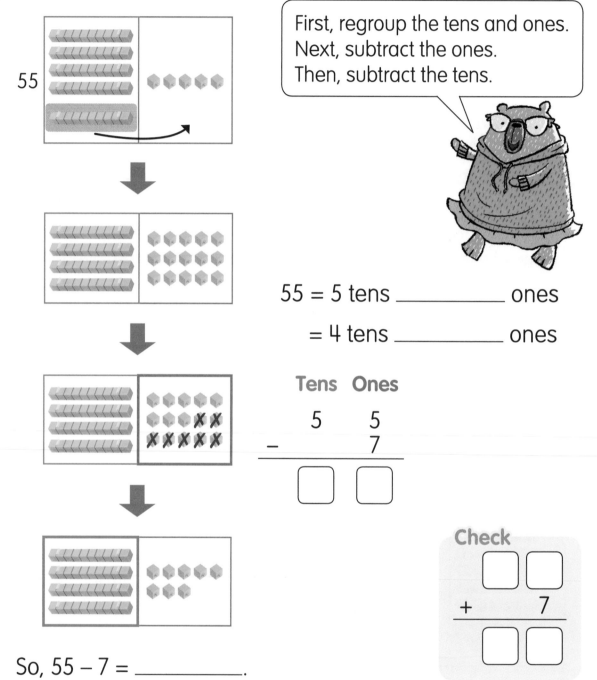

First, regroup the tens and ones.
Next, subtract the ones.
Then, subtract the tens.

55 = 5 tens _____ ones

= 4 tens _____ ones

Tens	Ones
5	5
−	7
☐	☐

So, 55 − 7 = _____.

Check

	☐	☐
+		7
	☐	☐

4 73 − 6 = _____

Tens	Ones
7	3
−	6
☐	☐

Check

☐	☐
+	6
☐	☐

5 64 − 8 = _____

Tens	Ones
6	4
−	8
☐	☐

Check

☐	☐
+	8
☐	☐

ENGAGE

Use 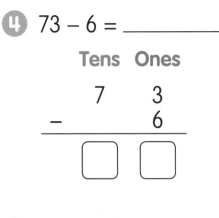 to show your work.

a Subtract 20 from 72.

b Subtract 23 from 72.

What do you notice?

Share your thinking with your partner.

72 − 23 = ?

① 54 − 38 = ?

You cannot take away 8 ones from 4 ones. So, you need to regroup.

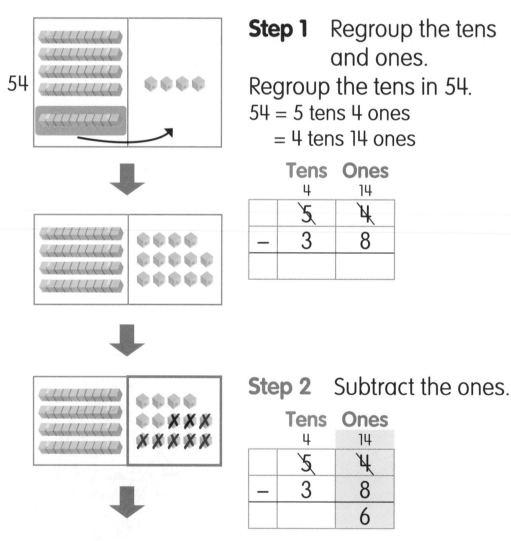

Step 1 Regroup the tens and ones.

Regroup the tens in 54.

54 = 5 tens 4 ones

= 4 tens 14 ones

	Tens	Ones
	4	14
	5̶	4̶
−	3	8

Step 2 Subtract the ones.

	Tens	Ones
	4	14
	5̶	4̶
−	3	8
		6

14 ones − 8 ones = 6 ones

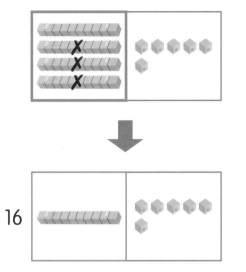

Step 3　Subtract the tens.

Tens	Ones
4	14
~~5~~	~~4~~
− 3	8
1	6

4 tens − 3 tens = 1 ten

16

So, 54 − 38 = 16.

Check

```
  1 6
+ 3 8
  5 4
```

🦉🦊 Math Talk

Austin subtracts 27 from 62.

Tens	Ones
6	2
− 2	7
4	5

Jasmine says that the way Austin subtracts is wrong.
Talk about what Austin does wrongly with your partner.
What is the correct way to subtract?

Hands-on Activity Subtracting two 2-digit numbers with regrouping

Work in groups.

Take a ✎ **, a** 🎲 **, and some** ▱ **.**

(1) Spin to get a number.
Write the number in the tens place
of the place-value chart.

Tens	Ones

(2) Roll the 🎲.
Write the number in the ones place of the
place-value chart.

(3) Subtract this number from 81 and solve.

(4) Ask your partner to use ▱ to check
the answer.

Tens	Ones
8	1
− ☐	☐
☐	☐

(5) Trade places.
Repeat (1) to (4).

a	Tens	Ones
	7	2
−	☐	☐
	☐	☐

b	Tens	Ones
	9	0
−	☐	☐
	☐	☐

c	Tens	Ones
	8	0
−	☐	☐
	☐	☐

TRY Practice subtracting ones and tens from a 2-digit number with regrouping

Regroup and subtract.

1 72 − 55 = ?

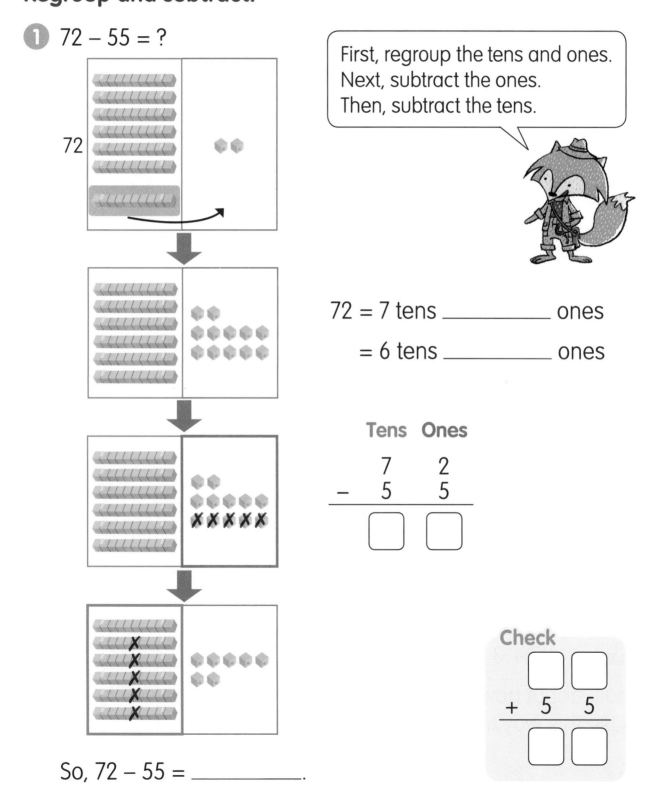

First, regroup the tens and ones.
Next, subtract the ones.
Then, subtract the tens.

72 = 7 tens _____ ones

= 6 tens _____ ones

Tens Ones

```
    7   2
−   5   5
  ┌──┐┌──┐
  └──┘└──┘
```

Check

```
  ┌──┐┌──┐
  └──┘└──┘
+   5   5
  ┌──┐┌──┐
  └──┘└──┘
```

So, 72 − 55 = _____.

2 73 − 37 = _____

Tens	Ones
7	3
− 3	7

☐ ☐

Check

☐	☐
+ 3	7

☐ ☐

3 71 − 56 = _____

Tens	Ones
7	1
− 5	6

☐ ☐

Check

☐	☐
+ 5	6

☐ ☐

MATH SHARING

Mathematical Practice **3** **Construct Viable arguments**

Pablo uses this way to subtract 27 from 62.

STEP 1 $27 + 3 = 30$

STEP 2 $62 − 30 = 32$

STEP 3 $32 + 3 = 35$

Talk about how this way works with your partner.
Use this way to subtract 28 from 73.

Name: _____   Date: _____

INDEPENDENT PRACTICE

Regroup.

1

$82 =$

Tens	Ones
8	

$=$

Tens	Ones
7	

2

$70 =$

Tens	Ones
	0

$=$

Tens	Ones
6	

Regroup and subtract.

3

Tens	Ones
4	4
−	9
☐	☐

4

Tens	Ones
5	3
−	7
☐	☐

5

Tens	Ones
6	6
− 2	8
☐	☐

6

Tens	Ones
7	3
− 1	8
☐	☐

7

Tens	Ones
7	2
− 3	3
☐	☐

8

Tens	Ones
9	0
− 1	6
☐	☐

Some eggs are about to hatch.
Subtract to find out which.
Then, color the eggs below that match your answers.

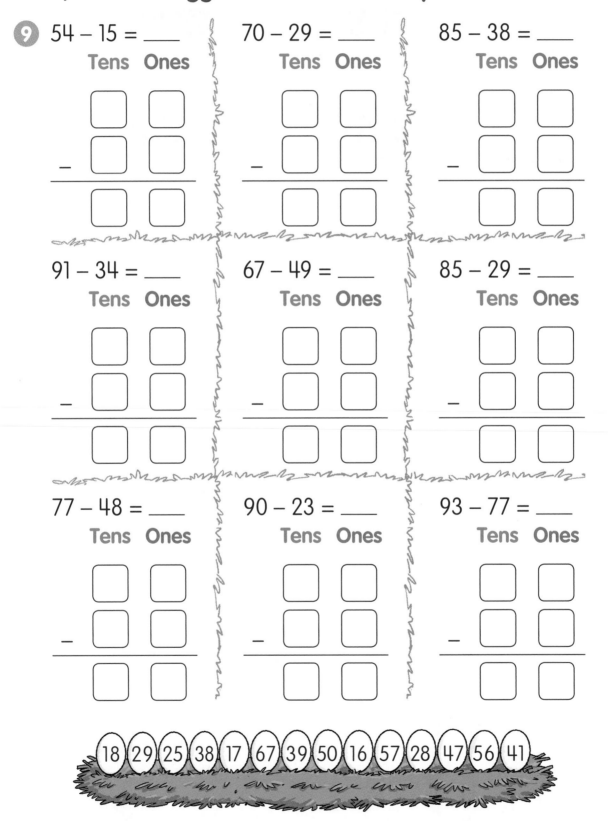

9 54 – 15 = ___

Tens Ones

70 – 29 = ___

Tens Ones

85 – 38 = ___

Tens Ones

91 – 34 = ___

Tens Ones

67 – 49 = ___

Tens Ones

85 – 29 = ___

Tens Ones

77 – 48 = ___

Tens Ones

90 – 23 = ___

Tens Ones

93 – 77 = ___

Tens Ones

18 29 25 38 17 67 39 50 16 57 28 47 56 41

Name: _____ Date: _____

Mathematical Habit 3 Construct viable arguments

Matthew adds 38 and 29.
He gives the answer as 57.
Did he add correctly?
Write down your thinking.

	Tens	Ones
	3	8
+	2	9
	5	7

Constance subtracts 26 from 81.
She gives the answer as 55.
Did she subtract correctly?
Write down your thinking.

	Tens	Ones
	8	1
−	2	6
	5	5

Problem Solving with Heuristics

1 **Mathematical Habit** **1** Persevere in solving problems

Complete each number sentence.
Use each number once.

| 25 | 30 | 45 | 70 | 100 | 75 |

Mathematical Habit **1** **Persevere in solving problems**

Complete each number sentence.
Use each number once.

| 24 | 26 | 40 | 50 | 64 | 90 |

3 **Mathematical Habit 1** Persevere in solving problems

	Tens	Ones
	6	☐
−	1	☐
	☐	3

What could the missing numbers be?
Write down three possible answers.

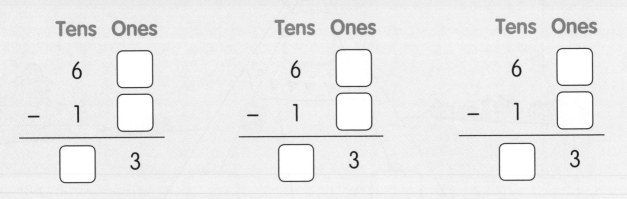

	Tens	Ones
	6	☐
−	1	☐
	☐	3

	Tens	Ones
	6	☐
−	1	☐
	☐	3

	Tens	Ones
	6	☐
−	1	☐
	☐	3

CHAPTER WRAP-UP

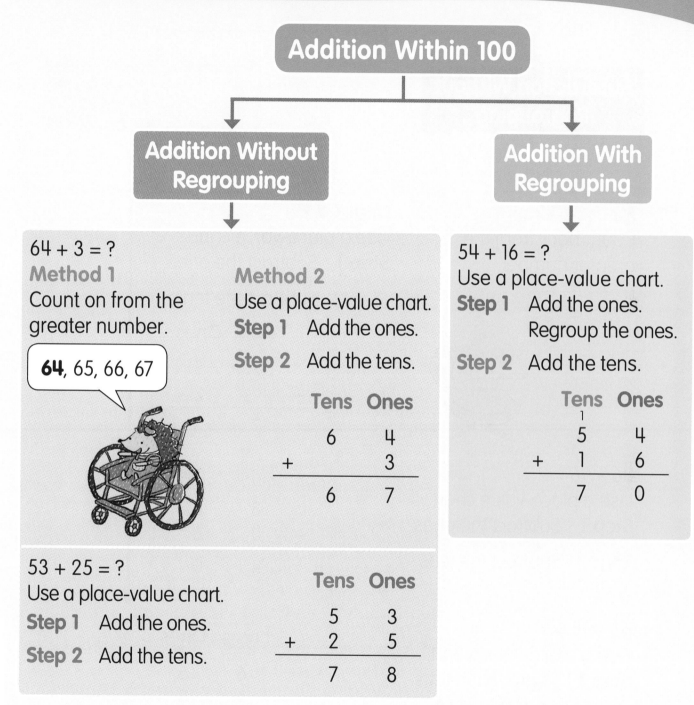

Addition Within 100

Addition Without Regrouping

64 + 3 = ?

Method 1
Count on from the greater number.

64, 65, 66, 67

Method 2
Use a place-value chart.
Step 1 Add the ones.
Step 2 Add the tens.

Tens	Ones
6	4
+	3
6	7

53 + 25 = ?
Use a place-value chart.
Step 1 Add the ones.
Step 2 Add the tens.

Tens	Ones
5	3
+ 2	5
7	8

Addition With Regrouping

54 + 16 = ?
Use a place-value chart.
Step 1 Add the ones.
         Regroup the ones.
Step 2 Add the tens.

Tens	Ones
1	
5	4
+ 1	6
7	0

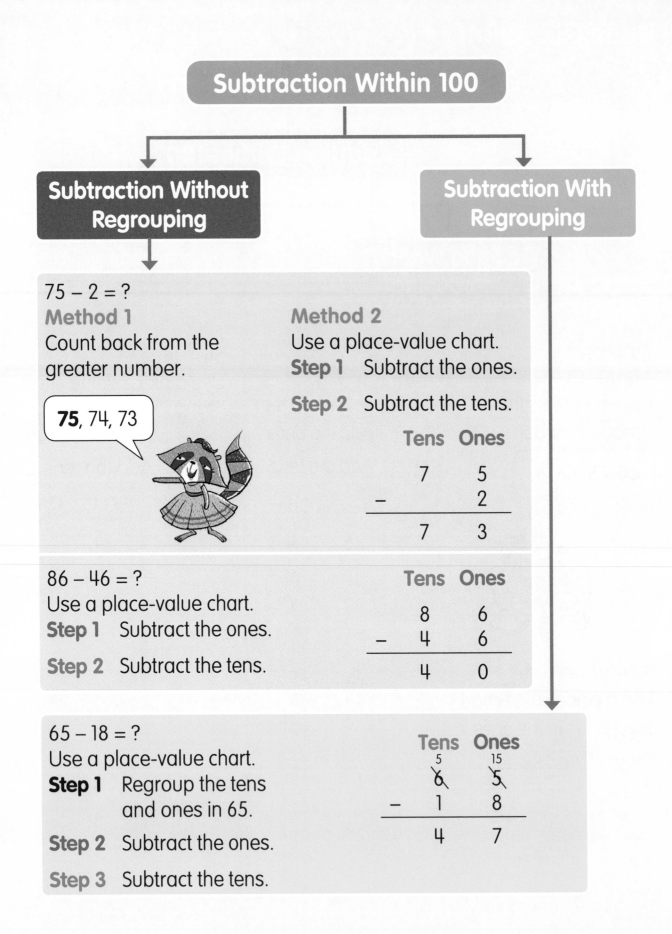

Subtraction Within 100

Subtraction Without Regrouping

75 – 2 = ?

Method 1
Count back from the greater number.

75, 74, 73

Method 2
Use a place-value chart.
Step 1 Subtract the ones.

Step 2 Subtract the tens.

Tens	Ones
7	5
–	2
7	3

86 – 46 = ?
Use a place-value chart.
Step 1 Subtract the ones.

Step 2 Subtract the tens.

Tens	Ones
8	6
– 4	6
4	0

Subtraction With Regrouping

65 – 18 = ?
Use a place-value chart.
Step 1 Regroup the tens and ones in 65.

Step 2 Subtract the ones.

Step 3 Subtract the tens.

Tens	Ones
5	15
6	5
– 1	8
4	7

Name: _____ Date: _____

Add.
Count on from the greater number.

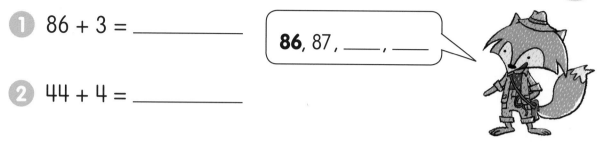

1 86 + 3 = _____

> **86**, 87, ____ , ____

2 44 + 4 = _____

3 51 + 20 = _____

Add.

4

Tens	Ones
5	3
+	5
☐	☐

5

Tens	Ones
	8
+ 6	0
☐	☐

6

Tens	Ones
7	1
+ 2	0
☐	☐

7

Tens	Ones
4	5
+ 4	2
☐	☐

Add and regroup.

8

Tens	Ones
6	4
+	9
☐	☐

9

Tens	Ones
	7
+ 5	4
☐	☐

10

Tens	Ones
3	2
+ 1	8
☐	☐

11

Tens	Ones
5	5
+ 1	6
☐	☐

12 39 + 53 = _____

Tens	Ones
☐	☐
+ ☐	☐
☐	☐

13 74 + 17 = _____

Tens	Ones
☐	☐
+ ☐	☐
☐	☐

Subtract.
Count back from the greater number.

14 79 – 3 = _____

79, 78 , _____ , _____

15 87 – 4 = _____

16 92 – 30 = _____

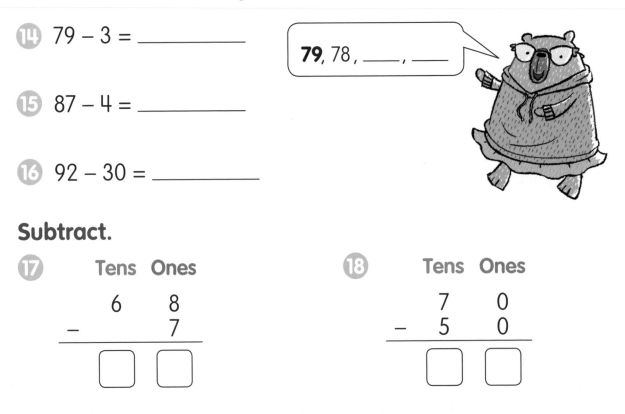

Subtract.

17

Tens	Ones
6	8
–	7
☐	☐

18

Tens	Ones
7	0
– 5	0
☐	☐

19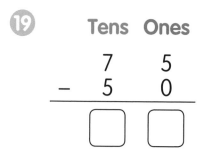

    Tens Ones

     7   5

  − 5   0

20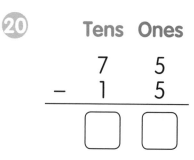

    Tens Ones

     7   5

  − 1   5

Regroup and subtract.

21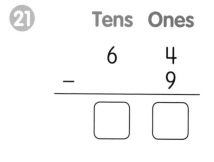

    Tens Ones

     6   4

  −   9

22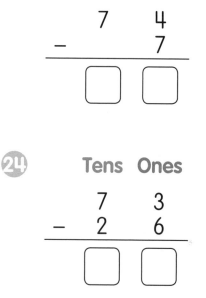

    Tens Ones

     7   4

  −   7

23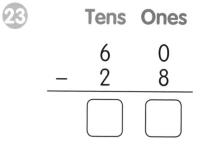

    Tens Ones

     6   0

  − 2   8

24

    Tens Ones

     7   3

  − 2   6

25 $92 - 9 =$ _____

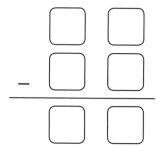

    Tens Ones

26 $85 - 27 =$ _____

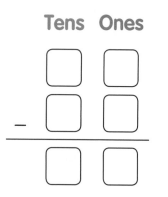

    Tens Ones

Assessment Prep
Answer each question.

27 Which cards give the answer 48?
Color the ducks.

	Tens	Ones
	2	3
+	2	5
	☐	☐

	Tens	Ones
	9	5
−	4	7
	☐	☐

	Tens	Ones
	5	0
−		2
	☐	☐

	Tens	Ones
	7	9
−	4	1
	☐	☐

28 Add or subtract.
Which answer is greater than 50?

Ⓐ

	Tens	Ones
	9	0
−	4	4
	☐	☐

Ⓑ

	Tens	Ones
	1	3
+	3	8
	☐	☐

Ⓒ

	Tens	Ones
	6	7
−	1	9
	☐	☐

Ⓓ

	Tens	Ones
	1	6
+	2	9
	☐	☐

Name: _____   Date: _____

Mixed Farming

Some farmers are working on a farm that plants crops and rears animals.

1 Farmer Cruz harvests 43 carrots.
Farmer Taylor harvests 44 carrots.
How many carrots do both farmers harvest in all?

43 + 44 = _____

Both farmers harvest _____ carrots in all.

2 There are some sheep on the farm.
29 sheep are grazing.
21 sheep are in the pen.

a How many sheep are there in all?

29 + 21 = _____

There are _____ sheep in all.

b Do you need to regroup to find the answer?
Explain.

3 There are 47 cows to be milked.
Farmer Walker milks 16 cows.

a How many cows does Farmer Walker still need to milk?

47 – 16 = _____

Farmer Walker still needs to milk _____ cows.

b How do you find the answer?

4 There are 60 ducks.
29 ducks are swimming.
The rest of the ducks are not swimming.

31 ducks are
not swimming

Farmer Lewis

a Is Farmer Lewis correct?
Subtract to check if she is correct.
Then, circle the correct answer.   Yes / No

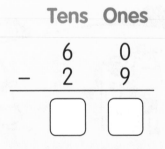

Tens	Ones
6	0
− 2	9
☐	☐

b Do you need to regroup to find the answer?
Explain.

© 2020 Marshall Cavendish Education Pte Ltd

5 There are 47 chicks in a farm.
Some eggs hatched.
There are 52 chicks in all now.

a How many eggs hatched?

47 + _____ = 52

_____ eggs hatched.

b How do you solve?
Explain.

Rubric

Point(s)	Level	My Performance
7–8	4	• Most of my answers are correct. • I show all my work correctly. • I explain my thinking clearly and completely.
5–6.5	3	• Some of my answers are correct. • I show some of my work correctly. • I explain my thinking clearly.
3–4.5	2	• A few of my answers are correct. • I show little work correctly. • I explain some of my thinking clearly.
0–2.5	1	• A few of my answers are correct. • I show little or no work. • I do not explain my thinking clearly.

Teacher's Comments

Graphs

Old MacDonald had a farm,
E-i-e-i-o
And on his farm he had some ducks,
E-i-e-i-o
With a quack, quack here,
And a quack, quack there,
Here quack, there quack,
Everywhere quack, quack.
Old MacDonald had a farm,
E-i-e-i-o

Key: Each ☆ stands for 1 animal.

How can you collect, organize, and show data in a picture graph and tally chart?

Name: _____ Date: _____

Showing information with pictures

Count.

There are 5 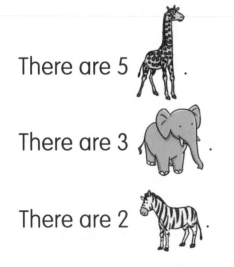 .

There are 3 🐘 .

There are 2 🦓 .

▶ **Quick Check**

Count.
Then, write each number.

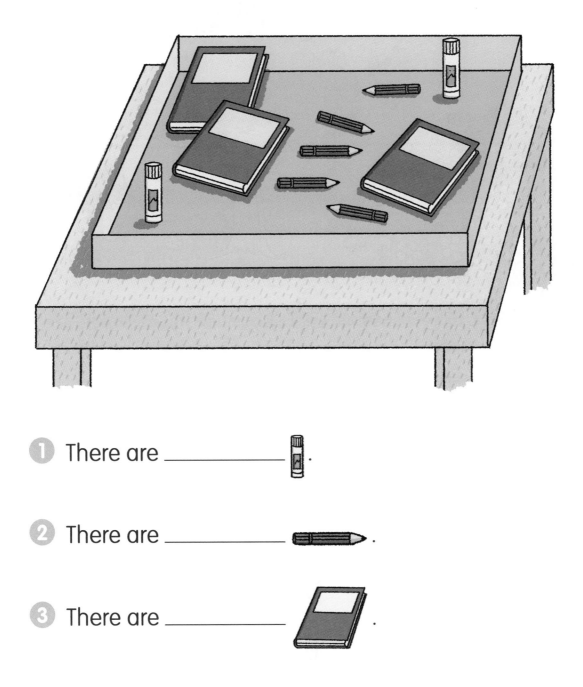

1 There are _____ .

2 There are _____ .

3 There are _____ .

Count.
Then, write each number.

④ There is _____  .

⑤ There are _____  .

⑥ There are _____  .

⑦ There are _____  .

⑧ There are _____  .

1 Simple Picture Graphs

Learning Objectives:
- Collect, organize, and show data as a picture graph.
- Understand the data shown in a picture graph.
- Understand the data shown in a picture graph using symbols.

New Vocabulary
data
picture graph
symbols
most
fewest
key

THINK

A store has some baseballs, basketballs, and volleyballs. The number of baseballs and basketballs are shown in the picture graph below.

Types of Balls at the Store

 🏀	**Basketball**	● ● ● ● ● ●
 ⚾	**Baseball**	● ● ● ● ● ● ● ● ● ●
 🏐	**Volleyball**	?

Key: Each ● stands for 1 ball.

There are more volleyballs than basketballs.
There are fewer volleyballs than baseballs.
Write three sentences about the number of volleyballs.

Take some 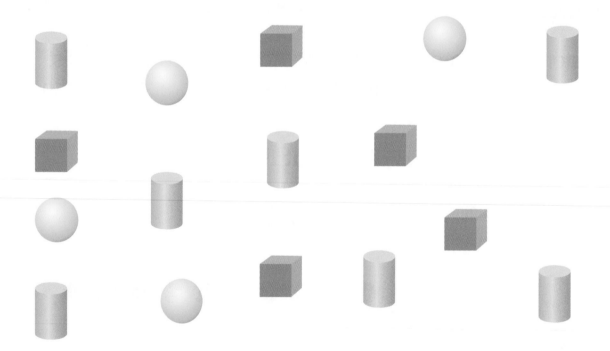 of different colors.
Arrange the 🎲 to show which color has the most and least.
Share your thinking your partner.

LEARN Collect **data** and show it as a **picture graph**

1 Wyatt has many different shapes.
Count the number of each shape.

Data is information that has numbers.
The information here is the number of shapes and
their types.

You can show data as a picture graph.

Shapes

Cube	Cylinder	Sphere

You can read and get information from a picture graph.

There are 5 cubes.
There are 7 cylinders.
There are 4 spheres.

A picture graph uses pictures or symbols to show data.

Wyatt has the most cylinders as shapes.
He has the fewest spheres as shapes.

He has 2 more cylinders than cubes.
He has 3 fewer spheres than cylinders.

There are 16 shapes in all.

"Most" means the greatest number.

"Fewest" means the least number.

Hands-on Activity Making a picture graph

Work as a class.

Your teacher will give you copies of 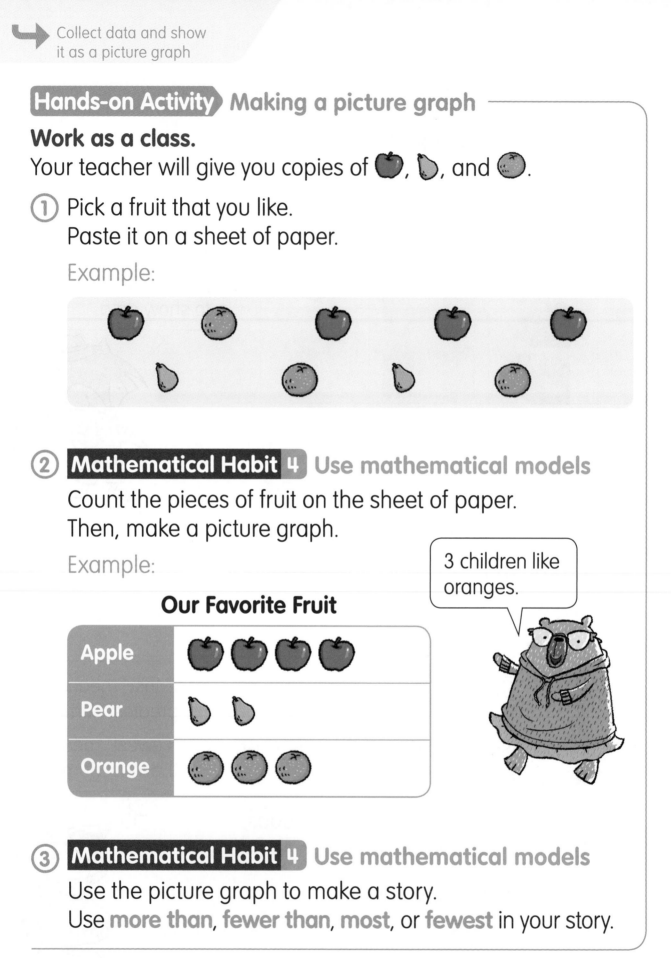, 🍐, and 🍊.

① Pick a fruit that you like.
Paste it on a sheet of paper.

Example:

② **Mathematical Habit 4** Use mathematical models

Count the pieces of fruit on the sheet of paper.
Then, make a picture graph.

Example:

Our Favorite Fruit

Apple	🍎 🍎 🍎 🍎
Pear	🍐 🍐
Orange	🍊 🍊 🍊

3 children like oranges.

③ **Mathematical Habit 4** Use mathematical models

Use the picture graph to make a story.
Use **more than**, **fewer than**, **most**, or **fewest** in your story.

TRY Practice reading and understanding data in a picture graph

Look at the picture graph.
Then, fill in each blank.
The picture graph shows the number of eggs laid by three hens.

Number of Eggs Laid

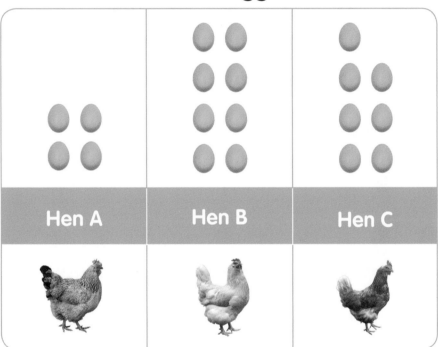

1. Hen A laid _____ eggs.

2. Hen B laid _____ eggs.

3. Hen C laid _____ eggs.

4. Hen _____ laid the most eggs.

5. Hen _____ laid the fewest eggs.

6. Hen C laid _____ more eggs than Hen A.

7. The hens laid _____ eggs in all.

Look at the picture graph.
Then, answer each question.
The picture graph shows some sea animals seen at a beach.

Sea Animals Seen at a Beach

Crab	
Starfish	
Jellyfish	

8 How many crabs are there? _____

9 How many jellyfish are there? _____

10 Which sea animal is seen most often? _____

11 Which sea animal is seen least often? _____

12 Are there more crabs or jellyfish? _____
How many more? _____

13 Are there fewer jellyfish or starfish? _____
How many fewer? _____

ENGAGE

Ask 10 friends which fruit they like best: apples, pears, or bananas.

Draw a picture graph to show your information.

Talk about how you did it with your partner.

LEARN Understand data shown in a picture graph

1. The picture graph shows the favorite toys of some children.

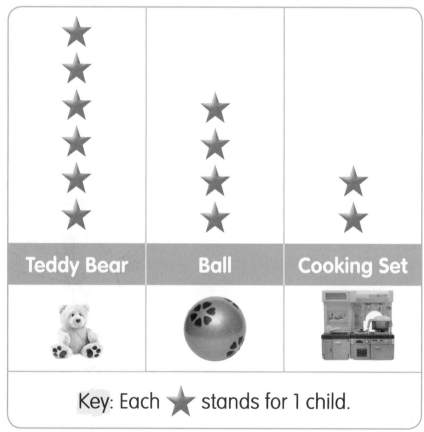

Our Favorite Toys

Key: Each ★ stands for 1 child.

The key shows what each picture or symbol stands for.

6 children like teddy bears.

2 more children like teddy bears than balls.

2 fewer children like cooking sets than balls.

The most popular toy is the teddy bear.

The least popular toy is the cooking set.

2 The picture graph shows the number of animals on
Sue's farm.

Animals on Sue's Farm

🐔	**Chicken**	X X X X X X
🐄	**Cow**	X X X
🦆	**Duck**	X X X

Key: Each X stands for 1 animal.

There are
3 cows.

There are
6 chickens.

There are as many
cows as ducks.

Math Talk

Use the picture graph
to make other stories
about the animals.

Your teacher will give you a bag of 🧊.
The bag has a 🟦, a 🟦, and a 🟦.

① Take a 🧊 from the bag.

② **Mathematical Habit 4** Use mathematical models

Draw a ⭐ to stand for the color of 🧊 you take.

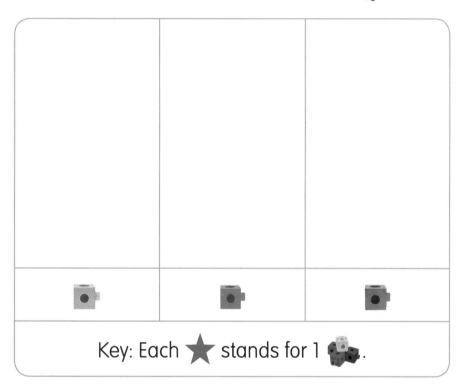

Key: Each ⭐ stands for 1 🧊.

③ Put the 🧊 you took back into the bag.

④ Repeat ① to ③ 10 more times.

⑤ Use your picture graph to make a story.
Share your story with the class.

TRY Practice reading and understanding data in a picture graph

Look at the picture graph.
Then, answer each question.
The picture graph shows the favorite colors of some children.

Our Favorite Colors

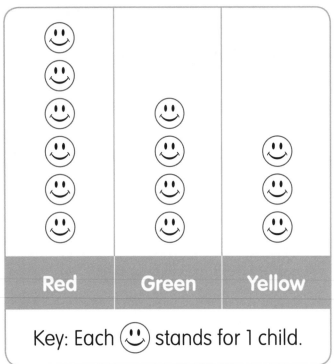

Key: Each ☺ stands for 1 child.

1. How many children like yellow? _____

2. How many more children like red than green? _____

3. How many fewer children like yellow than green? _____

4. Which is the most popular color? _____

5. Which is the least popular color? _____

INDEPENDENT PRACTICE

Look at the picture graph.
Then, fill in each blank.

The picture graph shows different types of vegetables in a kitchen.

Vegetables in a Kitchen

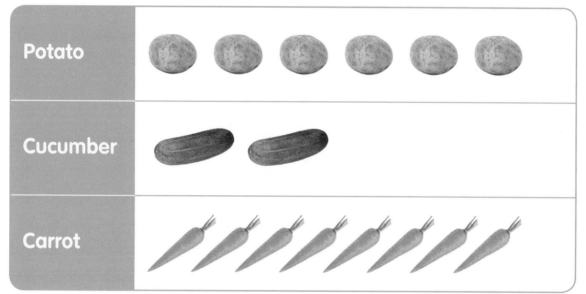

1 There are _____ potatoes.

2 There are _____ cucumbers.

3 There are _____ carrots.

4 There are _____ more potatoes than cucumbers.

5 There are _____ fewer cucumbers than carrots.

6 The number of _____ is the greatest.

7 The number of _____ is the least.

Look at the picture graph.
Then, fill in each blank.

The picture graph shows the different shapes used in a drawing.

Shapes used in a Drawing

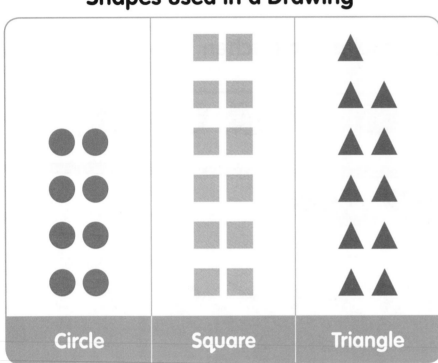

| Circle | Square | Triangle |

8 There are _____ squares.

9 There are 11 _____.

10 The shape used the most is the _____.

11 The shape used the least is the _____.

12 There are _____ fewer circles than squares.

Look at the picture graph.
Then, fill in each blank.
The picture graph shows some cars in a parking lot.

Cars in a Parking Lot

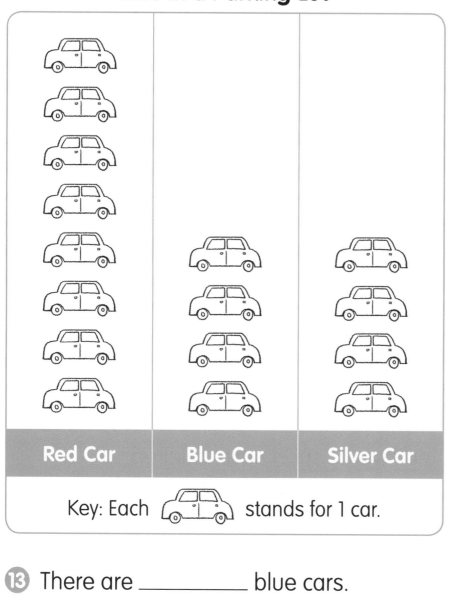

Key: Each stands for 1 car.

⑬ There are _____ blue cars.

⑭ There are _____ red cars and blue cars in all.

⑮ There are as many _____ cars as _____ cars.

⑯ How many cars are **not** blue? _____

Look at the picture graph.
Then, fill in each blank.
The picture graph shows the favorite sport of some children.

Favorite Sport

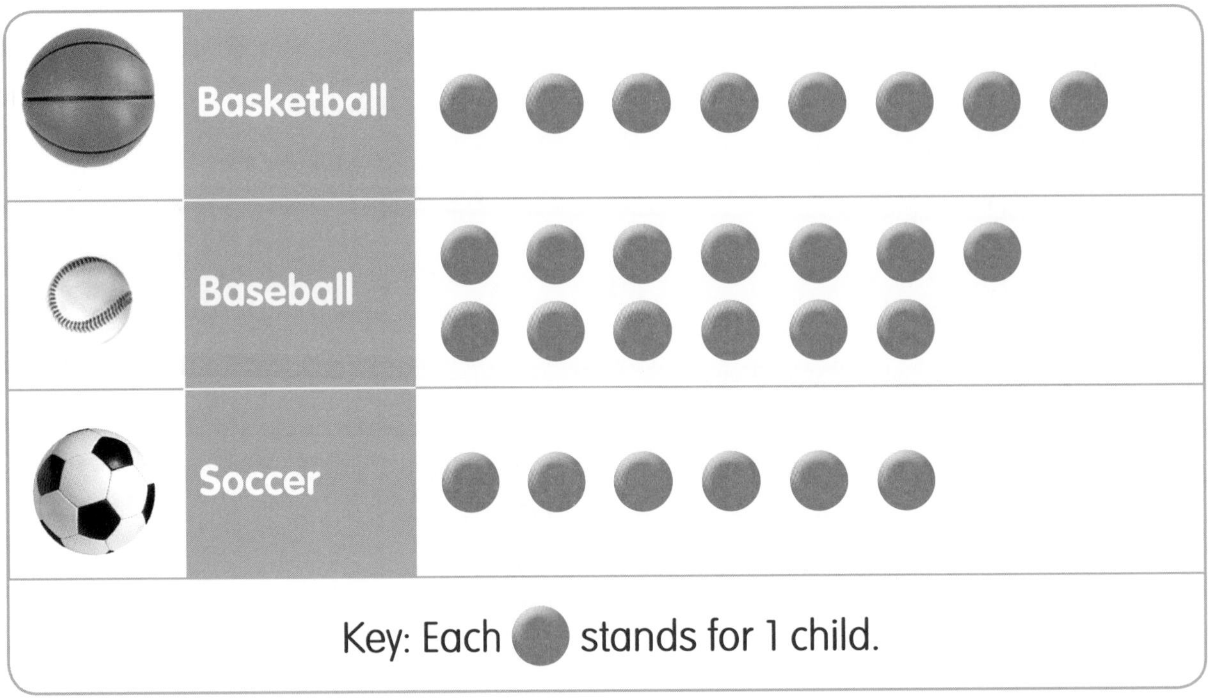

🏀	Basketball	● ● ● ● ● ● ● ●
⚾	Baseball	● ● ● ● ● ● ● ● ● ● ● ● ●
⚽	Soccer	● ● ● ● ● ●

Key: Each ● stands for 1 child.

17 Baseball is the favorite sport of _____ children.

18 _____ is the favorite sport of six children.

19 How many children chose basketball or soccer as their favorite sport? _____

20 Which is the most popular sport? _____

21 Which is the least popular sport? _____

Name: _____   Date: _____

 # Tally Charts and Picture Graphs

Learning Objectives:
- Make a tally chart.
- Show data in a tally chart as a picture graph.

> **New Vocabulary**
> tally mark
> tally chart

THINK

There are 18 students from Josiah's class taking part in Sports Day. Josiah makes a tally chart to show the information.

Type of Sport	Tally	Number of Students
Swimming	ⵌ I	6
Baseball	ⵌ II	7
Football	IIII	4

Josiah makes a mistake in his work.
What is the likely mistake he could have made?

ENGAGE

Collect data about your classmates who have brown eyes.
Draw tally marks | on the tally chart.
Then, complete the tally chart with this data.

Color of Eyes	Tally	Number of Classmates
Brown		
Not Brown		

LEARN Collect data and use a **tally chart** to organize it

1 Ms. Green has her class paste pictures of their favorite sport on the board.

Then, she makes a tally chart with this data.

She checks ✓ the favorite sport of each child and draws a
tally mark | on the tally chart.

baseball   tally mark

I check the favorite sport of one
child and draw a tally mark.

I draw four tally marks like this ||||.
To show five tally marks, I draw
the fifth mark across the first four
tally marks ||||.

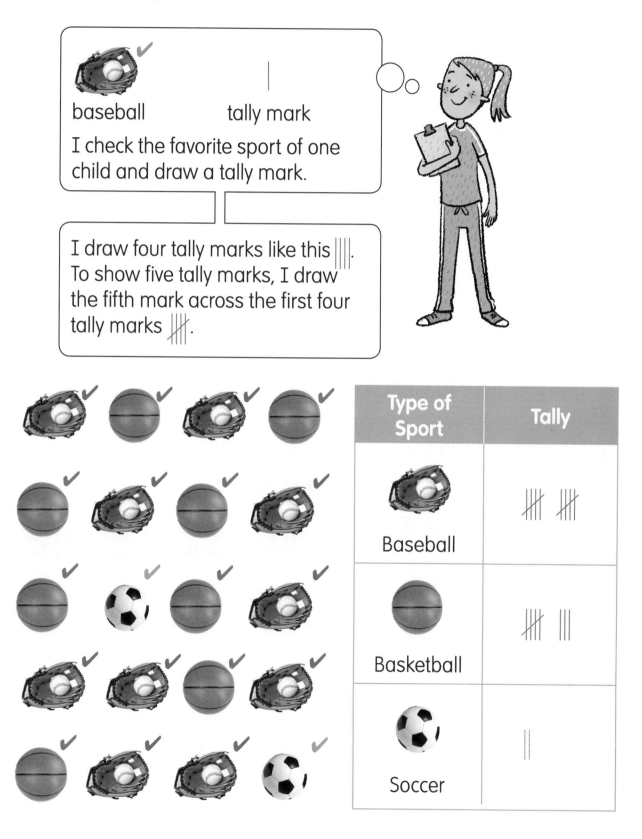

Type of Sport	Tally
Baseball	||||| |||||
Basketball	||||| |||
Soccer	||

This is Ms. Green's completed tally chart.
Then, Ms. Green counts the tally marks for each sport.

Type of Sport		Tally	Number of Children
	Baseball	|||| ||||	10
	Basketball	|||| |||	8
	Soccer	||	2

The tally chart shows the number of children who chose each sport as their favorite.

Ms. Green then uses a picture graph to show the data.

Favorite Sport

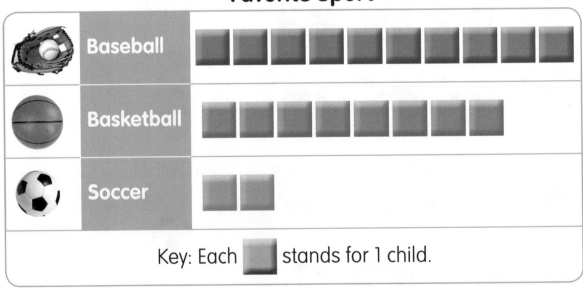

Key: Each [ ] stands for 1 child.

© 2020 Marshall Cavendish Education Pte Ltd

Hands-on Activity Using a tally chart to organize data

Your teacher will give you an empty bag.

① Take a ⬤, a ⬤, and a ⬤.
Place them in the bag.

② **Mathematical Habit 4** Use mathematical models

Take a 🔵 from the bag without looking.
Look at the color of 🔵 you took.
Then, draw a tally mark on the tally chart.

Color of 🔵	Tally	Number
⬤		
⬤		
⬤		

③ Put the 🔵 back into the bag.

④ Repeat ② and ③ 12 more times.

⑤ Complete the tally chart above.

⑥ a Which 🔵 is picked the most? _____

  b Which 🔵 is picked the least? _____

7 Use the data in the tally chart to make a picture graph.
Draw a 😊 to stand for the number of 🪙 you took.

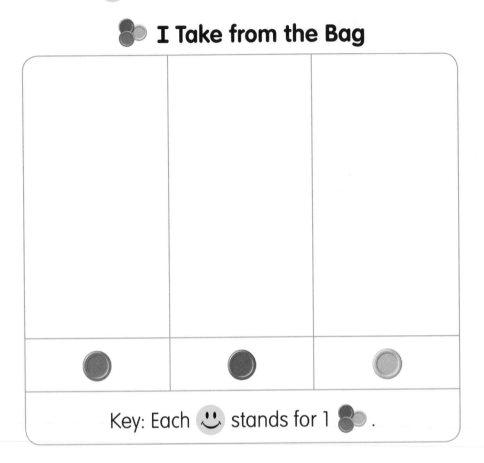

🪙 **I Take from the Bag**

Key: Each 😊 stands for 1 🪙 .

8 Use your picture graph to make a story.

© 2020 Marshall Cavendish Education Pte Ltd

TRY Practice making a tally chart and a picture graph

Sergio sees some animals at a safari.

Use a copy of this tally chart.
Count and make a tally mark for each animal.

1

Type of Animals		Tally	Number
	Buffalo		
	Zebra		
	Elephant		

Fill in each blank.

2 There are _____ zebras.

3 There are _____ animals in all.

Make a picture graph.
Use ★ to stand for 1 animal.

④ **Animals Sergio Saw at the Safari**

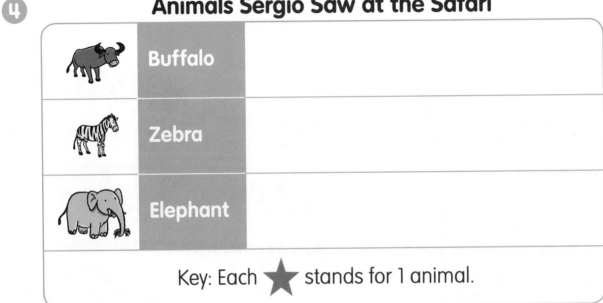

Key: Each ★ stands for 1 animal.

Use the picture graph in ④ to answer each question.

⑤ There are _____ zebras.

⑥ There are _____ buffaloes.

⑦ There are _____ elephants.

⑧ There are _____ more zebras than elephants.

⑨ There are _____ fewer elephants than buffaloes.

⑩ The number of _____ is the least.

⑪ The number of _____ is the greatest.

INDEPENDENT PRACTICE

Mario is making a tally chart and a picture graph.
The data is the different types of books he has.

Complete the tally chart.

1

Type of Books	Tally	Number
Math Book		
Puzzle Book		
Storybook		

Make a picture graph.
Use △ **to stand for 1 book.**

② **Books that Mario Has**

📘	Math Book	
📘	Puzzle Book	
📘	Storybook	
	Key: Each △ stands for 1 book.	

Fill in each blank

③ Mario has _____ math books.

④ He has _____ puzzle books.

⑤ He has _____ storybooks.

⑥ There are _____ more storybooks than puzzle books.

⑦ There are _____ fewer math books than storybooks.

⑧ The type of books Mario has the most is _____.

⑨ The number of _____ is the least.

⑩ Mario has _____ books in all.

Name: _____ Date: _____

Mathematical Practice 3 Construct viable arguments

Brody counted all the shapes he has.

Type of Shapes	Tally	Number
⬜ Square	|||||	6
⬤ Circle	|||| ||||	9
▲ Triangle	|||| |||	8

Brody made some mistakes in his tally chart.
Write all the mistakes he made.
What should the correct answers be?

Problem Solving with Heuristics

1 **Mathematical Practice** 1 Persevere in solving problems

The picture graph shows the number of rainy days in three weeks.

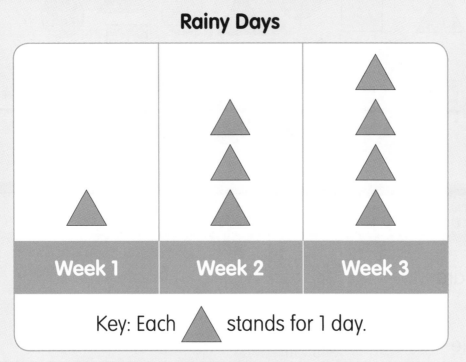

Rainy Days

| Week 1 | Week 2 | Week 3 |

Key: Each ▲ stands for 1 day.

a It rains the most in Week _____ .

b It rains the least in Week _____ .

c Week 4 has more rainy days than Week 1 but fewer than Week 2.

How many rainy days does Week 4 have? _____

2 **Mathematical Practice** **1** **Persevere in solving problems**

The picture graph shows the number of pets of some Grade 1 students in a class.

Pets of Grade 1 Students

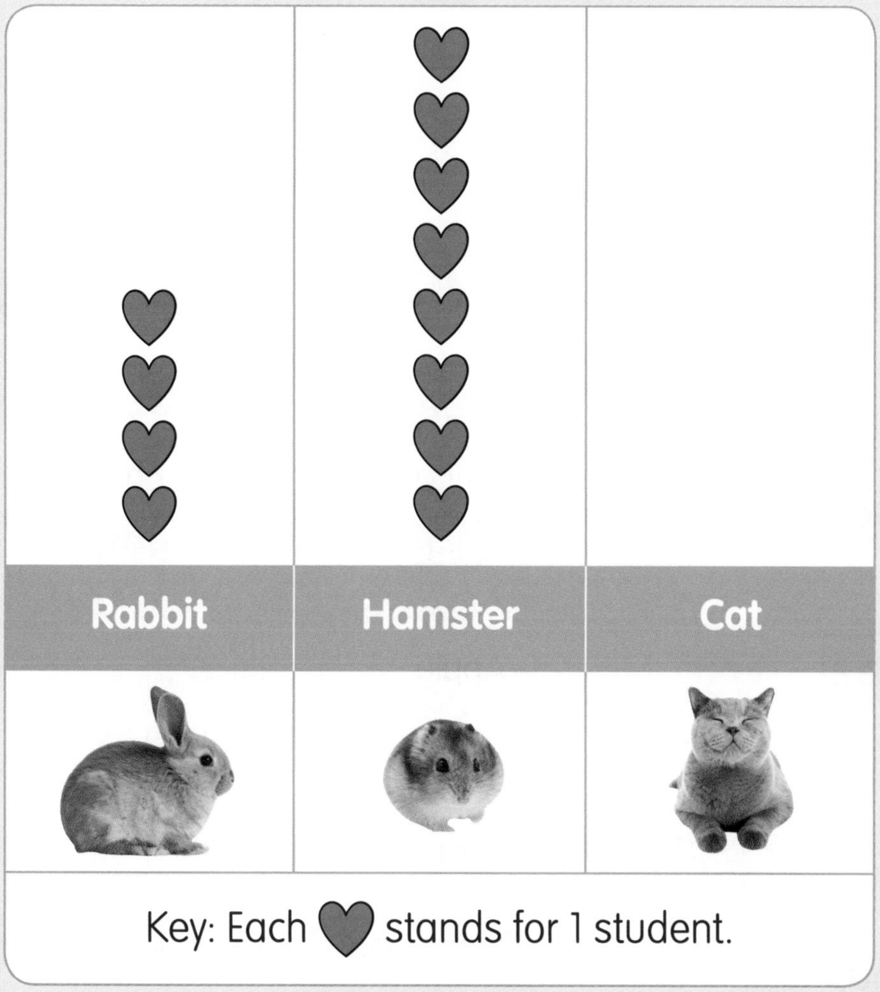

Key: Each ♥ stands for 1 student.

There are 18 Grade 1 students in the class.

How many students have cats as pets?

Draw ♥ in the picture graph to show the number.

How can you collect, organize, and show data in a picture graph and tally chart?

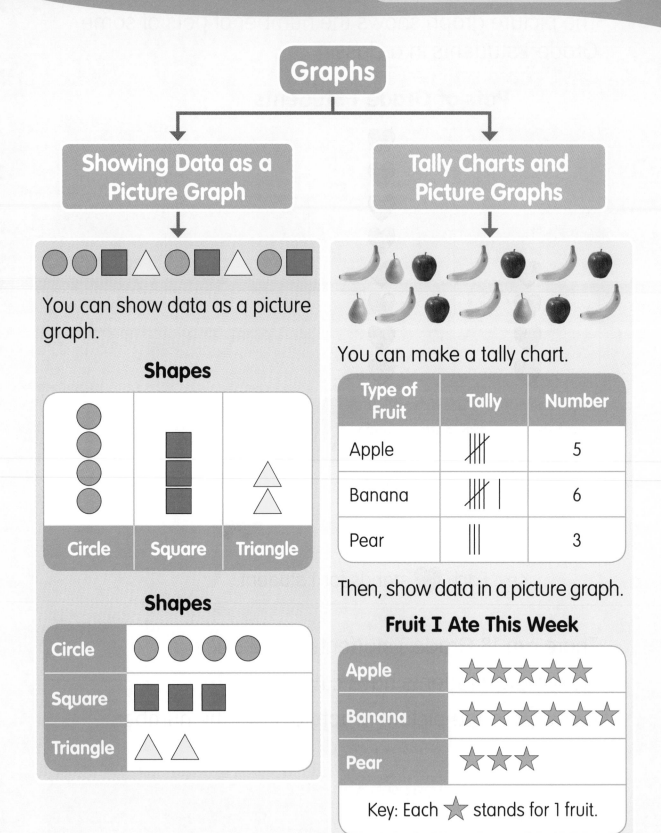

Graphs

Showing Data as a Picture Graph

You can show data as a picture graph.

Shapes

Circle	Square	Triangle

Shapes

Circle	
Square	
Triangle	

Tally Charts and Picture Graphs

You can make a tally chart.

Type of Fruit	Tally	Number
Apple	|||||	5
Banana	|||||		6
Pear	|||	3

Then, show data in a picture graph.

Fruit I Ate This Week

Apple	★★★★★
Banana	★★★★★★
Pear	★★★

Key: Each ★ stands for 1 fruit.

Name: _____   Date: _____

Look at the picture graph.
Then, fill in each blank.

The picture graph shows the number of people on a bus.

People on the Bus

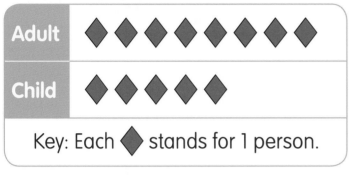

| Adult | ◆ ◆ ◆ ◆ ◆ ◆ ◆ ◆ |
| Child | ◆ ◆ ◆ ◆ ◆ |

Key: Each ◆ stands for 1 person.

1 There are _____ (more / fewer) children than adults.

2 There are _____ more adults than children.

Look at the tally chart.
Then, fill in each blank.

The tally chart shows some children's favorite musical instruments.

Instrument		Tally	Number of Children
	Piano	卌 ⦀⦀	9
	Guitar	卌 卌 ⫼	12
	Drum	卌 ⎮	6

3 _____ is the most popular musical instrument.

4 _____ is the least popular musical instrument.

A recycling project was carried out in class.
Some children brought bottles for recycling.
The tally chart shows the number of bottles each child brought.

5 **Complete the tally chart.**

Name	Tally	Number of Bottles
Anthony	ⅢⅡ ⅢⅡ	
Elizabeth	Ⅲ	
Jackson	ⅢⅡ Ⅱ	

6 **Make a picture graph.**
Use ● to stand for 1 bottle.

Bottles for Recycling

Anthony	
Elizabeth	
Jackson	

Key: Each ● stands for 1 bottle.

Use the picture graph in 6 to answer each question.

7 Who brought the fewest bottles? _____

8 How many fewer bottles did Jackson bring than Anthony?

_____

Look at the picture graph.
Then, fill in each blank.
Alexis is at a parking lot.
She makes a picture graph on the vehicles she sees.

Vehicles at a Parking Lot

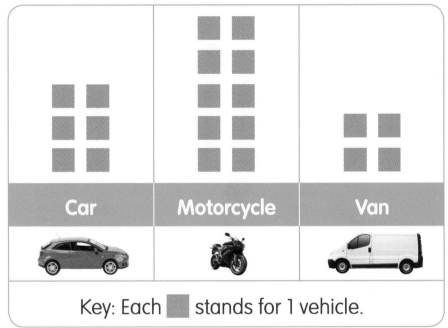

Key: Each ■ stands for 1 vehicle.

⑨ There are _____ cars.

⑩ The parking lot has the most _____ .

⑪ There are _____ more cars than vans.

⑫ There are _____ fewer cars than motorcycles.

⑬ There are _____ vehicles in all.

⑭ Some motorcycles leave the parking lot.
The number of motorcycles is now the same as the
number of vans.

_____ motorcycles leave the parking lot.

Assessment Prep

Answer each question.

A zookeeper counts the fruit that some monkeys eat.

15 a Count the pieces of fruit that the monkeys eat.
Then, complete the picture graph.

Fruit Monkeys Eat

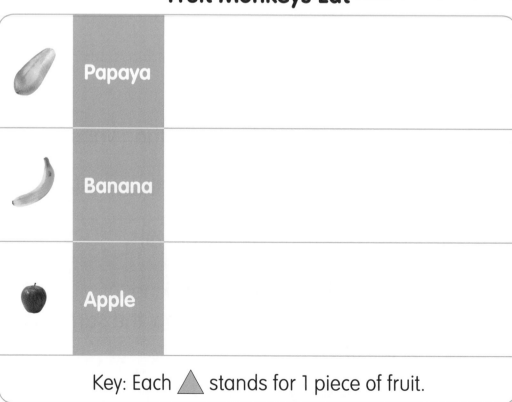

Key: Each △ stands for 1 piece of fruit.

b How many fewer papayas than bananas do the monkeys eat?

　Ⓐ 2

　Ⓑ 5

　Ⓒ 7

　Ⓓ 14

c How many pieces of fruit do the monkeys eat in all?

　Ⓐ 31

　Ⓑ 32

　Ⓒ 33

　Ⓓ 34

Eli counts the number of shapes he draws.
He makes a tally chart as shown below.

Type of Shapes		Tally
△	Triangle	‖‖ ‖‖
▢	Square	‖‖ ‖‖ ‖
⬤	Circle	‖‖ ‖

16 a How many squares are there?

(A) 9

(B) 10

(C) 11

(D) 12

b How many more triangles than circles are there?

(A) 2

(B) 3

(C) 5

(D) 9

c What is the total number of the two shapes Eli drew the most?

(A) 14

(B) 17

(C) 19

(D) 25

d Eli wants to have the same number of squares and circles.
How many more circles must he draw?

(A) 4

(B) 5

(C) 6

(D) 7

© 2020 Marshall Cavendish Education Pte Ltd

PERFORMANCE TASK

Name: ______________________ Date: ____________

Animals on a Farm

Farmer Parker has some goats, chickens, and ducks on her farm.

1 Complete the tally chart.

Type of Animals	Tally	Number
 Goat		
 Chicken		
 Duck		

2 Draw a picture graph.
Use ● to stand for 1 animal.

Animals on a Farm

	Goat	
	Chicken	
	Duck	

Key: Each ● stands for 1 animal.

Use the picture graph in **2** to answer each question.

3 Farmer Parker has _____ chickens.

4 Which animal does Farmer Parker have the most?

_____

5 Farmer Parker has _____ fewer goats than chickens.

6 Farmer Parker has 1 more _____ than _____ .

7 Farmer Parker has _____ animals in all.

Rubric

Point(s)	Level	My Performance
7–8	4	• Most of my answers are correct. • I show all my work correctly. • I explain my thinking clearly and completely.
5–6.5	3	• Some of my answers are correct. • I show some of my work correctly. • I explain my thinking clearly.
3–4.5	2	• A few of my answers are correct. • I show little work correctly. • I explain some of my thinking clearly.
0–2.5	1	• A few of my answers are correct. • I show little or no work. • I do not explain my thinking clearly.

Teacher's Comments

STEAM

Number Information

Numbers give us information called data.
Tally charts show data.
So do picture graphs.

Task

Collect data.
Work in pairs.

Your teacher will give you a bag of crayons.

1 Sort the crayons by color.

2 Make a tally chart to show the colors in your bag.

3 Use the data in your tally chart to make a picture graph.
Give your picture graph a title.

4 Listen as your teacher reads the story *Harold and the Purple Crayon*.

5 List Harold's adventures.

6 Use a purple crayon to draw a new adventure to add to the story.

7 Show your picture to the class.
Share your adventure.

How is money used in real life?

Counting to 100

a You can count on by tens.

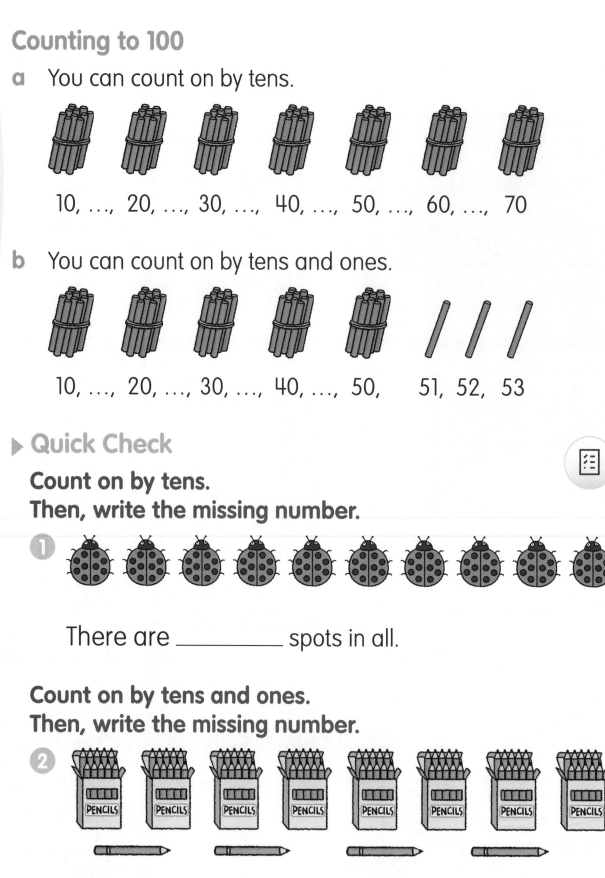

10, …, 20, …, 30, …, 40, …, 50, …, 60, …, 70

b You can count on by tens and ones.

10, …, 20, …, 30, …, 40, …, 50, 51, 52, 53

▶ **Quick Check**

Count on by tens.
Then, write the missing number.

1

There are _____ spots in all.

Count on by tens and ones.
Then, write the missing number.

2

There are _____ pencils in all.

Finding 10 more or less than another number

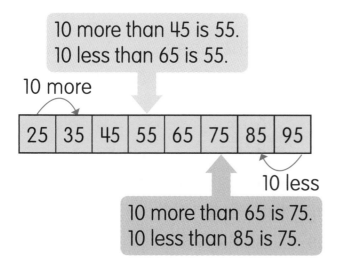

10 more than 45 is 55.
10 less than 65 is 55.

10 more

| 25 | 35 | 45 | 55 | 65 | 75 | 85 | 95 |

10 less

10 more than 65 is 75.
10 less than 85 is 75.

▶ **Quick Check**

Fill in each blank.
Use the counting tape to help you.

| 12 | 22 | 32 | 42 | 52 | 62 | 72 | 82 | 92 |

3 10 more than 32 is _____.

4 10 less than 82 is _____.

Fill in each blank.

5 10 more than 90 is _____.

6 10 less than 84 is _____.

Adding within 100

$36 + 38 = ?$

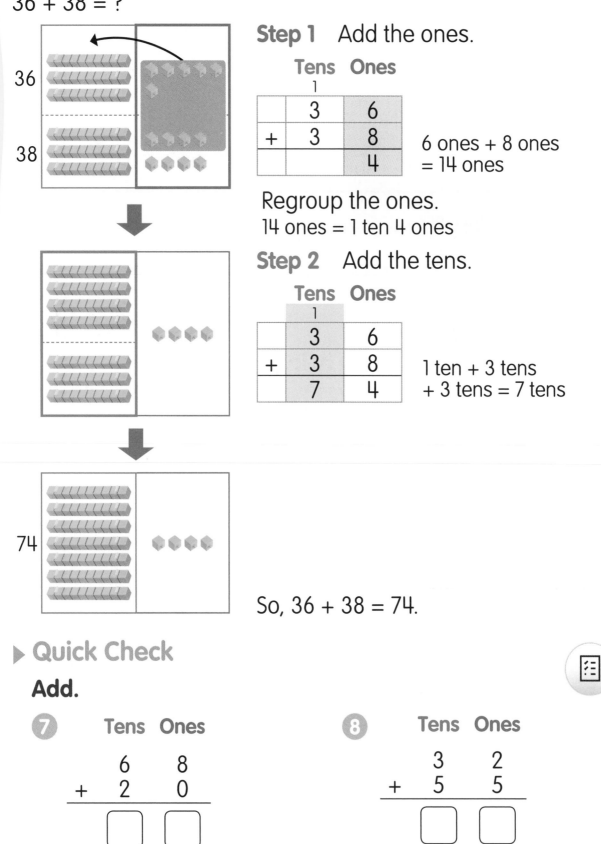

Step 1 Add the ones.

	Tens	Ones
	1	
	3	6
+	3	8
		4

6 ones + 8 ones
= 14 ones

Regroup the ones.
14 ones = 1 ten 4 ones

Step 2 Add the tens.

	Tens	Ones
	1	
	3	6
+	3	8
	7	4

1 ten + 3 tens
+ 3 tens = 7 tens

So, $36 + 38 = 74$.

▶ **Quick Check**

Add.

7

Tens	Ones
6	8
+ 2	0
☐	☐

8

Tens	Ones
3	2
+ 5	5
☐	☐

⑨

Tens	Ones
4	5
+	5

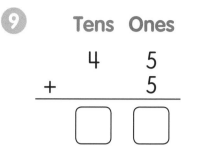

⑩

Tens	Ones
6	6
+ 2	5

Subtracting within 100

90 – 55 = ?

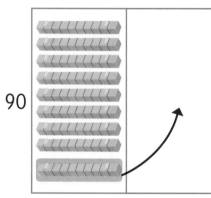

90

Step 1 Regroup the tens and ones.

Regroup the tens in 90.
90 = 9 tens 0 ones
    = 8 tens 10 ones

	Tens	Ones
	8 ̶9̶	10 ̶0̶
−	5	5

Step 2 Subtract the ones.

	Tens	Ones
	8 ̶9̶	10 ̶0̶
−	5	5
		5

10 ones – 5 ones
= 5 ones

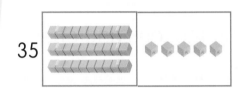

Step 3 Subtract the tens.

	Tens	Ones
	8	10
	9̶	0̶
−	5	5
	3	5

8 tens − 5 tens
= 3 tens

35

So, 90 − 55 = 35.

▶ **Quick Check**

Subtract.

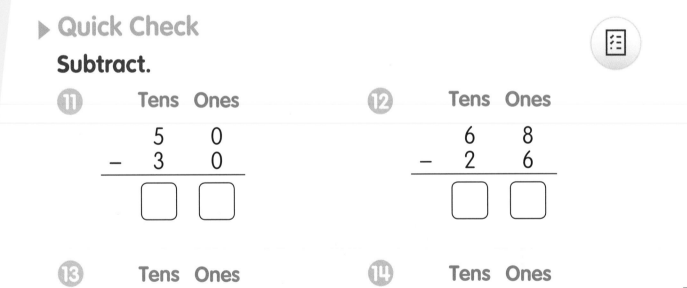

11.
Tens	Ones
5	0
− 3	0
☐	☐

12.
Tens	Ones
6	8
− 2	6
☐	☐

13.
Tens	Ones
8	5
−	9
☐	☐

14.
Tens	Ones
9	6
− 5	8
☐	☐

1 Penny, Nickel, and Dime

Learning Objectives:
- Recognize, identify, and name a penny, a nickel, and a dime.
- Understand that "¢" stands for cents.
- Count on to find the value of a group of coins.
- Exchange one coin for a set of coins of equal value.
- Use different combinations of coins less than 25¢ to buy items.

New Vocabulary
penny
nickel
dime
cent (¢)
value
exchange

THINK

Daniel has two bags of coins.
The total value of the coins in both bags is 50¢.
There are two dimes, two nickels, and two pennies in Bag A.
There are five coins in Bag B.
What are the five coins in Bag B?

ENGAGE

Your teacher will give you a 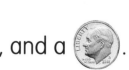, and a .

What do you notice about the coins?
What is the same?
What is different?
Share your thinking with your partner.

1 or

A penny has two faces.
A penny has a **value** of one **cent** or 1¢.

¢ means cents.

2 or

A nickel has two faces.
A nickel has a value of five cents or 5¢.

3

A dime has two faces.
A dime has a value of ten cents or 10¢.

Hands-on Activity Identifying the penny, nickel, and dime

Your teacher will give you some .

① Sort the coins into pennies, nickels, and dimes.

② Count how many of each type of coins you have. Then, complete the table below.

Type of Coins	Number
Penny	
Nickel	
Dime	

③ Answer each question.

a The number of _____ is the greatest.

b The number of _____ is the least.

Practice identifying the penny, nickel, and dime

Write the value of each coin.

 1 The value of a nickel is _____ ¢.

 2 The value of a dime is _____ ¢.

 3 The value of a penny is _____ ¢.

Write each number.

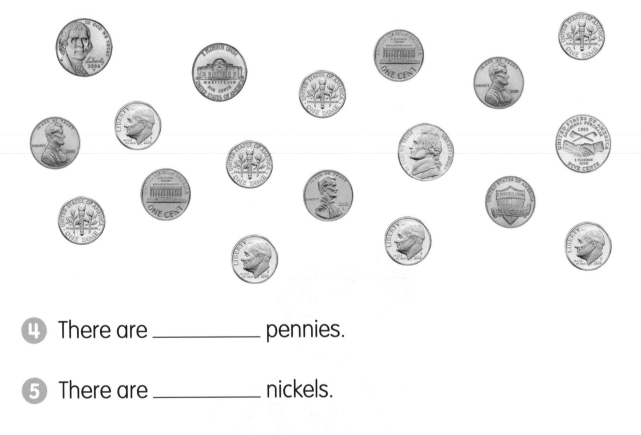

4 There are _____ pennies.

5 There are _____ nickels.

6 There are _____ dimes.

1. Arrange 20 nickels.
   Count by 5s.
   What is the last number?

2. Arrange 10 dimes.
   Count by 10s.
   What is the last number?

LEARN Count on to find the value of a group of coins of the same value

You can count on to find the value of the coins.

1.

Count on by 1s for pennies.
1, 2, 3, 4 cents

There are 4¢.

2.

Count on by 5s for nickels.
5, 10, 15 cents

There are 15¢.

③

Count on by 10s for dimes.
10, 20, 30 cents

There are 30¢.

Hands-on Activity Counting on to find the value
of a group of coins

Work in pairs.

Your teacher will give you some .

① Sort the by their types.

② Ask your partner to count on to find the value of each
group of coins.
Write your answers in the table.

Type of Coins	Value
Penny	¢
Nickel	¢
Dime	¢

③ Trade places.
Repeat ① and ②.

TRY Practice counting on to find the value of a group of coins

Write each missing number.

1

Count on by ____ s.

____, ____, ____, ____, ____, ____ cents

There are _____ ¢.

2

Count on by ____ s.

____, ____, ____, ____ cents

There are _____ ¢.

3

Count on by ____ s.

____, ____ cents

There are _____ ¢.

ENGAGE

A set of coins contains some pennies, nickels, and dimes.
Sarah picks four coins from the set.
Two of the coins she picks have the same value.
What are some of the likely total values of the four coins?
Use 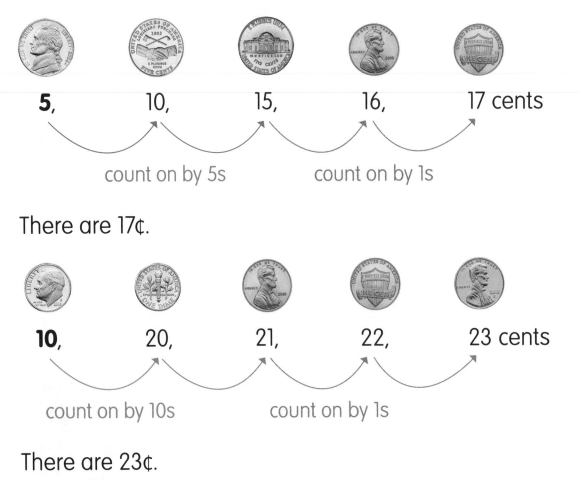 to help you.

LEARN Count on to find the value of a group of coins of different values

1 You can count on to find the value of a group of different coins.
Begin with the coin of a greater value.

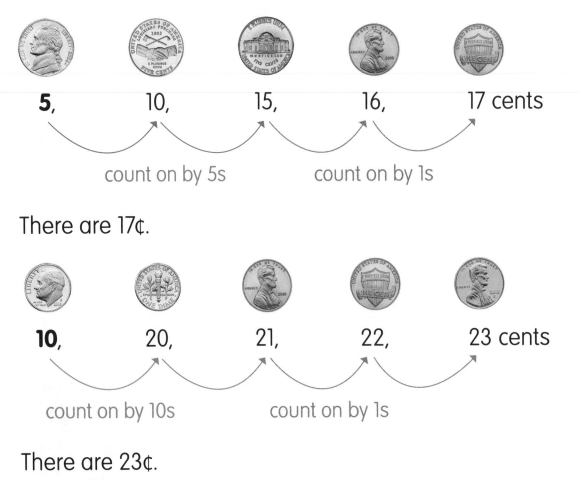

| **5**, | 10, | 15, | 16, | 17 cents |

count on by 5s   count on by 1s

There are 17¢.

| **10**, | 20, | 21, | 22, | 23 cents |

count on by 10s   count on by 1s

There are 23¢.

Work in groups of three.

Your teacher will give you some .

① Take some dimes and pennies.
Arrange the dimes and pennies in one row.
Place the dimes first, then the pennies.

② Ask a group member to count on to find the value of
the coins.

③ Ask the other group member to check the answer.
Do both group members get the same answer?

④ Trade places.
Repeat ① to ③ for the following.
a   pennies and nickels
b   nickels and dimes

Begin with the coins
of a greater value.

TRY Practice counting on to find the value of a group of coins

Write each missing number.

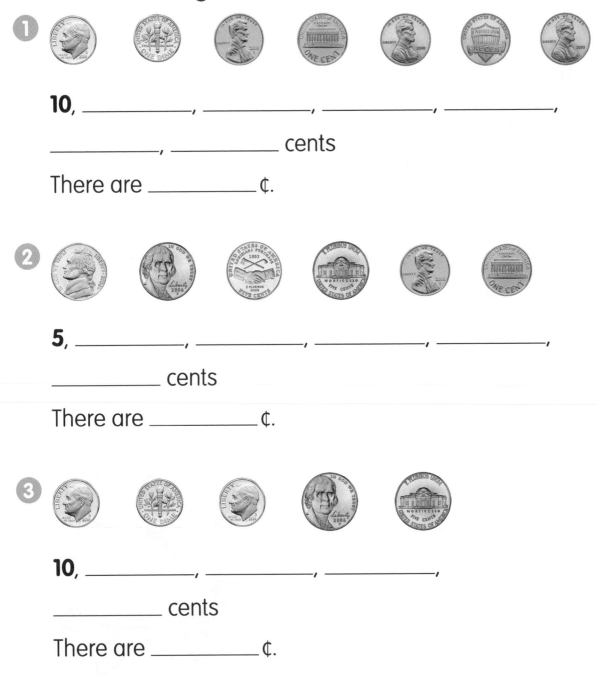

1 10, _____, _____, _____, _____,

_____, _____ cents

There are _____ ¢.

2 5, _____, _____, _____, _____,

_____ cents

There are _____ ¢.

3 10, _____, _____, _____,

_____ cents

There are _____ ¢.

ENGAGE

Tomas has six coins.

The six coins have an equal total value as one dime.

What coins does Tomas have?

Use to show the coins.

LEARN Exchange one coin for a set of coins of equal value

1 You can exchange a coin for other coins of equal value.

1 nickel   5 pennies

1 dime   2 nickels

Hands-on Activity Exchanging coins for a set of coins of equal value

Work in pairs.

Your teacher will give you some .

① Exchange 1 dime for pennies.

How many pennies do you get? _____

② Exchange 1 dime for pennies and nickels.
Each of you show how you exchange in different ways.
How many pennies and nickels do you get?
Write your answers in the table below.

Ways	Number of Pennies	Number of Nickels
1st Way		
2nd Way		

③ Repeat ② for 2 dimes.

Ways	Number of Pennies	Number of Nickels
1st Way		
2nd Way		
3rd Way		

TRY Practice exchanging one coin for a set of coins of equal value

Write each missing number.

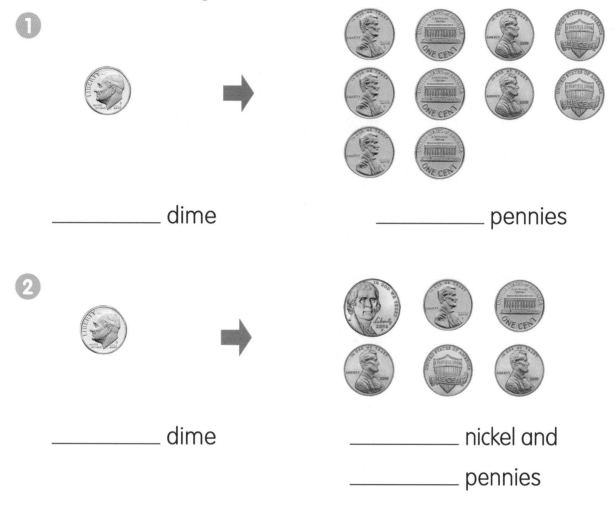

1

_____ dime

_____ pennies

2

_____ dime

_____ nickel and

_____ pennies

ENGAGE

Take some .

A file costs 18¢.

Show what you can use to pay for the file.

What coins did your partner use?

Did both of you use the same coins?

LEARN Use coins to show a given amount in different ways

1 You can use different groups of coins to show the same amount.

I can pay with 2 dimes and 1 penny.

I can pay with 1 dime, 2 nickels, and 1 penny.

I can pay with 4 nickels and 1 penny.

Work in pairs.

Your teacher will give you some .

① Use two ways to show how you can pay for each object shown below.

② Then, write the number of each type of coin used.

	Ways	Number of Pennies	Number of Nickels	Number of Dimes
18¢	1st Way			
	2nd Way			

	Ways	Number of Pennies	Number of Nickels	Number of Dimes
22¢	1st Way			
	2nd Way			

TRY Practice using different groups of coins to show the same amount of money

Fill in each blank.

①

10 ¢

a You can pay for the stamp with _____ pennies.

b You can also pay with _____ nickels.

2

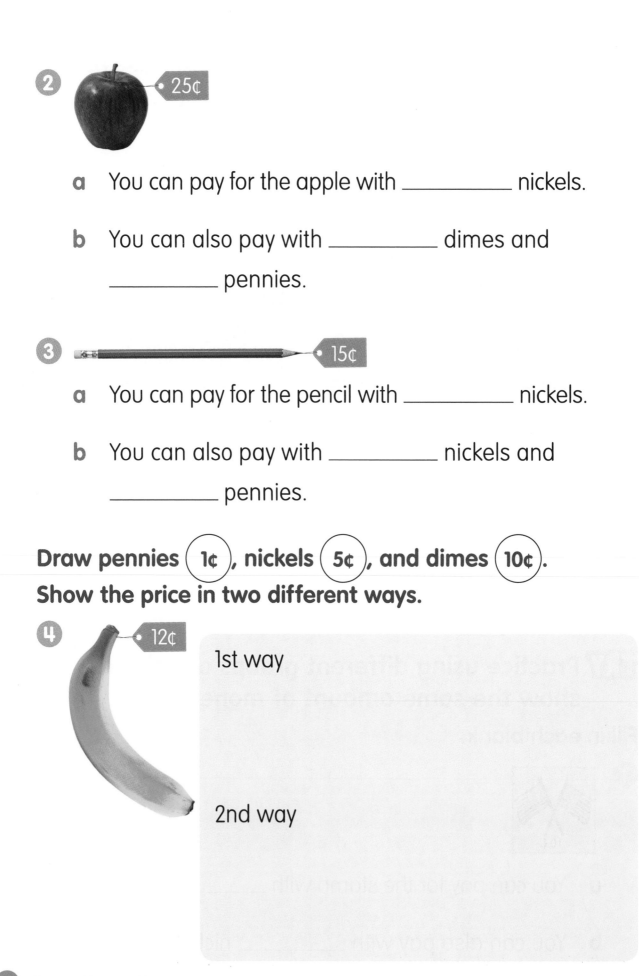

25¢

a You can pay for the apple with _____ nickels.

b You can also pay with _____ dimes and _____ pennies.

3

15¢

a You can pay for the pencil with _____ nickels.

b You can also pay with _____ nickels and _____ pennies.

Draw pennies (1¢), nickels (5¢), and dimes (10¢).
Show the price in two different ways.

4

12¢

1st way

2nd way

INDEPENDENT PRACTICE

Answer each question.

1. How many dimes are there in all? _____

2. How many more pennies than dimes are there? _____

3. How many fewer nickels than pennies are there? _____

Write each missing number.

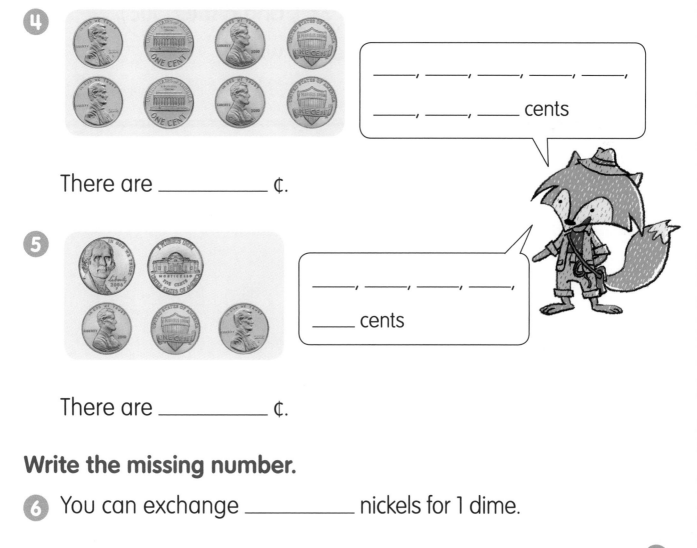

4. _____, _____, _____, _____, _____,

_____, _____, _____ cents

There are _____ ¢.

5. _____, _____, _____, _____,

_____ cents

There are _____ ¢.

Write the missing number.

6. You can exchange _____ nickels for 1 dime.

Write each price.

7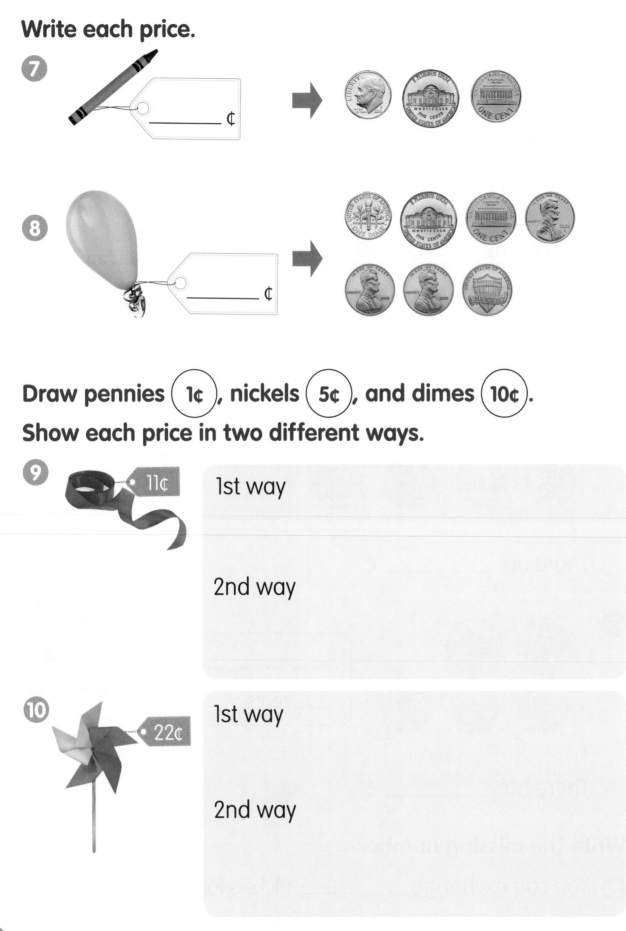

_____ ¢

8

_____ ¢

Draw pennies (1¢), nickels (5¢), and dimes (10¢).
Show each price in two different ways.

9 11¢

1st way

2nd way

10 22¢

1st way

2nd way

2 Quarter

Learning Objectives:
- Recognize, identify, and name a quarter.
- Exchange a quarter for a set of coins of equal value.

New Vocabulary
quarter

THINK

Amirah buys a small toy for 65¢.
She gives the cashier five coins.
How many nickels, dimes, and quarters does Amirah use?

ENGAGE

Tiana is buying a pencil.
The pencil costs 25¢.
Use  to show two ways to pay for the pencil.

LEARN Know the quarter

①

A quarter has two faces.
The quarter has a value of twenty-five cents or 25¢.

2 These are also quarters.

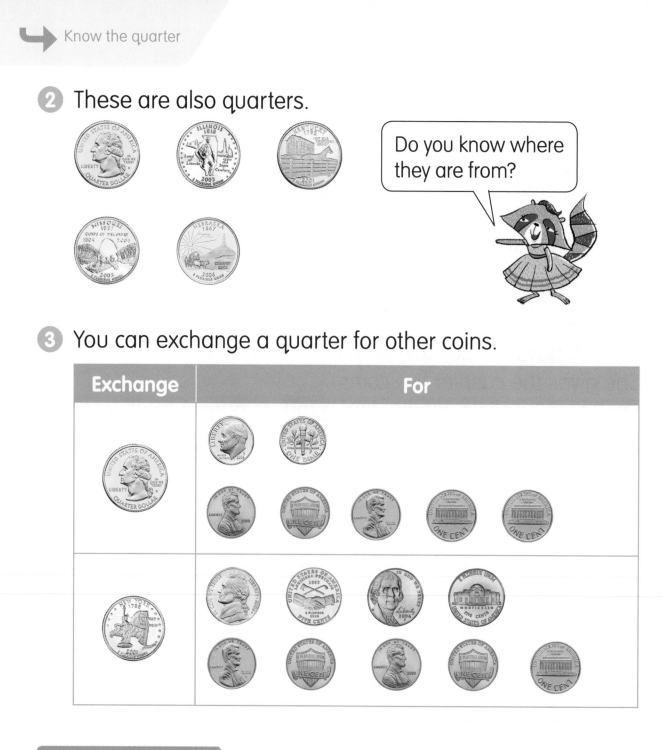

Do you know where they are from?

3 You can exchange a quarter for other coins.

Exchange	For

Hands-on Activity Exchanging a quarter for other coins of equal value

Work in pairs.

① Use 🪙🪙 to show how you exchange a quarter for:

   a pennies and nickels   **b** pennies and dimes

   c nickels and dimes

② Draw pennies (1¢), nickels (5¢), and dimes (10¢) in the table to show your answer.

Exchange	For
a	
b	
c	

③ Use different ways from ①.
Use 🪙 to show three more ways you can exchange a quarter for other coins.
Then, draw your answers in the table.

Exchange	For

© 2020 Marshall Cavendish Education Pte Ltd

TRY Practice exchanging a quarter for other coins of equal value

Fill in each blank.

1

The value of a _____ is _____ ¢.

2 You can exchange 1 quarter for _____ pennies.

3 You can exchange 1 quarter for _____ dimes and 5 pennies.

4 You can exchange 1 quarter for _____ nickels and 5 pennies.

Circle coins to make 2 quarters.

5

INDEPENDENT PRACTICE

Fill in each blank.

1 One _____ has a value of 25¢.

2 You can make _____ quarters with these coins.

3 You can exchange 1 quarter for 1 dime, _____ nickels, and 5 pennies.

4 You can exchange 1 quarter for 1 dime, 1 nickel, and _____ pennies.

Answer each question.

Set A   Set B

5 What is the value of the coins in Set A? _____ ¢

6 Which set has a greater value? _____

Draw pennies (1¢), nickels (5¢), dimes (10¢), and quarters (25¢).

Use different number of coins to match the price.

25¢

7 1 coin

8 3 coins

9 5 coins

10 8 coins

11 12 coins

3 Counting Money

Learning Objectives:
- Count money in cents up to $1 using the "count on" strategy.
- Choose the correct value of coins when buying items.
- Use different combinations of coins to show the same value.

THINK

Dominic has nine coins.

He wants to buy a pen that costs 92¢.

He has the exact amount of money to pay for the pen.

Six of the coins Dominic has are 1 quarter, 3 dimes, 1 nickel, and 1 penny.

What are the remaining three coins?

ENGAGE

Paulina has five coins.

The total value of the coins is 55¢.

What coins does Paulina have?

Use 🪙 to help you.

LEARN Count on to find the amount of money

1 You can count on to find the amount of money.

First, put the coins in order.

Then, count on from the coins of the greatest value.

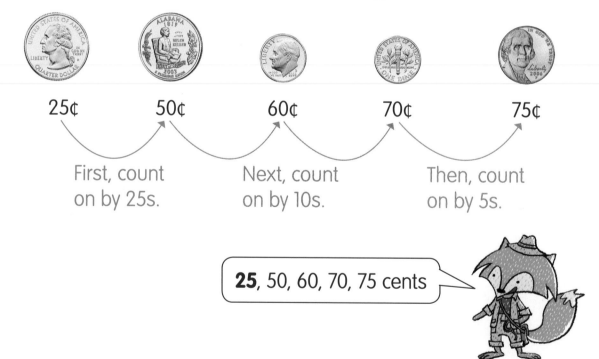

25¢	50¢	60¢	70¢	75¢

First, count
on by 25s.

Next, count
on by 10s.

Then, count
on by 5s.

25, 50, 60, 70, 75 cents

You count on by 25s for quarters, 10s for dimes,
5s for nickels, and 1s for pennies.

TRY Practice counting on to find the amount of money

Four children are buying some erasers.
Count on to find the price of each eraser.

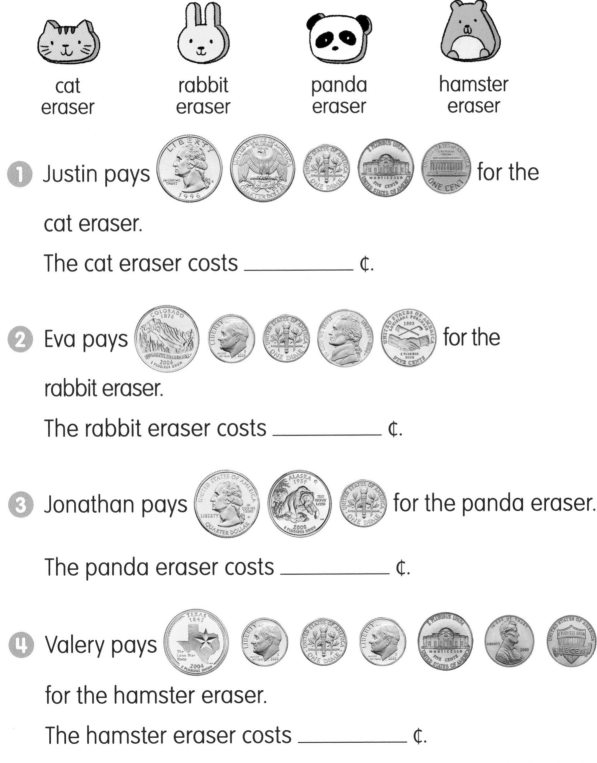

cat
eraser

rabbit
eraser

panda
eraser

hamster
eraser

1 Justin pays   for the

cat eraser.

The cat eraser costs _____ ¢.

2 Eva pays   for the

rabbit eraser.

The rabbit eraser costs _____ ¢.

3 Jonathan pays   for the panda eraser.

The panda eraser costs _____ ¢.

4 Valery pays

for the hamster eraser.

The hamster eraser costs _____ ¢.

Circle the coins to make 62¢.

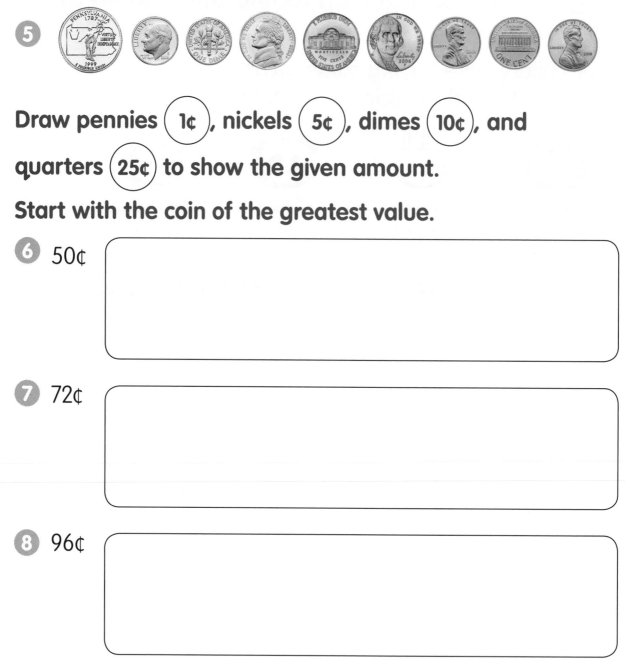

5

Draw pennies (1¢), nickels (5¢), dimes (10¢), and quarters (25¢) to show the given amount.

Start with the coin of the greatest value.

6 50¢

7 72¢

8 96¢

ENGAGE

Logan has some coins.

He wants to pay for an apple that cost 64¢.

Use to show two different ways to pay for the apple.

LEARN Use coins to show a given amount in different ways

1. Tristan wants to buy a pencil.
The pencil costs 55¢.

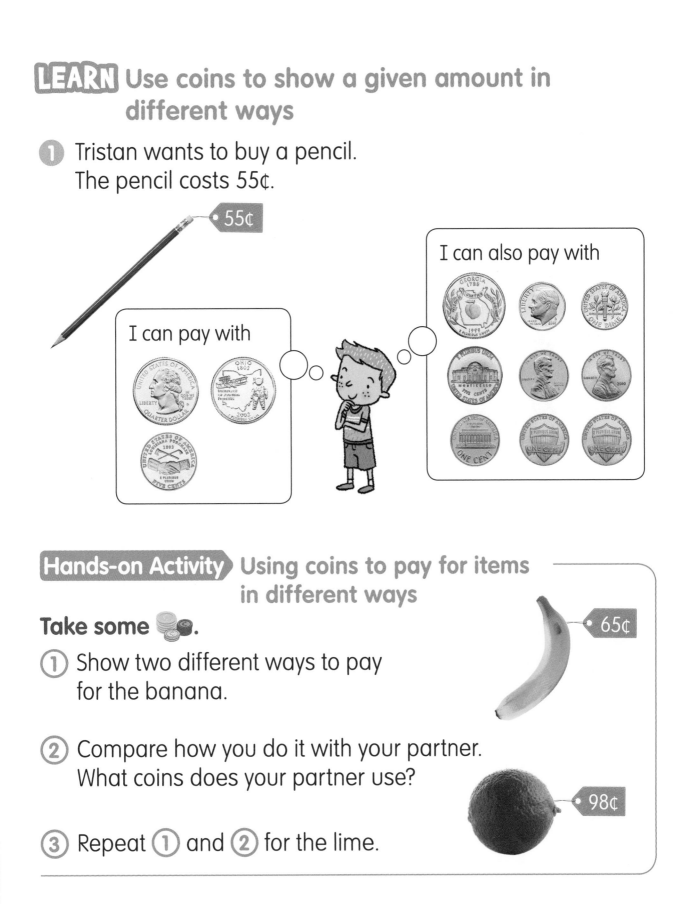

55¢

I can pay with

I can also pay with

Hands-on Activity Using coins to pay for items in different ways

Take some 🪙.

1. Show two different ways to pay for the banana.

65¢

2. Compare how you do it with your partner. What coins does your partner use?

98¢

3. Repeat ① and ② for the lime.

TRY Practice using coins to show a given amount in different ways

Draw pennies (1¢), nickels (5¢), dimes (10¢), and quarters (25¢).

Show each price in two different ways.

1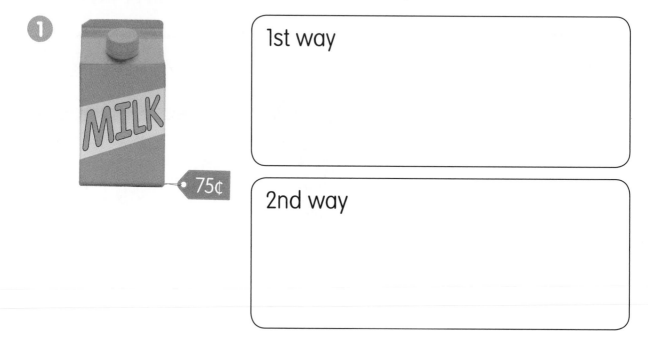

75¢

1st way

2nd way

2

85¢

1st way

2nd way

3

 46¢

1st way

2nd way

4

 99¢

1st way

2nd way

SAY HOW MUCH

41¢

? ? ?

What you need:

Players: 4
Materials: A bag, 2 quarters, 2 dimes, 2 nickels,
2 pennies

Place all the coins in the bag.

1. Each player picks a coin without looking.
   Do not show the coin to the other players.

2. On the count of three, all players place their coins on the table.

3. The first player to say the correct value of all four coins receives one point.

4. Place the coins back in the bag.
   Repeat 1 to 3.

Who is the winner?

The first player to get ten points wins.

INDEPENDENT PRACTICE

Count on to find each amount of money.

1

_____ ¢

2

_____ ¢

3

_____ ¢

4

_____ ¢

Arrange the coins in order from greatest to least value. Then, count on to find the total value of the coins.

5

The total value of the coins is _____ ¢.

Draw lines to match the correct purse to each item.

6

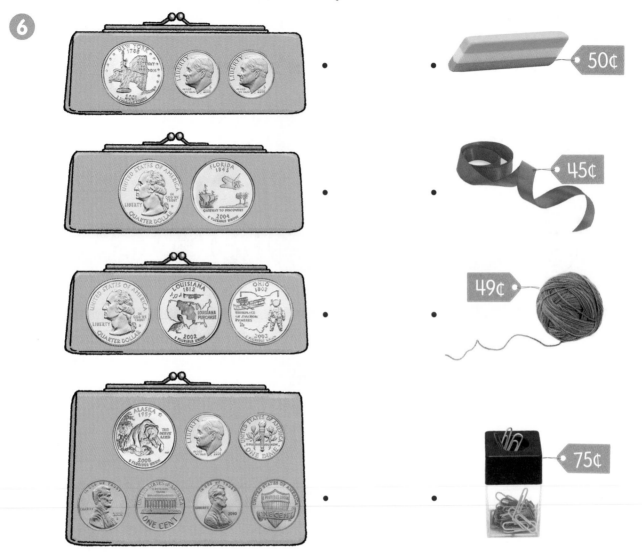

Use coins.
Write or draw two ways you can pay for the book.

7

67¢

1st way

2nd way

4 Adding and Subtracting Money

Learning Objectives:
- Add to find the cost of items.
- Subtract to find the change.
- Add and subtract money in cents (up to $1).
- Solve real-world problems involving addition and subtraction of money.

New Vocabulary
change

THINK

Claire has some dimes and quarters.
She has two more dimes than quarters.
The total value of the coins she has is 90¢.
How many dimes does Claire have?
How many quarters does she have?

ENGAGE

Shanti and Cooper have some quarters.
Shanti has two more quarters than Cooper.
The total value of the quarters is 100¢.
How much does Shanti have?
Use to help you.

LEARN Add and subtract money

1

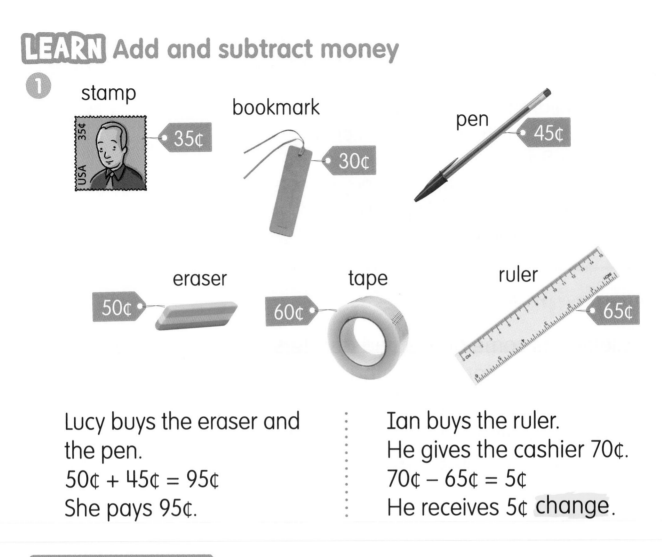

stamp 35¢

bookmark 30¢

pen 45¢

eraser 50¢

tape 60¢

ruler 65¢

Lucy buys the eraser and the pen.
50¢ + 45¢ = 95¢
She pays 95¢.

Ian buys the ruler.
He gives the cashier 70¢.
70¢ − 65¢ = 5¢
He receives 5¢ change.

Hands-on Activity Adding and subtracting money

Work in pairs.
Take some 🪙.

① **Mathematical Habit 1** Persevere in solving problems

You have 95¢.
Pick two items you want to buy from **LEARN**.
How much do your items cost in all?

_____¢ + _____¢ = _____¢

② Use 🪙 to pay your partner.

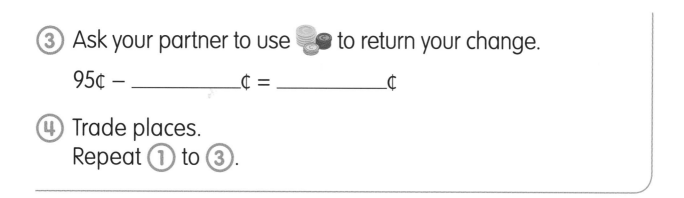

③ Ask your partner to use 🪙 to return your change.

95¢ − _____¢ = _____¢

④ Trade places.
Repeat ① to ③.

TRY Practice adding and subtracting money
Answer each question.

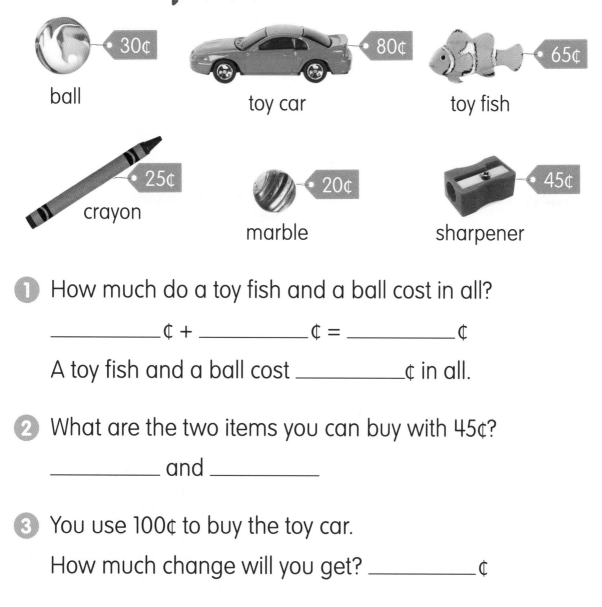

ball 30¢

toy car 80¢

toy fish 65¢

crayon 25¢

marble 20¢

sharpener 45¢

① How much do a toy fish and a ball cost in all?

_____¢ + _____¢ = _____¢

A toy fish and a ball cost _____¢ in all.

② What are the two items you can buy with 45¢?

_____ and _____

③ You use 100¢ to buy the toy car.

How much change will you get? _____¢

ENGAGE

Payton has some quarters and dimes.
She has 35¢ more than Ethan.
Ethan has 60¢.
What coins does Payton have?
Use  to help you.

LEARN Solve real-world problems involving money

Hugo, Kylie, Hannah, and Ali go to a store to buy erasers.
The picture shows some erasers sold in the store.

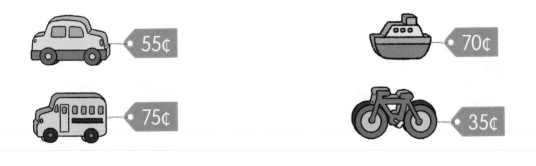

1 Hugo buys a car and a bicycle eraser.
How much does he spend in all?

STEP 1 Understand the problem.

How much does the car and
the bicycle eraser cost?
What do I need to find?

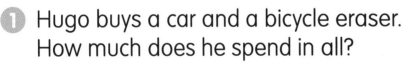

STEP 2 Think of a plan.
I can write an addition sentence.

STEP 3 Carry out the plan

55¢ + 35¢ = 90¢

Mike spends 90¢ in all.

STEP 4 Check the answer.

I can use to check my answer.

② Kylie buys the bicycle eraser.
She gives the cashier two quarters.
How much change does Kylie get?

25¢   50¢

Two quarters is 50¢

50¢ – 35¢ = 15¢
Kylie gets 15¢ change.

③ Hannah has 57¢.
She wants to buy the airplane eraser.
How much more money does Hannah need?

85¢ – 57¢ = 28¢
Hannah needs 28¢ more.

④ Ali buys the bus eraser.
He has a nickel left.
How much does Ali have at first?

How much is
a nickel?

75¢ + 5¢ = 80¢
Ali has 80¢ at first.

TRY Practice solving real-world problems involving money

Solve.

banana 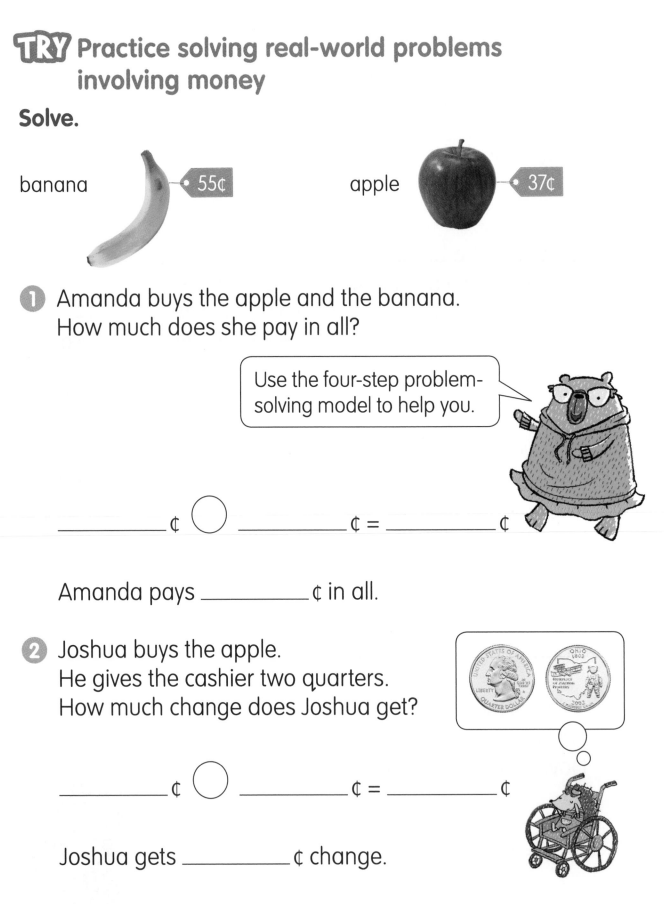 55¢

apple 37¢

1 Amanda buys the apple and the banana.
How much does she pay in all?

Use the four-step problem-solving model to help you.

_____ ¢ ◯ _____ ¢ = _____ ¢

Amanda pays _____ ¢ in all.

2 Joshua buys the apple.
He gives the cashier two quarters.
How much change does Joshua get?

_____ ¢ ◯ _____ ¢ = _____ ¢

Joshua gets _____ ¢ change.

3 Nolan has 28¢.
He wants to buy the banana.
How much more money does Nolan need?

_____ ¢ $\bigcirc$ _____ ¢ = _____ ¢

Nolan needs _____ ¢ more.

4 Trevon buys the banana.
Madelyn buys the apple.
How much less does Madelyn spend than Trevon?

_____ ¢ $\bigcirc$ _____ ¢ = _____ ¢

Madelyn spends _____ ¢ less than Trevon.

5 After buying the apple, Carolina has 8¢ left.
How much does Carolina have at first?

_____ ¢ $\bigcirc$ _____ ¢ = _____ ¢

Carolina has _____ ¢ at first.

These are some items on sale at a store.

bread bun — 60¢
bath tissue — 65¢
book — 90¢
nuts — 80¢
ball — 35¢
granola bar — 83¢
pencil — 20¢
sharpener — 75¢

Use  **to help you.**

1. Brooke wants to buy something to eat.
   She has 80¢.
   What can she buy?

2. Levi has 95¢.
   After buying something to eat, he has 15¢ left.
   What is the food that he buys?

3. Samantha has four quarters.
   Write down any two items she can buy.
   Then, find how much she spends.

INDEPENDENT PRACTICE

Solve.

1 Noah buys an eraser and a pencil.
The eraser costs 40¢ and the pencil costs 35¢.
How much does Noah spend in all?

_____ ¢ ◯ _____ ¢ = _____ ¢

Noah spends _____ ¢ in all.

2 A pen costs 50¢.
Layla buys the pen.
She has 15¢ left.
How much does Layla have at first?

_____ ¢ ◯ _____ ¢ = _____ ¢

Layla has _____ ¢ at first.

These are some items on sale at a store.

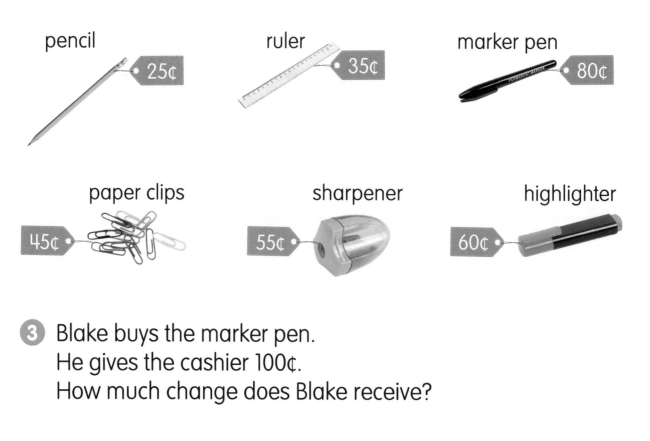

pencil   25¢

ruler   35¢

marker pen   80¢

paper clips   45¢

sharpener   55¢

highlighter   60¢

3 Blake buys the marker pen.
He gives the cashier 100¢.
How much change does Blake receive?

_____ ¢ ◯ _____ ¢ = _____ ¢

Blake receives _____ ¢ change.

4 Angel has 80¢.
She wants to buy two items.
Write down the items Angel can buy.

Mathematical Habit 1 Persevere in solving problems

Look around you.

Find three items you can buy with pennies, nickels, dimes, and quarters.

Write down what these items are.

Then, write how much they cost using pennies, nickels, dimes, and quarters.

Problem Solving with Heuristics

1 **Mathematical Habit 1** Persevere in solving problems

Look at the coins.

Which sentences are correct?

Color the ⬭.

> The value of the quarters is greater than the total value of the pennies, nickels, and dimes.

> You can exchange all the coins for 10 dimes.

> You can exchange all the coins for 3 quarters and 3 nickels.

> If you exchange the quarters for pennies, you will get a total of 55 pennies.

2 **Mathematical Habit 1** Persevere in solving problems

Evan has two coins under Cup A.
Audrey has four coins under Cup B.
The value of the coins in each cup adds up to 50¢.

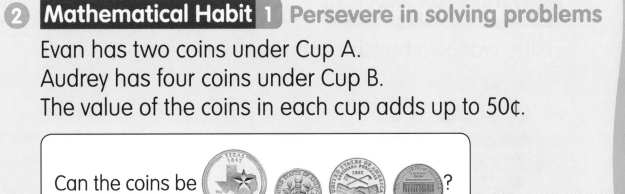

Can the coins be ?

a Which coins are under Cup A?

_____

b Which coins are under Cup B?

_____

3 **Mathematical Habit 1** Persevere in solving problems

Felipe wants to buy the notepad.

87¢

a Draw pennies (1¢), nickels (5¢), dimes (10¢), and quarters (25¢).

Show the price in three different ways.

b What is the least number of coins Felipe can use to buy the notepad? _____

c What is the greatest number of coins he can use to buy the notepad? _____

How is money used in real life?

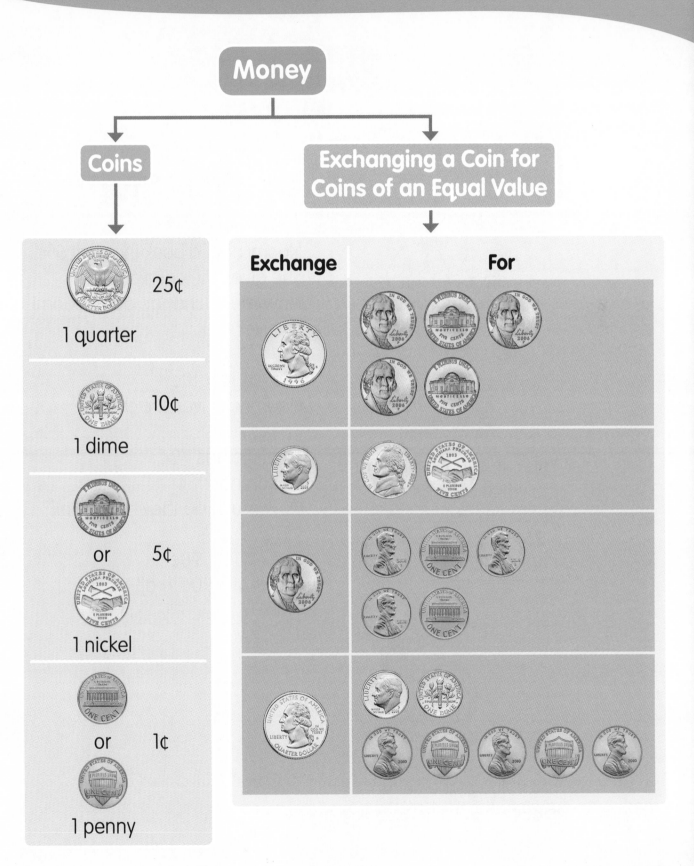

Money

Coins

1 quarter	25¢
1 dime	10¢
1 nickel or	5¢
1 penny or	1¢

Exchanging a Coin for Coins of an Equal Value

Exchange	For

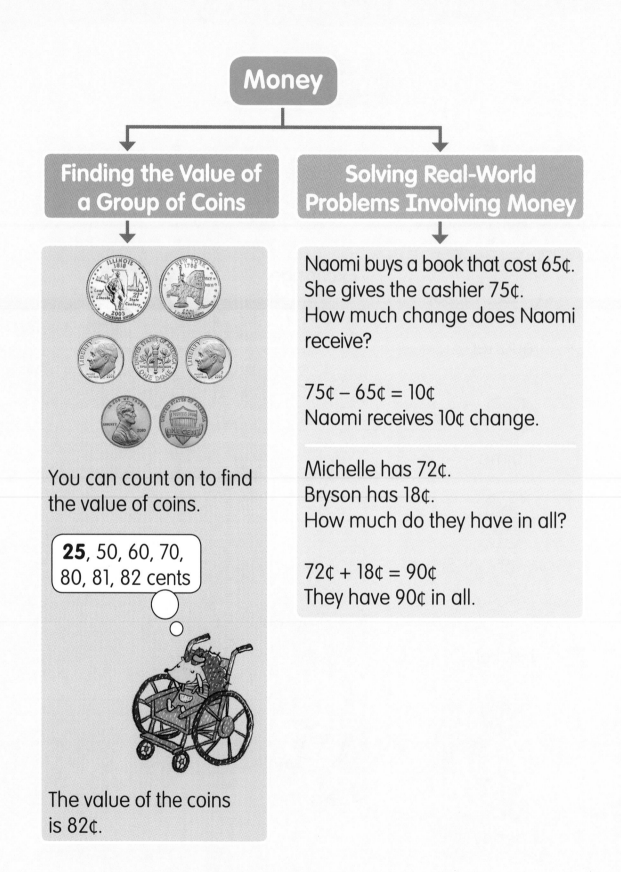

Money

Finding the Value of a Group of Coins

You can count on to find the value of coins.

25, 50, 60, 70, 80, 81, 82 cents

The value of the coins is 82¢.

Solving Real-World Problems Involving Money

Naomi buys a book that cost 65¢.
She gives the cashier 75¢.
How much change does Naomi receive?

75¢ − 65¢ = 10¢
Naomi receives 10¢ change.

Michelle has 72¢.
Bryson has 18¢.
How much do they have in all?

72¢ + 18¢ = 90¢
They have 90¢ in all.

Name: _____   Date: _____

Write the name of each coin.

 **1** _____

2  _____

3 _____

4  _____

Fill in each blank.
Write two ways to exchange a dime for coins of equal value.

5

Exchange		Number of Nickels	Number of Pennies
1 dime	1st way		
	2nd way		

Count on to find each amount of money.

6 is _____ ¢.

7 is _____ ¢.

8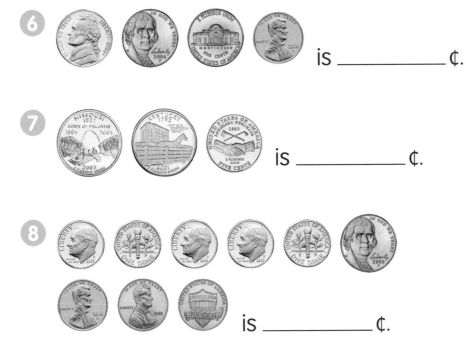

is _____ ¢.

Draw pennies (1¢), **nickels** (5¢), **dimes** (10¢), **and quarters** (25¢).

Show each price in two different ways.

9

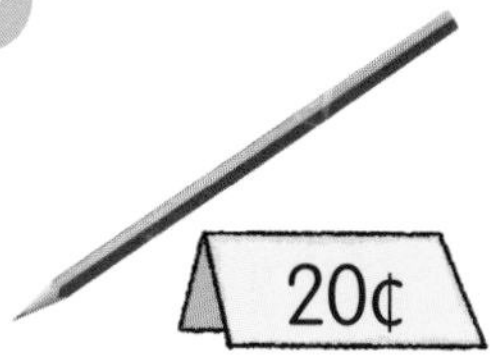

20¢

1st way

2nd way

10

95¢

1st way

2nd way

Add or subtract.
Then, fill in each blank.

11 73¢ + 17¢ = _____ ¢

12 38¢ − 19¢ = _____ ¢

Solve.

13 Landon buys a ruler that cost 65¢.
He gives the cashier 70¢.
How much change does Landon receive?

_____ ¢ ◯ _____ ¢ = _____ ¢

Landon receives _____ ¢ change.

14 Simone buys an exercise book for 52¢
and a pencil for 19¢.
How much does Simone spend in all?

_____ ¢ ◯ _____ ¢ = _____ ¢

Simone spends _____ ¢ in all.

Assessment Prep
Answer each question.

15 Vicente exchanged a quarter for some coins.
Which box shows the coins he may have exchanged for?
Make a ✔ in the box.

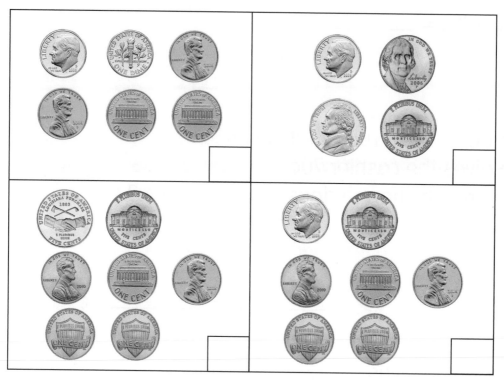

16 Which of the following shows a total value of 50¢?

Name: _____   Date: _____

Shopping at a Store

1 Faith has 67¢ to spend at the store.
She has just six coins.

a How many of each coin does Faith have?

b Faith's father gives her 2 more nickels and
4 more pennies.

Faith has _____ ¢ now.

2 Kim and Axel are shopping at the store.
Count on to find how much Kim and Axel have.

Kim

_____ ¢

Axel

_____ ¢

a Who has more coins? _____

b Who has more money? _____

c Kim wants to buy some stickers for 12¢.
Circle the coins she can use.

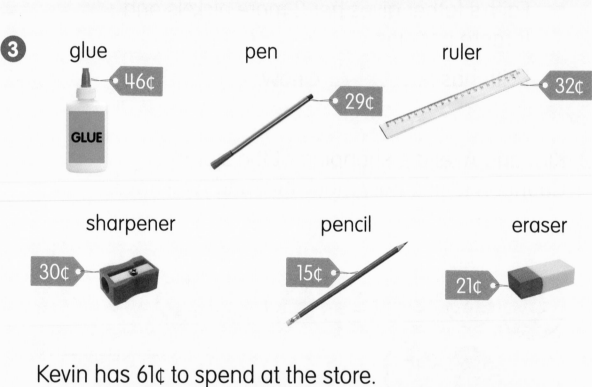

3 glue

46¢

GLUE

pen

29¢

ruler

32¢

sharpener

30¢

pencil

15¢

eraser

21¢

Kevin has 61¢ to spend at the store.
Which two items can Kevin buy if he spends exactly 61¢?
_____ and _____

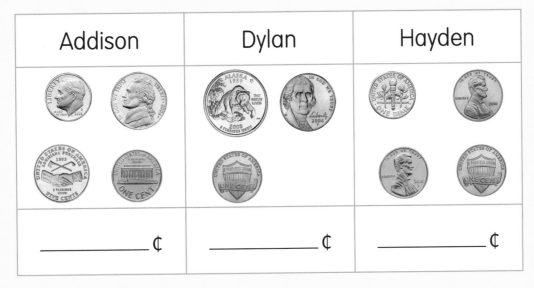

4 **a** How much does each child have?

Addison	Dylan	Hayden
_____ ¢	_____ ¢	_____ ¢

b _____ has the greatest amount of money.

c Addison and Hayden have _____ ¢ in all.

d Order the children's names by the amount of money they have from least to greatest.

_____, _____, _____
    least   greatest

Rubric

Point(s)	Level	My Performance
7–8	4	• Most of my answers are correct. • I show all my work correctly. • I explain my thinking clearly and completely.
5–6.5	3	• Some of my answers are correct. • I show some of my work correctly. • I explain my thinking clearly.
3–4.5	2	• A few of my answers are correct. • I show little work correctly. • I explain some of my thinking clearly.
0–2.5	1	• A few of my answers are correct. • I show little or no work. • I do not explain my thinking clearly.

Teacher's Comments

Glossary

A

- **about**

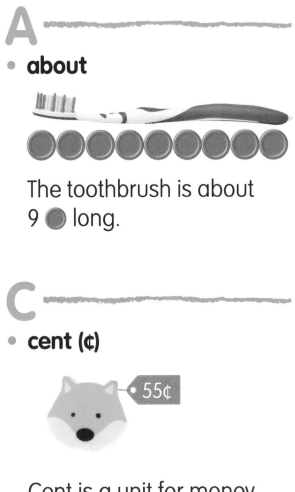

  The toothbrush is about 9  long.

C

- **cent (¢)**

  55¢

  Cent is a unit for money. "¢" stands for cents.

- **change**

  46¢

  Alonso buys the sharpener. He pays the cashier 50¢.
  50¢ − 46¢ = 4¢
  Alonso receives 4¢ change.

D

- **data**

  Data is information that has numbers.

Type of Sport	Tally	Number of Children
Baseball	‖‖‖ ‖‖‖	10
Basketball	‖‖‖ ‖‖‖	8
Soccer	‖	2

- **digit**

  A number is made up of digits.

  In the number 85, the digits are 8 and 5.

dime

A dime has a value of ten cents or 10¢.

E

eighty

Count	Number	Word
	80	eighty

exchange

You can exchange a coin for other coins of equal value.

F

fewest

Hen A	Hen B	Hen C

Hen A laid the fewest eggs.

fifty

Count	Number	Word
	50	fifty

G

- **groups**

There are 4 groups.
Each group has 4 hamsters.

H

- **heaviest**

Box B is heavier than Box A.
Box C is heavier than Box B.
Box C is the heaviest.

K

- **key**

Cars in a Parking Lot

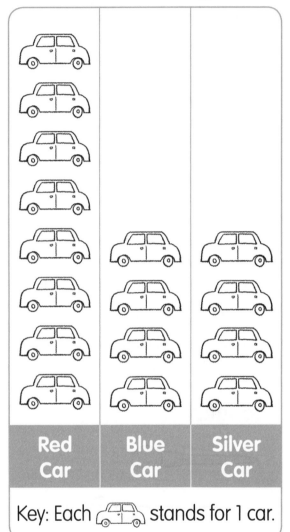

Red Car	Blue Car	Silver Car

Key: Each 🚗 stands for 1 car.

A key tells what each picture or symbol on a picture graph stands for.

L

lightest

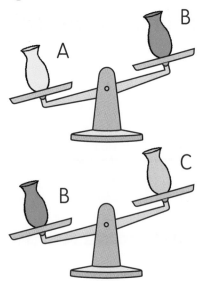

Vase B is lighter than Vase A.
Vase C is lighter than Vase B.
Vase C is the lightest.

longest

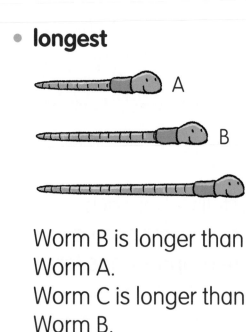

Worm B is longer than
Worm A.
Worm C is longer than
Worm B.
Worm C is the longest.

M

most

Our Favorite Toys

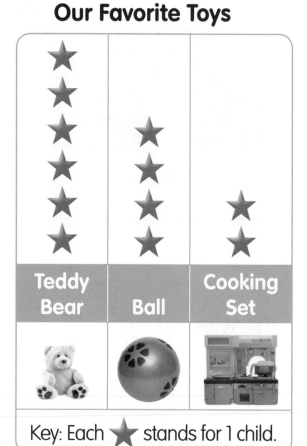

Key: Each ⭐ stands for 1 child.

The most popular toy is the teddy bear.

N

nickel

or

A nickel has a value of five cents or 5¢.

ninety

Count	Number	Word
	90	ninety

O

one hundred

Count	Number	Word
	100	one hundred

one hundred ten

Count	Number	Word
	110	one hundred ten

one hundred twenty

Count	Number	Word
	120	one hundred twenty

P

penny

or

A penny has a value of one cent or 1¢.

picture graph

Shapes

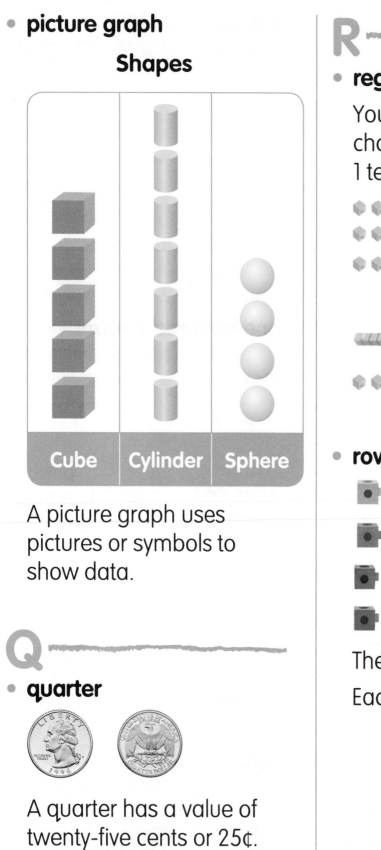

A picture graph uses pictures or symbols to show data.

quarter

A quarter has a value of twenty-five cents or 25¢.

regroup

You regroup when you change 10 ones to 1 ten or 1 ten to 10 ones.

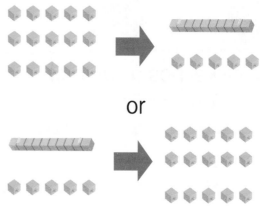

or

rows

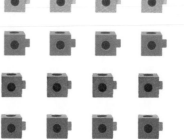

There are 4 rows of .
Each row has 4 .

S

same

Each group has 6 hearts.
The number of hearts in
each group is the same.

seventy

Count	Number	Word
	70	seventy

shortest

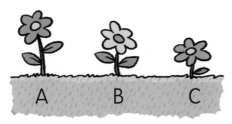

Flower B is shorter than
Flower A.
Flower C is shorter than
Flower B.
Flower C is the shortest.

sixty

Count	Number	Word
	60	sixty

starting line

You can use a start line to
compare the length of objects.

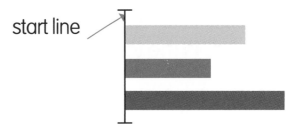

start line

symbol

A symbol is a picture that
represents data in a picture
graph.

Vehicles At A Car Park

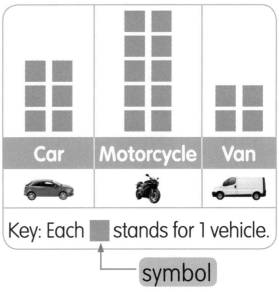

Car	Motorcycle	Van

Key: Each ▮ stands for 1 vehicle.

symbol

T

- ## tallest

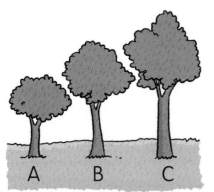

Tree B is taller than Tree A.
Tree C is taller than Tree B.
Tree C is the tallest.

- ## tally chart

Instrument	Tally	Number of Children
🎹 Piano	卌 IIII	9
🎸 Guitar	卌 卌 II	12
🥁 Drum	卌 I	6

A tally chart is used to collect data quickly.

- ## tally marks

A tally mark | is used to record each piece of data. Five tally marks is shown like this: 卌

卌 || stands for 7.

U

- ## unit

Each ⬛ stands for 1 unit.

The weight of the beans is about 9 units.

V

- ## value

The value of a coin tells us how much it is worth.

Index

Pages in **boldface** type show where a term is introduced

Photo Credits

1: © ValeStock/Shutter Stock, 1b: © © Elnur Amikishiyev/123rf.com, 1b: © Natalia Pauk/123rf.com, 19b: © MCE. Objects sponsored by Noble International Pte Ltd., 22t: © MCE. Objects sponsored by Noble International Pte Ltd., 27b: © MCE. Objects sponsored by Noble International Pte Ltd., 28: © MCE. Objects sponsored by Noble International Pte Ltd., 32tl: © Volodymyrkrasyuk/Dreamstime.com, 32tm: © Fabrizio Troiani/Dreamstime.com, 32tr: © Carroteater/Dreamstime.com, 47b: © MCE. Objects sponsored by Noble International Pte Ltd., 61b: © MCE. Objects sponsored by Noble International Pte Ltd., 62: © MCE. Objects sponsored by Noble International Pte Ltd., 63: © MCE. Objects sponsored by Noble International Pte Ltd., 64: © MCE. Objects sponsored by Noble International Pte Ltd., 65: © MCE. Objects sponsored by Noble International Pte Ltd., 66: © MCE. Objects sponsored by Noble International Pte Ltd., 67: © MCE. Objects sponsored by Noble International Pte Ltd., 68: © MCE. Objects sponsored by Noble International Pte Ltd., 69: © MCE. Objects sponsored by Noble International Pte Ltd., 76tl: © Kitchner Bain/Dreamstime.com, 76tm: © kriangkrainetnangrong/Shutter Stock, 76tr: © Elena Schweitzer/Shutter Stock, 76b: © MCE, 77: © MCE, 78: © MCE, 79t: © MCE, 79(m to b): © choness/iStock, 80t: © MCE. Objects sponsored by Noble International Pte Ltd., 81(t to m): © M.G. Mooij/123rf.com, 81(m to b): © MCE, 82b: © MCE, 83: Created by Fwstudio - Freepik.com, 84: © Jakub Gojda/123rf.com, 85mr: © MCE. Objects sponsored by Noble International Pte Ltd., 88: © MCE. Objects sponsored by Noble International Pte Ltd., 99: © Paolo De Santis/123rf.com, 99t: © Madlen/Shutter Stock, 99bl: © AlexussK/Shutter Stock, 99br: © arka38/Shutter Stock, 100(t to b): i) © MCE. Objects sponsored by Noble International Pte Ltd., ii) © Tanapon Samphao/Dreamstime.com, iii) © Passakorn Sakulphan/123rf.com, iv) © Charles Brutlag/123rf.com, v) © MCE. Objects sponsored by Noble International Pte Ltd., vi): © Garrett Aitken/Dreamstime.com, 102(t to b): i) © missisya/123rf.com, © Duncan Noakes/123rf.com, ii) © inbj/123rf.com, © 陈于达/123rf.com, iii) © Svetlana Foote/123rf.com, © Maksim Toome/123rf.com, © Sergey Petinov/123rf.com, iv) © Witoon Buttre/Dreamstime.com, © Nuttakit Sukjaroensuk/123rf.com, © Yurakp/Dreamstime.com, 104(m to b): i) © pockygallery/123rf.com, ii) © HSBortecin/Shutter Stock, iii) © Charles Brutlag/123rf.com, iv) © Tanapon Samphao/Dreamstime.com, 105: © MCE. Objects sponsored by Noble International Pte Ltd., 105b: © Mr.Teerapong Kunkaeo/Shutter Stock, 107tl: © Nikolai Sorokin/Dreamstime.com, 107tm: © Cloki/Dreamstime.com, 107m: © Tetiana Rozhnovska/Dreamstime.com, 107b: © Wabeno/Dreamstime.com, 108tl: © Hard Ligth/Shutter Stock, 108tm: © Jambals/Shutter Stock, 108m: © ivn3da/123rf.com, 108b: © pockygallery/123rf.com, 109b:

© Mr.Teerapong Kunkaeo/Shutter Stock, 111t: © MCE. Objects sponsored by Noble International Pte Ltd., 111mr: © Dmitrii Kiselev/123rf.com, 111br: © Mr.Teerapong Kunkaeo/Shutter Stock, 121m: © Igor Kovalchuk/Dreamstime.com, 121b: © Mr.Teerapong Kunkaeo/Shutter Stock, 122(t to b): i) © pockygallery/123rf.com, ii) © Igor Kovalchuk/Dreamstime.com, iii) © Amphaiwan/Dreamstime.com, iv) © Igor Kovalchuk/Dreamstime.com, v) © voennyy/123rf.com, vi) © Yvdavyd/Dreamstime.com, 123: © Mr.Teerapong Kunkaeo/Shutter Stock, 124(t to m): i) © Anton Starikov/Dreamstime.com, ii) © Garrett Aitken/Dreamstime.com, iii) © Marusea Turcu/Dreamstime.com, iv) © Yvdavyd/Dreamstime.com, 124bl: © Igor Kovalchuk/Dreamstime.com, 124bm: © Passakorn Sakulphan/123rf.com, 125: © Igor Kovalchuk/Dreamstime.com, 125: © Passakorn Sakulphan/123rf.com, 125tl: © Prapan Ngawkeaw/123rf.com, 125ml: © Kidsada Manchinda/123rf.com, 126: © Igor Kovalchuk/Dreamstime.com, 126tr: © MCE, 126tr: © Mr.Teerapong Kunkaeo/Shutter Stock, 126ml: © Mr.Teerapong Kunkaeo/Shutter Stock, 126bl: © MCE, 127: © Igor Kovalchuk/Dreamstime.com, 127tr: © Dmitrii Kiselev/123rf.com, 127mr: © Dmitrii Kiselev/123rf.com, 127b: © MCE, 128(t to m): i) © Broker/Dreamstime.com, ii) © Igor Kovalchuk/Dreamstime.com, iii) © Passakorn Sakulphan/123rf.com, iv) © Igor Kovalchuk/Dreamstime.com, v) © Passakorn Sakulphan/123rf.com, 128ml: © Maksym Bondarchuk/Dreamstime.com, 128mm: © MCE. Objects sponsored by Noble International Pte Ltd., 128mr: © Chattep Intaravichian/123rf.com, 128bm: © Chattep Intaravichian/123rf.com, 128br: © MCE. Objects sponsored by Noble International Pte Ltd., 129(t to b): i) © Nik Merkulov/123rf.com, ii) © Igor Terekhov/123rf.com, iii) © Carsten Reisinger/123rf.com, © MCE. Objects sponsored by Noble International Pte Ltd., iv) © MCE. Objects sponsored by Noble International Pte Ltd., v) © Oleg Vydyborets/123rf.com, vi) © Igor Kovalchuk/Dreamstime.com, vii) © Passakorn Sakulphan/123rf.com, viii) © Igor Kovalchuk/Dreamstime.com, ix) © Passakorn Sakulphan/123rf.com, 130(t to m): © MCE. Objects sponsored by Noble International Pte Ltd., 130tl: © Kidsada Manchinda/123rf.com, 130mm: © Kristin Smith/123rf.com, 130bl: © Amnach Kinchokawat/123rf.com, 130br: © Igor Terekhov/123rf.com, 131b: © MCE, 132tl: © Passakorn Sakulphan/123rf.com, 132tl: © Tirrasa/Dreamstime.com, 132m: © Satakorn/Dreamstime.com, 132m: © Passakorn Sakulphan/123rf.com, 132b: © Vladimir Liverts/Dreamstime.com, 132bl: © Natthapon Ngamnithiporn/123rf.com, 133: © Igor Kovalchuk/Dreamstime.com, 133: © Dmitrii Kiselev/123rf.com, 135t: © serezniy/123rf.com, 135t: © Olga Kovalenko/123rf.com, 135m: © MCE, 135m: © Andrei Kuzmik/Dreamstime.com, 136tl: © Igor Kovalchuk/Dreamstime.com, 140bm: © 123dartist/Shutter Stock, 140br: © tuulijumala/123rf.com,

141tl: © photogal/123rf.com, 141tm: © Dzmitry Kliapitski/123rf.com, 141ml: © Garrett Aitken/Dreamstime.com, 141mm: ©Udomosookl/iStock, 141bl: © Amnach Kinchokawat/123rf.com, 141bm: © Charles Brutlag/123rf.com, 142tm: © Oleg Vydyborets/123rf.com, 142ml: © missisya/123rf.com, 143tl: © Elena Schweitzer/Dreamstime.com, 143tm: © MCE, 143ml: © MCE, 143mm: © Witoon Buttre/Dreamstime.com, 143bl: © Elena Schweitzer/Dreamstime.com, 143bm: © MCE, 143br: © Witoon Buttre/Dreamstime.com, 144tr: © Kotema/Dreamstime.com, 144tr: © Tutye2001/Dreamstime.com, 144tr: © Amphaiwan/Dreamstime.com, 146(tl to tr): i) © Polina Ryazantseva/Dreamstime.com, ii) © Igor Terekhov/123rf.com, iii) © Iaroslav Danylchenko/123rf.com, iv) Polina Ryazantseva/Dreamstime.com, 146bl: © Veniamin Kraskov/Dreamstime.com, 146bm: © Dmitrii Kaztisyn/Dreamstime.com, 146br: © Toxitz/Dreamstime.com, 147(tl to tr): i) © Volodymyr Muliar/Dreamstime.com, ii) © tiero/123rf.com, iii) © Ivan Kuzmin/123rf.com, iv) © Volodymyr Muliar/Dreamstime.com, 147bl: © Sergey Kolesnikov/123rf.com, 147bm: © Svetlana Voronina/123rf.com, 147br: © MCE, 148tl: © boroda/123rf.com, 148tm: © Nbvf/Dreamstime.com, 148tr: © Maksym Narodenko/123rf.com, 149b: © MCE. Objects sponsored by Noble International Pte Ltd., 150: © MCE. Objects sponsored by Noble International Pte Ltd., 150tl: © Anton Starikov/123rf.com, 150ml: © Natthapon Ngamnithiporn/123rf.com, 151: © Houghton Mifflin Harcourt, 151: © MCE. Objects sponsored by Noble International Pte Ltd., 151tm: © Olga Popova/123rf.com, 151ml: © Design56/Dreamstime.com, 151mr: © Dzmitry Kliapitski/123rf.com, 153: © MCE. Objects sponsored by Noble International Pte Ltd., 153tl: © Maksym Narodenko/123rf.com, 153tm: © Sirichai Asawalapsakul/123rf.com, 153mm: © MCE, 154: © Dvmsimages/Dreamstime.com, 154ml: siraphol/123rf.com, 154tm: © Amphaiwan/Dreamstime.com, 155tl: © Polina Ryazantseva/Dreamstime.com, 155bl: © Chattep Intaravichian/123rf.com, 155br: © Kotema/Dreamstime.com, 156tl: © Pixelrobot/Dreamstime.com, 156tm: © Yurakp/Dreamstime.com, 156ml: © MCE. Objects sponsored by Noble International Pte Ltd., 156mm: © Yurakp/Dreamstime.com, 156b: © MCE. Objects sponsored by Noble International Pte Ltd., 156b: © 123dartist/Shutter Stock, 157(t to b): i) © Igor Kovalchuk/Dreamstime.com, ii) © pockygallery/123rf.com, © Pixelrobot/Dreamstime.com, © siraphol/123rf.com, iii) © Igor Kovalchuk/Dreamstime.com, © Houghton Mifflin Harcourt, iv) © Igor Kovalchuk/Dreamstime.com, v) © Houghton Mifflin Harcourt, 158(t to b): i) © Houghton Mifflin Harcourt, ii) © Aperturesound/Dreamstime.com, © Amphaiwan/Dreamstime.com, © Charles Brutlag/123rf.com, iii) © Houghton Mifflin Harcourt, © Igor Kovalchuk/Dreamstime.com, iv) © Houghton Mifflin Harcourt, v) © Igor Kovalchuk/Dreamstime.com, 159: © MCE. Objects sponsored by Noble International Pte Ltd., 161: © 123dartist/Shutter Stock, 161tl: © photoshkolnik/123rf.com, 161tm: © Elena Schweitzer/Dreamstime.com, 161mm: © Inna Kyselova/123rf.com, 162: © MCE. Objects sponsored

by Noble International Pte Ltd., 162tl: © kokoroyuki/123rf.com, 162ml: ©Olga Sapegina/123rf.com, 162mm: © Irogova/Dreamstime.com, 162bm: © 5second/123rf.com, 163: Created by Fwstudio - Freepik.com, 163(t to m): i) © philipus/123rf.com, ii) © Photoart11/Dreamstime.com, iii) © Helena Bilkova/Dreamstime.com, 164tl: © Tirrasa/Dreamstime.com, 164tr: © Nakit Jaroonsrirak/123rf.com, 164ml: © Jrtmedia/Dreamstime.com, 164mr: © Igor Kovalchuk/Dreamstime.com, 165t: © Dmytro Pauk/123rf.com, 167(mr to br): i) © gracethang2/Shutter Stock, ii) © Bryan Solomon/Shutter Stock, iii) © tanyar30/123rf.com, iv) © gracethang2/Shutter Stock, 168tl: © Production Perig/Shutter Stock, 168tm: © Aleksandr Belugin/123rf.com, 168tr: © Geniuskp/Dreamstime.com, 168b: © 123dartist/Shutter Stock, 168b: © MCE. Objects sponsored by Noble International Pte Ltd., 168b: © Enriscapes/123rf.com, 169t: © Nik Merkulov /123rf.com, 169t: © Exopixel/Dreamstime.com, 169m: © belchonock/123rf.com, 170t: ©Udomosookl/iStock, 170(t to m): © Chattep Intaravichian/123rf.com, 170(t to m): © MCE, 170m: © ivn3da/123rf.com, 170bl: © leedsn/123rf.com, 170br: © Charles Brutlag/123rf.com, 170b: © Igor Kovalchuk/Dreamstime.com, 171tl: © Mohammed Anwarul Kabir/Dreamstime.com, 171tm: © Ronny Fredriksen/Dreamstime.com, 171(ml to mr): i) © Dmitriy Syechin/123rf.com, ii) © ILYA AKINSHIN/123rf.com, iii) © Siwaporn Tharawattanatham/123rf.com, iv) © Dmitriy Syechin/123rf.com, 172tl: © Viktor Prymachenko/Dreamstime.com, 172tm: © Elena Schweitzer/Dreamstime.com, 172mm: © Valentina Razumova/123rf.com, 173(t to m): © Dvmsimages/Dreamstime.com, 173tl: © Jakkrit Orrasri/123rf.com, 173(m to b): © MCE. Objects sponsored by Noble International Pte Ltd., 173bl: © Jakkrit Orrasri/123rf.com, 174(ml to mr): i) © Nbvf/Dreamstime.com, ii) © Pixelrobot/Dreamstime.com, iii) © Yvdavyd/Dreamstime.com, iv) © Pixelrobot/Dreamstime.com, 174b: © Pixelrobot/Dreamstime.com, 176t: © Thanamat Somwan/Shutter Stock, 176m: © Igor Kovalchuk/Dreamstime.com, 176m: © Passakorn Sakulphan/123rf.com, 178l: © Madlen/Shutter Stock, 179l: © Anatoly Maslennikov/123rf.com, 181: © Jon Bilous/Dreamstime.com, 181br: © Mtlapcevic/Dreamstime.com, 182b: © Alla Zotova/123rf.com, 185: © MCE, 187b: © MCE, 188b: © MCE, 189: © MCE. Objects sponsored by Noble International Pte Ltd., 190: © MCE, 191: © MCE. Objects sponsored by Noble International Pte Ltd., 197t: © alekss/123rf.com, 197b: © robstark/123rf.com, 198t: © sunshinesmile/123rf.com, 202: © piotr_pabijian/Shutter Stock, 208bl: © rasslava/123rf.com, 210tl: © Pavlo Vakhrushev/123rf.com, 212tl: © Somchai Jongmeesuk/123rf.com, 213tl: © Jakub Gojda/123rf.com, 216: © piotr_pabijian/Shutter Stock, 221: Created by Fwstudio - Freepik.com, 221(t to m): i) © Remus Cucu/Dreamstime.com, ii) © Akinshin/Dreamstime.com, iii) © Jalcaraz/Dreamstime.com, 232t: © czalewski/123rf.com, 232b: © 2bears/Dreamstime.com, 233t: © hidesy/Shutter Stock, 236tr: © Igor Sokolov (breeze)/Shutter Stock, 237: © Grigorenko/Dreamstime.com, 295: Created by Fwstudio - Freepik.com, 311: © Maksim Mitsun/Dreamstime.com,

© 2020 Marshall Cavendish Education Pte Ltd

Published by Marshall Cavendish Education
Times Centre, 1 New Industrial Road, Singapore 536196
Customer Service Hotline: (65) 6213 9688
US Office Tel: (1-914) 332 8888 | Fax: (1-914) 332 8882
E-mail: cs@mceducation.com
Website: www.mceducation.com

Distributed by
Houghton Mifflin Harcourt
125 High Street
Boston, MA 02110
Tel: 617-351-5000
Website: www.hmhco.com/programs/math-in-focus

First published 2020

ISBN 978-0-358-10178-9

Printed in Singapore

2 3 4 5 6 7 8   1401   25 24 23 22 21 20
4500799762   B C D E F

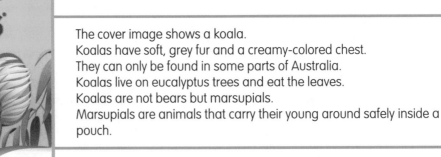

The cover image shows a koala.
Koalas have soft, grey fur and a creamy-colored chest.
They can only be found in some parts of Australia.
Koalas live on eucalyptus trees and eat the leaves.
Koalas are not bears but marsupials.
Marsupials are animals that carry their young around safely inside a pouch.